by Bryce G. Hoffman

can Icon: Alan Mulally and the Fight
e Ford Motor Company

T

RED TEAMING

How Your Business Can
Conquer the Competition by
Challenging Everything

BRYCE G. HOFFMAN

CROWN
BUSINESS

New York

Published in the United States by Crown Business, an imprint of the Crown
Publishing Group, a division of Penguin Random House LLC, New York.
crownpublishing.com

CROWN BUSINESS is a trademark and CROWN and the Rising Sun colophon are
registered trademarks of Penguin Random House LLC.

Crown Business books are available at special discounts for bulk purchases for sales
promotions or corporate use. Special editions, including personalized covers, excerpts
of existing books, or books with corporate logos, can be created in large quantities
for special needs. For more information, contact Premium Sales at (212) 572-2232 or
e-mail specialmarkets@penguinrandomhouse.com.

Library of Congress Cataloging-in-Publication Data has been applied for.

ISBN 978-1-101-90597-5
Ebook ISBN 978-1-101-90598-2
International Edition ISBN 978-1-5247-5998-8

Printed in the United States of America

Book design by Ralph Fowler Design
Illustrations by Mapping Specialists
Jacket design by Kalina Schoen

10 9 8 7 6 5 4 3 2 1

First Edition

To MSN and MSH,

and to my wife, Gretchen.

Thanks for being my red team.

Contents

Contents

Introduction

Know the enemy and know yourself; in a hundred battles you will never be in peril. When you are ignorant of the enemy, but know yourself, your chances of winning or losing are equal. If ignorant both of your enemy and yourself, you are certain in every battle to be in peril.

—Sun Tzu

On a cold, clear morning in March 2015, I eased my car past the hand-hewn stone walls and imposing iron gates of the old military prison at Fort Leavenworth, Kansas. When they used to talk about sending someone to break rocks at Leavenworth, they meant it. This was where the American military sent the baddest of its bad apples for more than a century. In 1875, the U.S. Army marched the first inmates out to what was still the frontier and forced them to build their prison around themselves, hewing it block by block from the native stone in a scene worthy of Kafka. Officially known as the United States Disciplinary Barracks, it served as the military's maximum security prison until it was deemed unfit even for the worst offenders. The main building had been torn down in 2002—and its inmates transferred to a modern, concrete penitentiary built at a more remote location on the base. I now found myself looking for a parking space on the fresh black asphalt that covered the area where the old cellblocks once stood. The rest of the original prison complex, from the walls and guard towers to the infirmary and workshops, still remained. Some of those buildings been converted into offices. Others, including a stone edifice that once housed the gallows, had been converted into classrooms. After a lengthy security check, I headed there, pressed my newly issued security pass to the electronic reader mounted next to the door of classroom 104, and tried to slip inside as discreetly as possible.

But it is hard to be discreet when you are the only civilian in a classroom full of soldiers.

There were a dozen other students, all wearing battle dress uniforms, and all of them turned in unison when I opened the door and eyed me suspiciously. Eleven were army majors, or soon to be promoted to that rank. One was an air force intelligence officer. Almost all of them had served multiple combat tours in Iraq and Afghanistan. Many wore the army's Combat Action Badge on their left breast, proof that they had been in the thick of it. Several sported paratroopers' jump wings. Some were highly decorated. One had a green beret sitting on top of his notebook. The room was occupied by an enormous U-shaped table with seats arranged around the outside edge. A name card was placed in front of each seat. Mine said MR. HOFFMAN. All the others said MAJOR SO-AND-SO.

"You must be important," said the officer to my left as I slipped into my seat.

"I assure you, I'm not," I said.

"Then why are you dressed that way?" he asked, eyeing my wool sport coat and slacks.

The only other person dressed *that way* was our instructor, Dr. Kevin Benson. He was a tall, lanky gentleman with a drooping white mustache that made him look like a frontier sheriff. But at least Benson was a retired colonel. And not just any retired colonel. He was, quite literally, the man who had written the invasion plan for Iraq. I felt like I was crashing a party I was not dressed for and had no business attending. But I was right where I needed to be if I was going to learn about *red teaming*—a revolutionary way to stress-test strategies and navigate an uncertain future I had first learned about from a zombie movie.

* * *

I don't like zombie movies. I never have. But several friends whose opinions I respect had recommended the 2013 film *World War Z*—and while I did not respect their opinions enough to actually go to the theater and see it, I did remember what they had said a few months later when I found myself laid up on the couch with a bad cold, scanning the list of new releases on Amazon Instant Video, looking for a way to kill the afternoon. *World War Z* was at the top of the list. It seemed suitably mindless, so I clicked on the "Play" button.

I couldn't tell you much about the movie—most of it was quickly lost in a decongestant haze—but one scene struck me like a shotgun blast to the face of an ambulatory corpse. Early on in the film, it emerges that only one nation, Israel, has managed to avoid the virally induced zombie apocalypse that has destroyed the rest of human civilization. Our hero, Brad Pitt, is sent to Jerusalem by what is left of the United States government to find out why. A senior Mossad officer meets Pitt at the airport and explains that his country decided to seal its borders after receiving reports of a fast-moving zombie plague in India. Other nations received the same hard-to-believe information but dismissed the reports as absurd. When Pitt asks why Israel decided to act upon them, the Mossad man credits the "Tenth Man Doctrine," which he says Israel adopted in the wake of the Yom Kippur War.

"In the month before October 1973 we saw Arab troop movements, and we unanimously agreed that they didn't pose a threat. Now, a month later, the Arab attack almost drove us into the sea. So, we decided to make a change," the Israeli explains. "If nine of us with the same information arrive at the exact same conclusion, it's the duty of the tenth man to disagree. No matter how improbable it may seem, the tenth man has to start thinking with the assumption that the other nine were wrong."

In this case, he was that tenth man, and he had managed to persuade his peers to close Israel's borders as a precaution, thereby preventing the zombie plague from infecting his country.

That didn't matter much in the movie; the zombies were at the Wailing Wall a few minutes later. However, it mattered a great deal to me—not because I spent a lot of time thinking about how to contain the undead, but because I spent a lot of time thinking about how companies could plan better, overcome groupthink, and avoid the curse of complacency that so often seemed to follow on the heels of success at big corporations.

Two years earlier, I had written *American Icon: Alan Mulally and the Fight to Save Ford Motor Company*. It had been a bestseller, and a number of CEOs in the United States and other countries had adopted my book as a manual for a new model of leadership—a forward-looking, data-driven approach to management that Mulally had used to save not only Ford but also Boeing. Many of those CEOs wanted to learn more about Mulally's method, and several had asked me to help them implement his ideas in their organizations. I quickly discovered that helping companies solve their problems was a more satisfying way to earn a living than writing about those problems. So I quit my job at the *Detroit News* after twenty years as a business journalist and launched a new career as a management consultant.

I knew Mulally's system worked. I'd seen it save Ford, and I had already helped a couple of companies use it to make dramatic improvements to their own operations. Yet I was worried that this system, by itself, was not enough. And I wasn't the only one. Bill Ford, the great-grandson of Henry Ford and the automaker's executive chairman, told me one fear still kept him up at night: Ford might come to take its newfound success for granted and lose the edge Mulally had honed so carefully. Yes, Mulally had saved Ford from bankruptcy and achieved record profitability. Yes, he had neutralized Ford's caustic corporate culture and replaced it with a collaborative, team-based management system. But as Bill Ford knew better than most, his company had squandered its success before, and he was worried it might do it again.

"It's something that I think about all the time," Ford told me. "How do we not go back to where we were? How do we stay lean and hungry? And how do we continue to foster innovation?"

Mulally's management system required senior executives to continually examine their plans and assumptions. However, I knew the longer those plans and assumptions remained valid, the harder it would be for the men and women at the top of the house to question them. Complacency is part of human nature. When things are going well, most of us prefer to assume they will continue to go well. Groupthink is also part of human nature. We are social creatures, and we put a bigger premium on conformity and cohesion than most of us would like to believe— particularly in large organizations, where staying on the right side of internal politics is often the key to job security and promotion. And while many people see big multinationals like Ford as fundamentally *dehumanizing,* I had spent enough time covering them as a reporter to know such organizations actually magnified human nature—sometimes to a troubling degree.

It was complacency and groupthink that had gotten Ford into trouble in the first place. Like its crosstown rivals, General Motors and Chrysler, Ford had taken the success it enjoyed in the decades after World War II for granted. Management and labor alike came to view that success as a birthright, rather than as something they had to go out and fight for every day. Even after foreign rivals figured out how to beat the American automakers at their own game, Detroit's Big Three continued to believe the lackluster cars they were producing remained competitive. That self-delusion extended from the boardroom all the way down to the factory floor, where the men and women who built those cars labored under the erroneous belief that their gold-plated wages and benefits were exempt from the business cycle and impervious to the pressures of globalization. It took a Great Recession to rouse Detroit from its reverie and shatter its belief that America's automakers were too big to fail.

Fortunately for Ford, Mulally arrived just ahead of that tidal wave of reality. He forced the company to take a hard look at its products and practices, and he borrowed enough money to fix them before the gates of the global credit markets slammed shut. GM and Chrysler were not so lucky. They went bankrupt and were only revived by the American taxpayers. Thanks to Mulally's leadership, Ford saved itself. But the question was, for how long?

As the person who wrote the book on Ford, it was a question I was being asked a lot as Mulally's retirement date approached and speculation began to swirl about his successor. I knew the system he put in place was capable of keeping Ford on the right trajectory, but only if the company continued to use it with the same unflinching honesty Mulally insisted upon. I suspected Mulally had driven the company's chronic complacency and groupthink into remission, but not eradicated those diseases entirely. So as Brad Pitt continued his quest to find a cure for the zombie plague, I found myself wondering whether this Tenth Man Doctrine might not be the cure for these all-too-actual maladies of business.

First, I had to find out if it was real.

* * *

I tracked down a former Israeli Defense Forces spokesman, Eytan Buchman, who helped separate fact from fiction.

"The Israeli military does indeed have a similar doctrine, but it is not called the Tenth Man Doctrine," he explained. "After the Yom Kippur War, the IDF's Intelligence Directorate created a red team, a devil's advocate team that can challenge prevalent assumptions within intelligence bodies."

Buchman described a small, elite organization that went by the code name *Ipcha Mistabra,* an Aramaic term used frequently in the Talmud that means something along the lines of, "on the contrary, the reality appears otherwise." Its motto was, "He who thinks, wins."[*]

So, it *was* real, but how did it work?

I knew what a devil's advocate was. What I didn't know, but soon learned, was that the devil's advocate was an actual office in the Roman Catholic Church. *Advocatus diaboli* is the popular title given to the *promotor fidei,* or "promoter of the faith," an important officer of the Sacred Congregation of Rites whose job is to challenge all nominations for sainthood through a skeptical analysis of the candidate's character and supposed miracles. While this function has changed over time, the Catholic Church still employs hostile witnesses as part of the process of vetting potential saints. In 2002, for example, the Church called atheists Christopher Hitchens and Aroup Chatterjee to testify against Mother Teresa during her beatification proceedings. Hitchens later complained that he had not been paid for this service and had, therefore, represented the Devil pro bono.

While that might seem a bit comical to laypeople, I could see how a similar approach could be used to stress-test military planning assumptions.

Or a new product strategy.

Or a merger proposal.

Or a business plan.

But what was this "red team" that Buchman referred to?

---

[*]This motto is a riff on the tagline of Britain's vaunted Special Air Service, or SAS, commandos: "He who dares, wins."

RED TEAMING

Before covering the automobile industry in Detroit, I had spent much of the 1990s covering the high-tech industry in Silicon Valley. There, I had heard the term *red team* used in reference to the "white hat" hackers companies paid to break into their computer networks in order to expose vulnerabilities so that those holes could be patched before the more nefarious "black hat" hackers discovered them. These red teams were widely employed to help protect sensitive computer networks and the data stored on them. But they did not seem to be what Buchman was referring to when he used the term *red team*.

It turns out there are many different types of red teams. In addition to the *cybersecurity red teams* I encountered in Silicon Valley, there are *penetration testing red teams* that probe the physical security of everything from secret government installations to corporate research-and-development laboratories. For example, U.S. Department of Homeland Security red teams send agents armed with fake bombs through airport screening lines to see if the Transportation Safety Administration's inspectors can catch them (too often, they cannot). Both military and business war-gamers use *threat emulation red teams* as stand-ins for the enemy. That enemy can be a rogue state or a rival company. Finally, there are *decision support red teams,* which use critical and contrarian thinking to stress-test strategies, plans, and theories. These were the sort of red teams Buchman was talking about, and as I learned more about them, I became convinced that this sort of red teaming was exactly what companies needed to dispel groupthink and complacency and cope with a rapidly changing—and increasingly uncertain—world.

* * *

The Israelis may have been the first to see the potential of red teaming, but they were not the last. The terrorist attacks of September 11, 2001, and the disastrous wars that followed humbled the American military and intelligence agencies, prompting them to seek out new ways of thinking and alternative methods of analysis.

It was a sobering time for America's generals and spymasters. The fall of the Soviet Union and the U.S.-led coalition's stunning victory in a one-sided war with Iraq in 1991 had convinced them that America's technological superiority and mastery of information would guarantee her security at home and victory abroad for the foreseeable future. In the ruins of the twin towers and the short-lived victories in Afghanistan and Iraq, they discovered just how wrong they had been.

U.S. intelligence agencies and military planners were determined to avoid making similar mistakes in the future by thinking more deeply and more skeptically about the challenges and opportunities that faced America around the world. To that end, they began pulling together an array of critical thinking and groupthink mitigation techniques, and they began assembling red teams tasked with using these tools to evaluate their strategies and plans. These red teams were soon offering alternative interpretations of intelligence in Washington and challenging existing strategies for combating insurgents in Afghanistan and Iraq.

The penetrating insights and sobering analyses offered by these red teams raised a lot of eyebrows—not just in the United States, but also around the world. As reports generated by U.S. red teams were shared with allied forces, other countries saw the value of this contrarian approach and were eager to emulate it. Soon, the British, Canadians, and Australians had established their own red teams.

When they did, they turned to the cutting-edge red team training program the U.S. Army had created at Fort Leavenworth for inspiration and guidance. It had emerged as the gold standard for red team instruction. Even the rival U.S. Marine Corps sent its officers there for training. So did other government agencies, such as the Department of Homeland Security, Customs and Border Protection, and the Drug Enforcement Administration. If I wanted to learn everything there was to learn about red teaming, this was the place to do it. No one from outside the government or military had ever been allowed to take the army's full red teaming course, but I was determined to be the first.

I called the Pentagon, and asked if I could enroll.

* * *

The army's initial answer was, not surprisingly, no. But if my twenty-plus years as a journalist had taught me anything, it was never to take *no* for an answer. So I reached out directly to the head of the program, a retired army colonel named Steve Rotkoff. He had been one of the first officers to propose the idea of decision support red teaming back in 2004, and from what I had heard, he was its most ardent evangelist. If anyone in the military would help me, I was sure it would be him.

By the time I called Rotkoff, I had read everything I could find about red teaming, including the *U.S. Army Red Team Manual,* which Rotkoff had helped write. The more I read, the more I became convinced the army had developed something of real business value. Here was a systematic way to make critical and contrarian thinking part of the planning and decision-making process of a large organization. If it worked in such a rigidly hierarchical and bureaucratic organization as the army, I knew it could work in corporations, too. And when I discussed what I had learned about red teaming with my corporate clients and senior executives at companies whose insights I valued, they were just as interested and intrigued as I was.

"When can you start teaching us how to do this?" one CEO asked me when I was still trying to figure out exactly what red teaming actually entailed. "We need red teaming *now.*"

I had never encountered an idea that generated such immediate and universal interest. But it was the response I got from my contacts at Amazon and Google that convinced me red teaming could be something game-changing.

Amazon and Google are famous (or infamous, if you happened to be one of their competitors) for disrupting entire industries. Other companies study them closely, desperate to catch a glimpse of the secret of their success. When I described red teaming to my friends at Google and Amazon, they all said the same thing: *This sounds really familiar. This sounds a lot like how we do things.*

"We don't call it red teaming. In fact, we don't have a name for it at all," said one friend who was fairly high up in Amazon. "But we do a lot of what you're describing as part of our internal planning process. We always have. It's just something that Jeff [Bezos] instilled in us—something he made part of our DNA from the very beginning. It is a big part of the reason why we are so effective at looking at other companies and figuring out how to do what they do better. I'm often asked by other companies—particularly older, established companies—how they can be more like Amazon. And I never know what to tell them. I mean, I don't want to be a jerk and tell them, 'The only way you can do that is to tear everything down and start over again from scratch, because that's how we've always done things around here since the very beginning.' But until now, that's the best answer I could come up with. It sounds like you've found a better one. Maybe red teaming is a way to teach these companies to think more like us."

I told Rotkoff about the enthusiasm for red teaming in business circles. I told him how important I thought it could be to companies struggling to contend with new competitors, new technologies, and the new realities of business in the twenty-first century. I told him I wanted to write a book that explained red teaming in a way companies could make sense of so they could start using this approach to deal with those challenges and opportunities. And I told him that everyone I talked to who knew anything about red teaming told me his school was the best place in the world to learn about this revolutionary approach.

Rotkoff offered to do what he could to help.

"Let me make a few phone calls," he said.

* * *

Steve Rotkoff is nobody's idea of an army officer. He is a Jewish New Yorker of middling height and above average girth, with bushy eyebrows and a thick Brooklyn accent. His children describe him as a cross between Homer Simpson and Vito Corleone.

"I don't fit the G.I. Joe model the army likes," he acknowledges. "I also don't like to sugarcoat things."

Rotkoff was born in Flatbush in 1955. His father was an advertising guy from the *Mad Men* era who ran his own agency in the city. It was a small firm, with five or six employees, and the family's fortunes varied with the amount of work coming through the front door. Business was good when Rotkoff turned twelve, and the family left Brooklyn for Croton-on-Hudson. But it was bad when it came time to decide on a college.

"You're a smart boy," Rotkoff's father told him when he was a junior in high school. "Get a scholarship someplace."

The next day, a West Point cadet showed up at Croton-Harmon High School to extoll the merits of the United States Military Academy. When Rotkoff learned that West Point was not only free to attend but actually *paid* its cadets, he asked how he could apply. When he got accepted, his parents were relieved. But the rest of his family was dismayed.

"Why would you want to be a *Cossack*?!" they demanded, referring to the Russian irregulars who had driven his family and countless other Jews out of Eastern Europe. As a result, they now viewed all soldiers with a mix of contempt and fear. Rotkoff assured his relatives he had no intention of becoming a Cossack. He had a plan. He would go to West Point for two years, save his cadet's salary, then transfer to a civilian school before he incurred any obligation to the army. Then would come law school and a good job with a respectable firm in Manhattan.

"Unfortunately for my family, I discovered that West Point does a tremendous job of propagandizing you once you are there. They remind you that you can *transfer* from Harvard, but you can only *quit* West Point. It is a very effective strategy, because most of the people who enroll in West Point are not quitters—and neither was I," Rotkoff recalled. "I told my family that I would just serve the minimum five years that I now owed the army, then resign my commission, go to law school, and become a lawyer. But once I became an army officer, I found I really liked it, too."

It helped that Rotkoff's first supervisor, Major Jack Jacobs, was another Jew from Brooklyn who shared Rotkoff's sarcastic sense of humor. Jacobs also happened to be one of only three Jews to receive the Congressional Medal of Honor since the end of World War II. As a result of his heroism in Vietnam, he had also come home with two Silver Stars, three Bronze Stars, and two Purple Hearts. Jacobs became Rotkoff's mentor and showed him that he could flourish as a Cossack.

Rotkoff found his niche in military intelligence. It was the one place where his sharp intellect was rewarded and his sharp tongue was tolerated. Rotkoff's success as an intelligence officer prompted Uncle Sam to pay for three master's degrees. The army even sent him to its elite School of Advanced Military Studies, whose graduates were known as "Jedi knights." By September 11, 2001, Rotkoff had made colonel and was in command of the 504th Military Intelligence Brigade at Fort Hood, Texas. On that fateful day, he was at Fort Huachuca in Arizona with other senior intel officers for meetings with the new head of the army's Intelligence Center. Rotkoff was heading for the showers after his morning workout in the base gym when the first plane hit the World Trade Center. He huddled around the locker room television with a group of other half-naked men and watched his city burn. A few hours later, he was on a military jet back to Fort Hood with orders to prepare his brigade for war.

While those preparations were still under way, Rotkoff was asked by Major General James "Spider" Marks to help oversee intelligence for the ground invasion of Iraq. Marks had been tapped by General David

McKiernan, the commander of the Coalition ground forces then assembling in the Arabian Desert, to be his staff intelligence officer. Rotkoff had been two years behind Marks at West Point, and Marks thought he was one of the brightest officers in the army. He asked Rotkoff to be his deputy, telling him he needed someone by his side who was not afraid to speak his mind: "You have complete authority to be strident and borderline disruptive and insubordinate."

It was an offer Rotkoff could not refuse.

Rotkoff threw himself into the task of planning the invasion. His entire career had been leading up to this moment. He was excited, but he was also worried. Rotkoff could not shake a nagging feeling that everything was moving too fast. He and his team were still scouring satellite photos, looking for Saddam Hussein's elusive weapons of mass destruction to make sure that they could not be used against Coalition forces when the first tanks began lining up just south of the Iraqi frontier. By the time those tanks crossed the Line of Departure on March 20, 2003, Rotkoff had come to believe that the United States was making a big mistake—a mistake that might have been avoided if only the nation had taken more time to think the whole thing through a little more carefully, to challenge its assumptions about the region and its people, and to ask the tough questions that no one had bothered to ask until it was too late.

Rotkoff gave vent to his feelings in his war journal, which became a book of haiku:

> *Where is WMD?*
> *What a kick if he has none*
> *Sorry about that*

> *Saddam Fedhayeen*
> *Where the hell did they come from?*
> *Everyone missed it*

We knew how to fight
Not so, building a NATION
We may lose the PEACE

Two years later, after watching the victory he and his fellow soldiers had won so easily unravel with almost equal haste, Rotkoff would help convince the army's top generals to create a system to ensure that never happened again. They would call that system *red teaming*.

*   *   *

Rotkoff called me back in February 2015 to inform me that I had to report to Fort Leavenworth in one month to begin my red team training.

"I finally found the right lawyer to give me the right *fatwa*," Rotkoff said with a chuckle, apologizing for the short notice. "Things take a long time to happen in the army, but when they finally do happen, they happen fast."

I would have a lot to do during the next four weeks. Rotkoff had managed to get me not just into the red teaming program, but into the red team leader course, which was responsible for training the officers who would head up the army's red teams. That meant three months of training at the University of Foreign Military and Cultural Studies.

"I have to warn you, this is a very intense program," Rotkoff told me before I set out for Kansas. "We push our students to really question themselves, to challenge their own thinking and think critically about their own experiences. Many of your classmates will have had some pretty intense experiences downrange, and most of them will be redeploying as soon as you guys graduate. So this is not going to be your typical grad school seminar."

It wasn't. It was a lot better—once everyone got used to having a civilian in their midst.

* * *

Having failed to achieve anything resembling a discreet entrance on the first day of class, I was grateful that Dr. Benson wasted little time getting down to business. Instead of worrying about me, my classmates were soon focused on the "Classroom R.O.E."—or *rules of engagement,* as the major sitting next to me explained. He would spend a lot of time translating military acronyms for me over the next few months. As I learned in the introductions that followed, these men—and one woman—had seen firsthand the missteps that had spurred the military to develop red teaming. They knew what those mistakes had cost. Some of them had paid dearly for them themselves. There was no hidden cost to war for these people; they knew the full tally and had helped cover the bill. They were a far cry from the fist-pumping, *hooah*-shouting stereotype of the American G.I. They were skeptical, critical, and analytical. In other words, they were ideally suited to become red teamers.

When my turn came to introduce myself, I told them how I had become interested in red teaming, why I thought it would prove so valuable for business, and how I hoped to share its secrets with the wider world. I asked for their permission to record our classroom sessions. Nobody objected. Later that day, when we were checking out our textbooks at the base library, one of the intel officers in my class tapped me on the shoulder.

"You have an interesting story," he said with a wicked smile. "Former journalist, now a business consultant. It's the exact sort of cover story a spy would use."

"Damn!" I hissed. "I thought I had you all fooled."

Everybody broke out laughing, and I knew my fears about being accepted in the class were entirely misplaced. The next day, the class voted to forgo their uniforms for the next three months to make me feel more at home.

And I did feel at home. I wasn't just accepted by my classmates; I also became good friends with several of them. Over the next few months,

I got to know them well, and their unique perspectives helped me better appreciate and understand why red teaming was so valuable, and so necessary. Our nightly reading assignment averaged more than two hundred pages. We read books on the psychology of human thought and decision making written by eminent scholars such as Daniel Kahneman and Gary Klein. We studied manuals of intelligence analysis penned by former spies such as Richard Heuer and Morgan Jones. We read books on anthropology, religion, and history. Of course, we studied war plans and read military classics by the likes of Carl von Clausewitz and Antoine-Henri Jomini, but we also read a lot of business books by authors such as Michael Lewis and Peter Senge. Just as I had figured out the business world could learn a lot from the military, the military had figured out it could learn a lot from the world of business.

* * *

Halfway through my course, I got a call from Alan Mulally. I told him I was with the army at Fort Leavenworth, and he wanted to know what I was doing down there in his home state of Kansas. I told him about red teaming and the army's effort to make its plans and strategies better.

"That is the core of my management system: It's not just about looking at the risks, but also about looking at the opportunities, and building that into the operating rhythms of the company so that the senior leadership team is continually checking this," he told me. "Because your competitors are changing, the technology is changing, and you're *never* done. You always need to be working on a *better* plan to serve your customers and grow your business."

Mulally had retired from Ford in the summer of 2014, and since leaving the automaker he had been traveling around America and talking with CEOs of many of the country's largest corporations, and what he had become even more convinced of is the need for this sort of rigorous questioning.

"It's an exciting thing. It's a healthy thing. If you ask those sorts of questions about what you are doing, then you don't wake up at night with the anxiety that I'm seeing everywhere," he said. "Right now, everybody is looking out for the next Uber. Everybody is worried about being disrupted. But rather than worry about that, why not just make that part of the job and work it into the operating rhythm of the company?"

I told Mulally that was exactly what red teaming was all about, and I shared some of the tools and techniques I was learning from the military.

"That type of approach is essential," Mulally said. "The companies that I've seen that are moving ahead in the world are *never* satisfied with where they are. They're always looking for a better plan. They're never satisfied with where their products and services are today. If you combine red teaming with my Working Together Management System, you've got something *really* powerful—because that is what *working together* is all about!"

* * *

We graduated in June 2015. Like the rest of my classmates, I received my official red team leader certificate from the U.S. Army. Unlike them, I went home to Michigan, while they reported to their next assignment, in Iraq, South Korea, or some classified location in Africa. But I continued my research and education into red teaming.

I studied with the U.S. Marine Corps and talked to the leading red team thinkers from the British Ministry of Defence and NATO. I sought out the men and women who had done pioneering work in the intelligence community, as well as red teamers from other branches of government. I met with the cognitive psychologists whose work had provided the scientific foundations for red teaming and talked to executives from companies that were beginning to use elements of red teaming to plan better, make sounder decisions, and even pick better investments. As I did this, I began piloting these tools and techniques with my consulting clients, helping companies in the United States and around the world use red teaming to improve their plans and make better strategic decisions. In the process, I refined the methods I learned from the military and intelligence communities, adjusted these techniques to meet the unique demands of business, and incorporated new tools that were already in use in the private sector.

This book reflects all of those learnings—and there have been a lot of them. But the biggest one is this: Red teaming works. It works for small California tech start-ups and Japanese sovereign wealth funds. It works for old, iconic corporations and innovative disruptors. It works for nonprofits and hedge funds. And it can work for your company, too, if you let it.

Hard Lessons: The Origins of Red Teaming

*Failure is only the opportunity to begin
again, this time more intelligently.*

—Henry Ford

If American military red teaming has an origin story, it began one
night in November 2002, when a white, windowless van pulled up
in front of the headquarters of Coalition Forces Land Component
Command at Camp Doha in Kuwait. The converted warehouse was
one of the few permanent structures on the rapidly expanding base,
which was growing like a gathering storm just over the horizon from
the Iraqi border. Inside, Colonel Steve Rotkoff was waiting with his
boss, Major General James "Spider" Marks, the head of military intelligence for the allied ground forces, and Major General James Thurman,

the head of operations. All three men were outfitted for war, wearing sand-colored battle dress with Beretta 9mms strapped to their thighs. Rotkoff had no idea where they were going. Since he had been told to bring his helmet, he knew they were headed off base. But both generals had their own drivers and never traveled outside the wire without their personal security details. Those were nowhere in sight. However, as the three men crunched across the gravel to the waiting van, Rotkoff could see two Americans in civilian clothes waiting in the front seats. The guy riding shotgun had a carbine on his lap.

CIA, Rotkoff thought. *I guess this is their show.*

Nobody said a word as the door slammed shut and the van lurched forward, spraying gravel in its wake. As they approached the main gate, General Marks turned to Rotkoff.

"We're headed into Kuwait City. We're going to meet somebody that the CIA is bringing in for us to talk to," he said. "Your job is to take notes."

Rotkoff nodded.

The van drove to a corrugated metal building somewhere on the outskirts of the city. A heavy steel door rolled up to let them in, along with the smell of hot sand, which permeated everything in Kuwait. Another door opened at the opposite end of the building to admit an identical windowless white van, which pulled up alongside theirs as both the building's doors crashed shut. The door of the other van slid open to reveal a bearded Iraqi cleric wearing a black turban and billowing black robe. He gathered his robes around him and emerged, followed by his interpreter. One of the CIA men made the introductions as the rest of the agents took up their positions at the building's doors and fingered the safeties on their carbines.

The imam's name was Sayyid Abdul Majid al-Khoei. He was a prominent Shi'ite leader from the holy city of Najaf. The CIA informed the army officers that he was going to be "our man in Iraq." They had arranged the meeting so that Marks and Thurman could interview al-

Khoei. He would provide valuable local information to help them fine-tune the invasion plan.

As Rotkoff looked around, he realized the building was the very definition of the word *nondescript*. If it had a purpose other than this meeting, all traces of it had been removed. The space now contained only a small table set with bottled water and surrounded by half a dozen chairs. Three were simple, padded folding chairs; the other three were high-backed leather swivel chairs that seemed to have been swiped from some corporate office. The imam was shown to one of those. The generals took the other two. The interpreter and Rotkoff were left with their choice of folding chairs. Rotkoff took the one to the left of Marks and pulled out his notebook. As he did, al-Khoei reached into his robe and produced a fistful of fat, Cuban cigars, which he offered to everyone at the table with a smile. Marks and Rotkoff shook their heads. They did not smoke. General Thurman did. He took one, then two when he saw the brand.

"What do you want to know?" al-Khoei asked with a smile as he lit one and puffed on it.

The generals looked at each other and then began a rapid-fire barrage of questions.

"What are the highways like in Iraq?"

"How well are they maintained?"

"What are the roads like when you get into Baghdad?"

"What about your hometown, Najaf?"

"How wide are the streets?"

"Can we get tanks in there?"

They asked a lot of questions about the dams that tamed the Tigris and Euphrates. They were worried Saddam Hussein would blow them to flood the southern part of the country and slow the Coalition's advance. Did al-Khoei think that was likely?

"Perhaps," he said, with what Rotkoff perceived as a growing impatience with the line of questioning.

"How about the Iraqi army?"

"Will the men stand and fight?"

"How can we encourage them to surrender?"

"What should we say to them in our propaganda?"

"Is there a particular message that would resonate with them?"

The imam continued to answer the generals' questions, but Rotkoff could tell he was getting more and more frustrated. *We're asking the wrong questions,* he thought as he studied the cleric's face. But his job was just to take notes.

After about an hour of these questions, al-Khoei had had enough. He raised his hand and cut Thurman off midquestion.

"Stop," the imam said firmly. "Let me ask *you* a question."

"Okay," the general agreed. "Go ahead."

"Once you've toppled Saddam and freed my country, how long do you intend to stay?"

Thurman and Marks explained that the U.S. military planned to pull out of Iraq a year after the liberation of Baghdad. Iraq would not be that different from France after World War II. It had an educated population. It had industry that could be rebuilt. And it had oil and natural gas to pay for it all. The Americans were confident that the Iraqi people would pick themselves up, dust themselves off, and continue their march of progress right where they had left off when Hussein decided to invade Kuwait back in 1990. Foreign troops would just get in their way.

The imam looked at each of the men without speaking, then took a long drag on his cigar and exhaled a rolling cloud of smoke along with a deep sigh as he leaned back in his chair.

"Saddam tortured my father," he began, speaking slowly to make certain the translator missed nothing. "Saddam killed my brother. Saddam imprisoned my mother."

For the next five minutes, al-Khoei listed each member of his extended family that had been killed, tortured, raped, or imprisoned on the orders of the Iraqi dictator.

"I tell you all this so that you know that I am no friend of Saddam

Hussein's," al-Khoei said when he had finished this litany of atrocities. "But if that is your plan, you need to call the invasion off. You need to take all of your tanks, all of your planes, all of your men, and go home. Just let us continue to die our slow death under Saddam—because, believe me, what you will unleash if you go ahead with your plan will be much, much worse."

Marks and Thurman were visibly shaken by the cleric's words.

"Why?" Marks asked after a long, awkward moment.

"Because you do not understand Iraq," al-Khoei said.

For the next hour, he proceeded to school them. He explained how Saddam Hussein and his Ba'ath Party had spent decades playing clan against clan, tribe against tribe, religious faction against religious faction. He told them about the British occupation of Iraq after World War I, how the wounds suffered during the decades of colonial oppression had still not fully healed for many of his countrymen. He told them about the guns every Iraqi family kept hidden in their homes, about the underground criminal networks that even Saddam's secret police had been unable to choke off, and about the fault lines of informal power relationships among families and tribes that American military planners had not even begun to factor into their calculus of postwar Iraq.

"You are wrong. This is not going to be the liberation of Paris with pretty girls throwing flowers at your feet," al-Khoei warned. "This is going to be post-Tito Yugoslavia. *Everybody* is going to kill *everybody*."

The two American generals looked at each other and shook their heads.

"How long do you think we should be prepared to stay in your country?" Thurman asked warily.

The imam pulled out another cigar, lit it, and took another long drag.

"How long have you been in Germany? Sixty years?" he asked. "That should be about right. It's going to take two generations to change Iraq. Maybe then you can leave."

It was a long ride back to Camp Doha. For a while, nobody said anything. They were dumbstruck. They had thought the whole thing through a hundred times or more, from the moment they would unleash hell on Baghdad until the day the last American soldier boarded the plane for home. But there was so much that they had not even considered. Finally, Thurman broke the silence.

"I can't believe he thinks we're going to be there for sixty years," the general said.

Marks and Rotkoff just shook their heads.

Rotkoff started writing his report that night. He had taken copious notes, and he left nothing out. It was all there—everything the imam had warned them about. Marks and Thurman read it over the next morning and e-mailed it directly to the two men in charge of the invasion, Coalition Forces Land Component Commander General David McKiernan and his boss, Central Command, or CENTCOM, commander General Tommy Franks. They forwarded it to the White House, where it was presumably included in President George W. Bush's daily intelligence briefing. Rotkoff waited for word that the invasion was being put on hold, that everything was being reconsidered in light of this important new information. But nothing happened.*

Rotkoff's report had no impact at all on the invasion plan. Nobody mentioned it again. It was quickly forgotten as the generals became consumed with the thousand details that needed to be sorted out before the invasion could begin. America was not ready for this war. Neither were her allies. There was so much to do, and so little time to think. Yet, Rotkoff could not stop thinking about what the imam had said.

He was still thinking about it four months later as he watched the jets scream toward Baghdad, heavy with their payloads of shock and awe. He was thinking about it three weeks later as he listened to General

---

*It is worth noting that Colonel Kevin Benson, my instructor at the University of Foreign Military and Cultural Studies, was never even informed of this meeting or given a copy of the report—even though he and his staff were responsible for planning the invasion and occupation of Iraq.

McKiernan curse the overzealous tankers pulling down the statue of Saddam Hussein in Baghdad's Firdos Square. And he was still thinking about it the day after that when word arrived at headquarters that Imam al-Khoei had been murdered by a mob outside the Imam Ali Shrine in his home city of Najaf—an assassination ordered by rival Shi'ite cleric Muqtada al-Sadr, one of the first of what would ultimately be tens of thousands of internecine killings that would paint Iraq red with blood, just as al-Khoei had predicted that night in the CIA safe house in Kuwait City.

"It was the first realization that things were really going to be as bad as he said they were going to be," Rotkoff later told me. "People always talk about watershed events. This was a watershed event in my life. I was a different person after this."

That person would go on to challenge the way the army planned, the way the army made decisions, even the way the army thought. He would help create an entirely new way of doing all these things—a revolutionary new approach the army would call *red teaming*.

Never Again

Thirty years earlier, and a few hundred miles to the west, two armies were massing on another border.

At 2:00 p.m., on October 6, 1973, hundreds of Egyptian jets screamed into Israel, strafing airbases, bombing command posts, and lighting up Israeli air defense batteries with their rockets. Five minutes later, almost two thousand Egyptian howitzers, guns, and mortars began pummeling the fortified Israeli positions east of the Suez Canal. Then came the water cannons, massive high-pressure pumps that cut through the towering sand wall the Israelis had erected on the eastern bank like a wave through a sand castle. Beneath those plumes of water, rubber rafts filled with commandos oared across the canal. By the time they reached the other side, Egyptian combat engineers had already begun erecting pontoon bridges, and Egyptian tanks were soon streaming through gaps cut by the water cannons. Beyond that rampart lay the heavily fortified Bar-Lev Line, which was supposed to hold for at least a day—hopefully two—giving the Israelis time to mount a counterattack. The Egyptians breached it in less than two hours. As the stunned defenders emerged from their bunkers waving white handkerchiefs, columns of Egyptian tanks poured around them like an onrushing flood, pushing the overwhelmed Israeli Defense Forces back across the Sinai Peninsula toward Jerusalem.

At the same moment some 250 miles to the northeast, Syrian paratroopers backed by MiG fighter-bombers launched an airborne assault on Mount Hermon, Israel's sophisticated electronic surveillance installation that served as its "Eyes on the Golan." Those eyes were quickly put out, and hundreds of Syrian artillery pieces began raining shells down on the Israeli defensive line that stretched along the Golan Heights. As more jets joined the fray, five Syrian divisions slammed into that line. The outnumbered Israelis held their ground through the night, but by morning, the Syrians had broken through. In the early hours of October 7, as the first Syrian tanks crested an escarpment overlooking the Sea of Galilee, Israeli Defense Minister Moshe Dayan told his generals to get ready to blow bridges over the Jordan River. Then he called Prime Minister Golda Meir.

"The Third Temple is going under," he told her.

It was code. It meant Israel was falling.

According to some reports, Meir responded by giving Dayan permission to activate the country's nuclear arsenal. A dozen bombs were assembled. If Israel was going down, it would take the Arab world with it. But the Arab advance began to lose steam before the order to arm the warheads was given.

Over the next two weeks, Israeli troops, supported by rushed shipments of weapons and ammunition from the United States, halted the Egyptians and Syrians and began to push their armies back. A cease-fire went into effect on October 25.

The Yom Kippur War did little to shift the boundaries in the Middle East, but it shook Israel to its very foundations. The Israeli government established a special commission headed by Shimon Agranat, chief justice of the country's Supreme Court, to figure out how preparations for such a massive military operation had gone undetected. As the commission soon learned, they had not.

Israel's Military Intelligence Directorate, AMAN, had been quite aware of the troop buildup in Syria and Egypt. AMAN's director, Eli Zeira, had given Meir and her cabinet regular briefings about the latest developments in both countries in the days leading up to the attack. But he and other members of her national security team had shrugged those troops movements off as saber rattling—even after King Hussein of Jordan took the unprecedented step of flying to Tel Aviv in his helicopter to personally warn the prime minister that an invasion was imminent.

The Israelis knew the Egyptians had begun calling up their reserves on September 27. It was reported on Egyptian radio and television networks. Over the next three days, Israeli soldiers on the eastern bank of the Suez watched through their binoculars as Egyptian bulldozers on the other side began plowing roads through the sand to the water's edge. Israeli reconnaissance flights came back with pictures of bridging material being moved to the western bank of the canal. Meanwhile, Israeli pilots flying along the Syrian border counted two thousand tanks being rolled into forward positions along the frontier. Yet Meir and her cabinet concluded that the Arabs were just trying to pressure Israel to give back the territory it had seized from them in the last war. They had played similar games before, and responding to their empty threats had been costly and needlessly alarming for the populace.

The Israelis told the U.S. Central Intelligence Agency as much when the Americans began urging them to prepare their defenses. But the CIA was not so sure. The CIA told the Israelis that, this time, Egypt and Syria did not appear to be bluffing. So did Israel's own spy agency, the Mossad. On September 30, Mossad told AMAN that a reliable intelligence source in Egypt had warned that what the Egyptians were publicly calling a training exercise would culminate in an actual attempt to cross the Suez Canal. Zeira dismissed all these reports as "baseless." He assured Meir and the rest of the cabinet that the Arabs knew Israel could defeat their armies in a single day.

On October 2, the Egyptian press reported the country's army had been placed on full alert. Yet, at a cabinet meeting on October 3, Zeira told Meir the probability of war was still "low."

By October 4, Israeli reconnaissance flights could clearly see the massive buildup of men, tanks, and guns taking place on the Egyptian side of the Suez. Moreover, the Soviets—allies of Egypt and Syria—had begun evacuating dependents and other nonessential personnel from the two Arab states. But the Israelis remained unconvinced.

In the early hours of October 5, Mossad's best Arab source called his handler and spoke the code word *radish,* which meant war was imminent. The chief of Mossad was so worried, he flew to Europe to meet with that source in person to confirm it. Once he had, the Mossad chief contacted Zeira directly and told him war *was* coming. A few hours later, the Russians provided their own confirmation by ordering all their ships in Arab ports to put to sea immediately. Reluctantly, Meir put the Israeli Defense Forces on heightened alert that morning, but stopped short of calling up its reserves. This was critical, because Israel has a small standing army. Its defense strategy relies on its ability to rapidly activate its enormous reserves, which then included just about every Jewish man and woman of fighting age in the country. Meir and her cabinet decided to let them stay asleep as they continued to monitor developments through the night.

At 4:00 a.m. on October 6, the Mossad called Zeira to inform him that their man in Cairo had just provided the exact time of the attack: The invasion would begin at 2:00 p.m. that afternoon. When Golda Meir met with her military advisers later that morning, they finally agreed war was likely. With just hours to spare, she issued the order to call up the reserves.

The Agranat Commission blamed these colossal intelligence failures on something called "The Concept." The Concept was a product of Israel's stunning victory in the 1967 Arab-Israeli War. That victory made the nation's military leaders overconfident in their own abilities and dismissive of their foes. So did the success of subsequent Israeli intelligence operations, which led them to believe they knew exactly what the Arabs were thinking. And what the Arabs were thinking, per the The Concept, was this:

1. Because of the staggering losses they had suffered at the hands of the Israeli Air Force in the previous wars, the Egyptians would not try to invade Israel again until they were certain their air force could control the skies.

2. Syria would never attack Israel alone; it would only do so in partnership with Egypt in order to force Israel to fight on two fronts.

For six years, The Concept had proven true. Yes, there had been isolated military clashes between Israel and its neighbors. Yet, while the Arabs had tried to make the Israelis think they were about to attack more than once, there had been no invasion. What began as a theory had become an axiom—and each time that axiom proved correct, those who questioned it looked more foolish. So people stopped questioning The Concept, even in the face of overwhelming evidence to the contrary. As David T. Buckwalter, a professor of national security affairs at the U.S. Naval War College, would later write:

> By October 1973 the "concept" had been "proven." It was a given that Egypt would not go to war while still inferior in the air. Therefore, although the Israelis believed Syria was preparing for some sort of military action, by the tenets of the "concept," Syria would not attack.

But there was a problem with The Concept. It assumed the only way Egypt could control the skies was by building a better air force. What the Israelis did not know was that Egypt had given up on that idea. Instead, the Egyptians had embraced a new military technology: mobile surface-to-air missiles. The Soviets had developed some very sophisticated ones, and they had been willing to sell them to Egypt at a good price. The Egyptians realized that, armed with enough of these mobile rockets, they could form a formidable air defense shield over their men and tanks—a shield that could advance with them across the Suez Canal, through the Sinai, and on into Israel. Egypt and Syria had also been buying SCUD missiles from the Soviets, giving them the ability to strike deep into Israel without risking their vulnerable bombers. The Israelis were aware of these purchases but ignored them. Why? Because they were looking for airplanes.

The Concept was a textbook example of how groupthink and complacency can lead to disaster. To make sure the disaster of the Yom Kippur War was not repeated, the Agranat Commission made several recommendations. One of these was the formation of a special "devil's advocate" office inside AMAN that would be tasked with challenging all future concepts and assumptions.

After that office was established, it became known by the code name *Ipcha Mistabra* (which, as I mentioned in the Introduction, means "on the contrary, the reality appears otherwise" in Aramaic). Its job is to pick apart the reports generated by AMAN's regular analysts and produce papers that argue the opposite of whatever the prevailing opinion is inside the directorate. *Ipcha Mistabra* also prepares worst-case scenarios and alternative futures analyses that are used to inform Israel's long-term military planning. Its job is not necessarily to be right; its job is to force the organization as a whole to think harder and question its own assumptions.

According to a 2007 report by the Brookings Institution, "the staff in the devil's advocate office is made up of extremely experienced and talented officers who are known to have a creative, 'outside the box' way of thinking." These men and women are "highly regarded" by their peers and superiors, and "their memos go directly to the office of the Director of Military Intelligence, as well as to all major decision makers."

The directorate's regular analysts are also encouraged to write "different opinion" memos that challenge the conclusions of their departments if they disagree with them. This practice is officially sanctioned, and Brookings found that analysts do not face retaliation or criticism for exercising this privilege.

The Israelis did not call it *red teaming* when they first decided to institutionalize this sort of contrarian thinking back in the 1970s, but red teaming is exactly what *Ipcha Mistabra* does—and it has proven extraordinarily effective. The office is credited with helping the Israelis avoid another surprise attack like the one that almost cost them their country in 1973. Some of Israel's brightest military thinkers have called for the expansion of its use throughout the country's armed forces.

"It's taken quite seriously—at least inside the Intelligence Directorate," says former IDF officer Eytan Buchman. "It's now enshrined in the way the IDF operates."

A Failure of Imagination

As with Israel, it would take a surprise attack to show America the limits of its intelligence analysis. After the terrorist attacks of September 11, 2001, toppled the twin towers of the World Trade Center, cut a furrow of destruction through the Pentagon, and cost thousands of Americans their lives, the United States formed its own version of the Agranat Commission to find out how America's intelligence agencies and vast national security apparatus had failed to detect and derail the terrorist plot. The National Commission on Terrorist Attacks Upon the United States, also known as the 9/11 Commission, found that:*

---

*The 9/11 Commission was established by President George W. Bush on November 27, 2002. Former New Jersey governor Tom Kean was ultimately tapped to head the commission on December 15, 2002. Its first hearings were not held until March 31, 2003. The 9/11 Commission released its final report on July 22, 2004.

The 9/11 attacks were a shock, but they should not have come as a surprise. Islamist extremists had given plenty of warning that they meant to kill Americans indiscriminately and in large numbers. . . . During the spring and summer of 2001, U.S. intelligence agencies received a stream of warnings that al-Qaeda planned, as one report put it, "something very, very, very big." Director of Central Intelligence George Tenet told us, "The system was blinking red."

So why were these warnings ignored? The commission concluded that "the most important failure was one of imagination."

The CIA did not wait for the 9/11 Commission's report to begin setting things right. As survivors were still being pulled from the rubble of the World Trade Center, Tenet ordered the formation of a new team with orders to "think unconventionally" about the security challenges that now faced the United States. Tenet called the group the "Red Cell."

"Tenet decided to form a group of contrarian thinkers to challenge conventional wisdom in the intelligence community and mitigate the threat of additional surprises through 'alternative analysis,'" wrote national security expert Micah Zenko in a 2015 piece for *Foreign Policy* magazine, which offered a rare glimpse inside this secretive organization.

According to the CIA, the "Red Cell takes a pronounced 'out-of-the-box' approach and produces memos intended to provoke thought rather than to provide authoritative assessment." Those memos changed the way the CIA thought, and the Red Cell was deemed so effective that the 2004 Intelligence Reform and Terrorism Prevention Act mandated red teaming for all U.S. intelligence agencies.

By then, the U.S. Army had also begun developing its own version of red teaming.

The term *red team* dates back to the early 1800s, when the Prussian army began using *Kriegsspiel,* or "war gaming," to train its officers. One group of officers would develop a battle plan, while another group would assume the role of the enemy and try to thwart it. The idea was to expose flaws or weaknesses in Prussian tactics in the safety of the war room rather than wait for them to be revealed upon the battlefield. These tabletop simulations used wooden blocks as stand-ins for military units. Because most Prussian soldiers wore blue uniforms, the home team was represented by blue game pieces. The enemy force was represented by red markers and referred to as "the red team." It was their job to probe for weaknesses in the Prussians' plans and strategies. The name stuck.

The U.S. Army developed its own version of *Kriegsspiel* in the late 1800s. But war gaming in the United States was largely limited to training young officers; it was not used to stress-test actual strategies or plans. That started to change during the Cold War, when red teams were established by the Rand Corporation to see how the Soviets might respond to American moves on the geopolitical chessboard. By the late 1990s, some in the Pentagon were beginning to see a need for the military to start red teaming itself. America's easy victories in the first Gulf War and two Balkans campaigns had not just dispelled the specter of defeat that had haunted the country since Vietnam, but also made many of her military leaders feel invincible.

"The Department of Defense was becoming overconfident to the point of hubris about its ability to dominate future military operations," recalls then Deputy Assistant Secretary of Defense for Requirements, Plans, and Counterproliferation Policy James Miller.* "Many in the military seemed to think we were on the verge of creating long-term technological supremacy against all adversaries and that would be fundamentally decisive in all future military confrontations."

Miller was not one of them. He believed the United States could not afford to take anything for granted on the battlefield. During the war in Kosovo, he had set up threat emulation red teams to gauge how Yugoslavian president Slobodan Milosevic might respond to the NATO air campaign. Those teams were effective, but Miller thought they would have been even more effective if they had been allowed to challenge the

---

*Miller later became undersecretary of defense for policy during the Obama administration.

NATO plan itself. After he left the Pentagon in 2000, Miller helped establish the Defense Adaptive Red Teaming program, or DART, at Hicks & Associates, a consulting firm that helped the Pentagon conduct war games. DART provided not only opponents for those simulations, but also contrarian analysis of military doctrine and policies.

"Much of the work focused on concepts. We would tear them apart, either through a war game or analytically," Miller said. "There was a lot of interest among senior leaders in the military in what we were doing."

The September 11 terrorist attacks took that interest to a whole new level. In 2003, a Pentagon task force recommended expanding red teams beyond their traditional threat emulation role to provide contrarian analysis and "challenge emerging operational concepts in order to discover weaknesses before real adversaries do."

That was exactly what Steve Rotkoff was doing in Iraq.

Thinking Differently

In February 2003, about a month before the invasion, Colonel Rotkoff and General Marks were approached by U.S. Marine Corps Major General Robert "Rusty" Blackman, the chief of staff at the Combined Forces Land Component Command Headquarters at Camp Doha. Blackman asked if they remembered how Saddam Hussein had ordered the destruction of the Kuwaiti oil fields as his forces retreated from that country during the first Gulf War in 1991. They did. Those fires had created not only an environmental catastrophe, but also serious problems for Coalition forces. The thick, black smoke had played havoc with their laser range finders and made it hard to see Iraqi troops when they decided to fight.* The smoke slowed the Coalition's advance, caused at

---

*The smoke from the oil fires was later citied as a major factor in the Battle of Phase Line Bullet, one of the only times the Iraqis managed to repulse an American assault during the entire war.

least one helicopter crash, and was believed to have been the source of many of the health problems that would later afflict Gulf War veterans. General Blackman wanted to make sure none of that happened this time around. He asked Marks and Rotkoff to come up with a plan for preventing the Iraqis from setting fire to their own oil fields.

Rather than approach this problem from a military perspective, Rotkoff's team called the oil field experts at Boots & Coots and asked them how one would go about blowing up an oil well if one were so inclined. They learned the most effective way was to shut down the well and plant a subsurface charge. But that would mean halting oil production. A simpler alternative was to just pack a bunch of explosives around the well and blow it up while it was still pumping. This was an important piece of information, because though Iraq was officially subject to an international oil embargo, Rotkoff and his team knew Saddam Hussein was selling oil on the black market—a lot of it—and using the proceeds of those sales to fund his regime.

"That was Saddam's only real revenue stream. That was how he was paying everyone to stay loyal. So we knew that he was going to wait until the last possible minute to blow the oil fields and that he was going to do it with surface charges that would take some time for his men to set. We also knew that he expected us to start this war like we had the last one, with a massive amount of aerial bombardment, which meant he believed he would have plenty of advance warning before he had to give that order," Rotkoff said. "At that time, the plan did in fact call for more than a week of aerial bombing before our first tanks crossed the Line of Departure. We proposed that they change the plan so that the ground invasion began *before* the air campaign. That way, we could race in and be through the oil fields—almost all of which were on the southern border—before his men even had time to rig the wells."

At the same time, Colonel Kevin Benson and his team of war planners were trying to figure out how to maintain some element of surprise in the opening hours of the ground war with almost 400,000 Coalition soldiers massed on the Iraqi border. Sending those troops over the frontier ahead of the jets would solve that problem as well, because the Iraqis expected the war to begin in the air. Rotkoff and Benson worked together to sell the idea to the higher-ups. It all made perfect sense to the generals in charge of the land forces, but the proposal did not go over well with the U.S. Air Force. It wanted to spearhead the invasion, not leave it to the ground-pounders to claim the glory. There were heated discussions among the different services and their counterparts in the allied forces. Finally, a compromise was reached that called for a short, intense air assault on Iraq, followed by a ground invasion a few hours later.

The strategy worked; the Iraqis had time to blow up only a couple of oil wells before the fields were overrun and captured.*

"That was a real success. It changed the whole beginning of the war, and we avoided the environmental disaster, the mobility problems, and all of that other stuff," Rotkoff said. "We didn't know it at the time, but we were red teaming."

In fact, Rotkoff spent part of every Sunday red teaming in the weeks leading up to the invasion. While he and the other members of Marks's intelligence staff spent most of their waking hours preparing the daily intelligence briefing for General McKiernan, there was no briefing on Sundays. It was supposed to be a day of rest. However, Rotkoff found he could not rest with the preparations for war in full swing. Instead, he started inviting the best and brightest members of his intelligence team to informal weekly gatherings that he called "Sunday Afternoon Prayer Sessions."

"The object was to discuss something that was unexamined, something that we did not have time to talk about during the week," Rotkoff explained. "I was frustrated by the fact that we were so embedded in the moment that we had no time to think about anything other than

---

*This "G-Day before A-Day" strategy took the Iraqis so completely by surprise that the army, in its official history of the war, compared it to the celebrated "left hook" maneuver that had helped the United States and her allies win such an easy victory in the first Gulf War.

moving a piece of paper from here to there. I was worried that there were things that we were missing. I wanted people to think—really *think* about what we were doing."

Participation was by invitation only, and Rotkoff invited only men and women who had demonstrated their ability to think critically. He held the meetings in a SCIF, or sensitive compartmented information facility, a room-size "cone of silence," the walls of which were filled with sophisticated electronic jamming equipment to ensure that nothing that was said or done inside could be heard or intercepted by anyone on the outside. He wanted the people he invited to be able to discuss anything—even the most sensitive topics—without reservation or hesitation. Rotkoff provided pizza and fake beer. The real thing was forbidden in Kuwait. But he let the participants set the agenda and decide what they wanted to discuss.

The most important discussion of all began right before the war started, when one of the regular members of Rotkoff's prayer group, Lieutenant Colonel Steve Peterson, asked if he could have the entire afternoon to talk about something that had been troubling him.

"I've been thinking a lot about a question that I don't think anybody in the intelligence community has been asking as we go into this fight," Peterson said hesitantly as he addressed the prayer group that Sunday. "How does Saddam win?"

Rotkoff's jaw literally dropped.

"I had been in most of the briefings leading up to the war. I had been in briefings at CENTCOM in Qatar. I'd been in briefings with V Corps in Europe. I'd been in briefings at the Pentagon in Washington. And I had *never once* heard anyone ask that question," Rotkoff said. "I mean, it would have been considered ludicrous. Saddam *couldn't* win. He was about to go up against the biggest military machine on the face of the planet. We were going to crush him. It was just a matter of how and how long it would take. Those were the only questions anyone was asking. Until now."

Peterson outlined a worst-case scenario unlike anything Rotkoff or anyone else in the room had considered. The Iraqi dictator would not stand and fight. He would go to ground and order his loyal Ba'athists to do the same. He would have members of his Republican Guard create caches of weapons and ammunition around the country. Then he would have them shed their uniforms and disappear into Iraq's crowded cities. They would tap into Iraq's criminal networks, its underground economy and black markets. They would make connections, build cells, and wait. They would wait until the Americans and their allies were confident that they had won the war, that the country had been pacified, that Saddam Hussein and his henchmen were no longer a threat. Then, they would strike.

"It all came to pass. It all happened just like Peterson had described. The only thing he got wrong was that Saddam wasn't around to lead it," Rotkoff told me over lunch one day in Kansas City twelve years later, still shaking his head at what it had cost America and her allies in blood and treasure. "We knew he was right then, too. We had stumbled upon something that really needed to be considered as part of our war planning. So we developed a briefing and showed it to Spider [Marks]. He was excited about it, and asked us to share it with McKiernan. McKiernan was also impressed and had us put together a package that he sent up to [General Tommy] Franks. It sort of died there. It never went beyond that. I don't know why. But I did know that I wanted to make sure stuff like that was duly considered next time we went to war."

Rotkoff soon got his chance to make sure stuff like that was.

Red Team University

In August 2003, General Peter Schoomaker took over as army chief of staff. A legendary Special Operations commander who had little patience for the bureaucracy of what he called "the big army," Schoomaker was appalled by the military's own failure of imagination. Though generals had warned the American people the "war on terror" would last for years, nobody had really believed it. As a result, Schoomaker inherited an army that was low on ammunition, low on soldiers, and desperately in need of new thinking. He put out an appeal for fresh ideas.

One of the best came from Rotkoff. He had retired after Baghdad fell and returned to Washington. There, he had been hired to lead a "lessons learned" team for the head of Army Intelligence, Lieutenant General Keith Alexander. Rotkoff and his group at the Pentagon used the Sunday Afternoon Prayer Sessions as a model. They proposed establishing a standing team of contrarian thinkers who would be tasked with subjecting the army's strategies and plans to a critical, independent analysis.

"The army has, historically, had an engineering mind-set. Army officers like to decide as quickly as possible on what the desired end state is so that they can begin figuring out how to get there. The problem is that, in the environment that we're in and with the world changing as rapidly as it does, you can't ever stop thinking. You have to be open to the fact that maybe—just *maybe*—you've got it wrong," Rotkoff said. "I told them how we created this space for real, meaningful conversations to take place about our strategies and plans. I knew what could come from that, and that was why I was so evangelical about it—because I knew it could really make a difference if we let it."

General Schoomaker loved the idea. To him, it sounded a lot like the way Special Forces operated. Unfettered by the army's bureaucratic decision-making processes, they would have one team develop a plan and then give that plan to another team to rip apart. Schoomaker ordered the creation of red teams throughout the army. He also ordered the establishment of a new school to train a cadre of red teamers and red team leaders to staff them.

The army set up its red team training school at Fort Leavenworth, Kansas, in 2004. In addition to housing the military's maximum security prison, the base was home to the army's Command and General Staff College and its elite School of Advanced Military Studies. As the "intellectual center of the army," it was the obvious choice to host what the army had decided to call the University of Foreign Military and Cultural Studies. The name was supposed to disguise the real purpose of the new school. But most people in the army still referred to it as "Red Team University," or, given the military's love of acronyms, simply UFMCS.*

The school's first director was a retired colonel, Greg Fontenot. Like Rotkoff, Fontenot was a warrior-philosopher bent on changing the army from within. But they were cast from two very different molds. If Rotkoff was a cross between Vito Corleone and Homer Simpson, Fontenot was a saner version of Colonel Kurtz from *Apocalypse Now,* with a bit of George S. Patton thrown in for good measure. A hard-charging tank commander who moonlighted as a military historian, Fontenot was not afraid to speak his mind—at times to his detriment. Fontenot led a tank battalion in Desert Storm and served as director of the School of Advanced Military Studies before leading an armored brigade in Bosnia in 1995. There, his lack of self-censorship caught up with him. Fontenot scuttled his chances of making general after he let a *Wall Street Journal* reporter know what he really thought of the various factions in the Bosnian civil war. The army allowed him to quietly return to the United States and serve out his career as the head of its Battle Command Training Program. The army hired him back as a civilian war-gamer,** before tapping him to lead the new school.

"They told me they wanted to train people to be devil's advocates and critique the army's planning from the inside," Fontenot recalled. "I was given a year to figure out how to do it."

Fontenot started assembling a team to develop the curriculum. He knew Rotkoff had been involved in putting together the red teaming

*UFMCS was set up under the auspices of the army's Training and Doctrine Command's Intelligence branch. Branch director Maxie McFarland was responsible for overseeing the implementation of the new red teaming program and selecting the school's first director.

**In this capacity, Fontenot had actually participated in a couple of the DART red teaming exercises.

proposal at the Pentagon, so he asked him to help. Then Fontenot hired him as the lead instructor for the first class. As different as the two men were, they shared a belief that the army needed to change the way it made big decisions.

Putting It to the Test

Their boss, General David Petraeus, agreed. As commander of Fort Leavenworth and its Combined Arms Center when UFMCS was being set up, he became an early fan of red teaming. The "surge" Petraeus led after taking command of the Multi-National Force in Iraq in early 2007 was one of the first examples of how this new approach would shape U.S. military strategy.

By the end of 2006, Americans were weary of the war in Iraq. So were the Iraqis. All of Imam al-Khoei's dire predictions had come to pass, and the sectarian violence he warned the Americans about back in 2002 was destroying what was left of the nation. More and more Coalition soldiers were dying as they struggled to maintain some semblance of order in a country that was tearing itself apart. The obvious solution, and the one favored by most Americans, was for the United States to cut its losses and withdraw completely. However, contrarian analysis revealed some big problems with that strategy. While it might appease the electorate at home, it would further damage America's reputation in the world and create a security nightmare for the Iraqis. The country might collapse and create a haven for terrorists. So, instead of pulling American troops out, General Petraeus requested that thirty thousand more be sent in to restore something resembling peace in the country. This, he argued, was the best way for America to get out.

But Petraeus did not just ask for more troops. He also changed the way those troops operated. Instead of hunkering down on fortified bases and only emerging for aggressive, heavily armed patrols that invited confrontation, Petraeus ordered his soldiers out among the population. Coalition troops were soon separating Sunnis from Shi'ites, patrolling with Iraqi forces the most dangerous neighborhoods of Baghdad and other cities, and working among the people to resolve the myriad of problems that prevented a return to normal life in Iraq. Fighting side by side with Iraqi troops, Coalition forces also went after the insurgents where they lived, drove them out, and reclaimed whole swaths of the country. Petraeus would later say that "the surge that mattered most in Iraq was not the surge of forces. It was the surge of ideas, which guided the strategy that ultimately reduced violence in the country so substantially."

And it *did* work—at least until politicians in Washington intervened, declared victory prematurely, and began pulling U.S. troops out of Iraq before the work Petraeus had them doing was finished. The country's subsequent descent into chaos did not represent a failure of the surge but rather painful proof that it had been the right strategy all along. Even politicians who had opposed the troop buildup would later acknowledge as much.

This illustrates a fundamental point about red teaming: It only works when there is buy-in from the top. That has not always been the case in the U.S. military. But in the areas in which it has been allowed to work, red teaming has helped the army respond far more effectively to emerging threats, leverage new technology, and cope with rapidly changing geopolitical realities. Because much of the work of army red teams remains classified, it is hard to offer more specifics about the many ways it has changed the military's thinking. However, the broad outlines of the work army red teams are doing says much about the way it has been embraced by senior generals.

In late 2010, the army brought in a red team leader to analyze its plan for the final withdrawal of U.S. forces from Iraq in 2011. This was a critical moment for the army, which wanted to leave the country with as little drama as possible and avoid any scenes that might remind people of America's humiliating departure from South Vietnam in 1975. The red team helped fine-tune the plan, and it worked. The army has also used red teams to critique its strategies, from the Korean Peninsula to central Africa, and it has made critical adjustments because of those analyses. In 2016, Rotkoff himself lead a red team review of the United States' strategy for countering the so-called Islamic State for the chairman of the Joint Chiefs of Staff, who was so impressed with the results that he has since called Rotkoff back to lead several more red team exercises on critical strategic issues. And the army's use of red teaming has not been limited to war planning; it has even used red teaming to rework its ethics policy.

Perhaps the most compelling proof of red teaming's value to the army is that at a time when massive reductions in military spending have left senior American officers questioning whether they will have the resources to fight the next war, the red team training program at Fort Leavenworth has actually been expanded.

"Red teaming has become part of army doctrine, but even more important, the tools and techniques we teach here at UFMCS have become part of all the conversations about every new task and every new mission," says Rotkoff, who took over as director of UFMCS after Fontenot retired in 2013. "Our ideas are now being reflected back to us every day in the million small decisions that are made at a local level. And those small decisions are *transforming* the army and making it better able to cope with the challenges of the twenty-first century."

Red Teaming Becomes a Movement

As word of the army's success with red teaming spread, other branches of the military began sending their officers to UFMCS to learn about it. The Marines were so impressed that, in 2010, they started their own red team training program at the Marine Corps University in Quantico, Virginia.

"We're able to help mitigate groupthink," said Lieutenant Colonel

Brian McDermott, who leads the standing Marine red team in Quantico. "We're able to help the staff and the commander better understand the operating environment."

The air force and the navy have sent officers to Fort Leavenworth for red team training and have used ad hoc red teams to review important policy decisions. In 2016, the air force conducted a red teaming exercise to evaluate its plan for incorporating women into combat roles. U.S. Special Operations Command, or SOCOM—the joint organization in charge of America's elite units such as the army Special Forces, Marine Raiders, and Navy SEALs—has made red teaming an integral part of its own planning process.

Allied countries, seeing the impact of red teaming in the U.S. military, also began sending their officers to Fort Leavenworth for training. Many of those countries have since established their own red teaming programs. The British were one of the first. Like their American allies, they had learned some very tough lessons in Iraq and Afghanistan—lessons they were determined not to repeat.

"Six or seven years ago, the Ministry of Defence was having a bit of a heart-searching moment, and it decided that it might *possibly* have made a couple of bad decisions," retired British Army brigadier Tom Longland, then head of the ministry's red teaming program, told me in 2015. "There was a big drive on how we were making decisions. Part of the drive came into the idea of evidence-based decision making, which sounds fine—in fact, it is very difficult to argue against. But you've got to have tools to decide upon the value of the evidence and make the decisions, which of course is where we came in."

The *we* that Longland referred to was the Development, Concepts and Doctrine centre at the U.K. Defence Academy in Shrivenham. It is the military's think tank, serving the British Army, Royal Navy, and Royal Air Force. Traditionally, its job has been to produce doctrine and develop concepts. The centre was initially just tasked with producing a red teaming manual for Her Majesty's armed forces. But its role quickly expanded, and it is now the official red team for the Ministry of Defence.

"We essentially apply red teaming techniques in an analysis of the paper, the plan, the philosophy that's being put forward," Longland explained. "We've done them for the structure of the Royal Navy. We did it for the reorganization of the Ministry of Defence. We did it for the defense review. You can do it for almost anything—and you *should*."

The Canadian Armed Forces, the Australian Department of Defence, and the New Zealand Defence Force have also created red teams. So has NATO, though the North Atlantic Treaty Organization calls its program *alternative analysis*.

"We have too much groupthink," said Johannes de Nijs, head of NATO's alternative analysis program at Allied Command Transformation Headquarters in Norfolk, Virginia. "We have to think differently about things that we are doing right now. We have to be innovative and transformative about ways in which we, in the military, are operating."

The success of red teaming has sparked interest outside the military, too. In the United Kingdom, the Department of Works and Pensions established a red team to review welfare reform. In the United States, the State Department, the Agency for International Development, the Federal Bureau of Investigation, the Department of Homeland Security, and other agencies have all asked the army to help them make red teaming part of their planning processes.

In 2012, one of the classes at Fort Leavenworth was asked to work with local, state, and federal law enforcement agencies to red team security plans for the upcoming Major League Baseball All-Star Game in Kansas City. The class identified the telecommunications network that allowed all of these agencies to communicate with one another as a critical weakness. It could find no contingencies in the plan for what to do if terrorists succeeded in scrambling it.

"That's impossible," insisted one of the FBI agents. "We don't need to worry about that."

Before he had even finished explaining how sophisticated the bureau's communications network was, one of the majors in the class—who happened to be a signals intelligence officer with army Special

Forces—had found a jammer for sale on Amazon that was capable of taking down the whole network. He printed out the product description and handed it to the FBI agent. The FBI immediately began working on a contingency plan.

Another class red teamed Kansas City's controversial airport expansion plan. The results were so eye-opening that the mayor wrote a letter to the general in charge at Fort Leavenworth, and asked if all of Kansas City's major initiatives could be subjected to similar scrutiny in the future.

Later, the Federal Reserve Bank of New York heard about red teaming and used its quasi-governmental status to persuade the army to send red teamers from Fort Leavenworth to help it, too.

As major corporations began hearing whispers about the work being done at Fort Leavenworth, they asked if they could pay the army to red team their strategies and plans, or at least send their people to the university to learn how to red team for themselves. While the answer was no, the army gave me the green light. And in the coming pages, I will share everything I learned there with you.

CHAPTER 2

What Is Red Teaming?

Want of foresight, unwillingness to act when action
would be simple and effective, lack of clear thinking,
confusion of counsel until the emergency comes, until self-
preservation strikes its jarring gong—these are the features
which constitute the endless repetition of history.

—Sir Winston Churchill

O n August 11, 2015, Larry Page, the cofounder of Google, sent a letter to his staff announcing one of the most stunning developments
in the recent history of the high-tech industry: Google was creating a
new company, Alphabet Inc. It would be a new type of conglomerate,
and Google itself would become one of its many subsidiaries. It was
a radical restructuring that nobody saw coming, least of all Google's
employees. In his memo to them, Page explained the rationale behind
the move:

We've long believed that over time companies tend to get
comfortable doing the same thing, just making incremental

changes. But in the technology industry, where revolutionary ideas drive the next big growth areas, you need to be a bit uncomfortable to stay relevant.

That is what red teaming does. Red teaming challenges your plans and the assumption upon which they are based. Red teaming forces you to think differently about your business and consider alternative points of view. Red teaming makes critical and contrarian thinking part of your company's planning process and gives you a set of tools and techniques that can be used to stress-test your strategy. Red teaming helps you better understand your customers and your competitors. Red teaming helps you scan the business environment for both threats and opportunities. Red teaming shows you the dangers that lie ahead—and how to turn them to your advantage. Red teaming may make your organization a bit uncomfortable, but it will also help you stay relevant, keep ahead of your competition, and cope with an increasingly uncertain world.

As the U.S. Department of Defense explains:

Red teams are established by an enterprise to challenge aspects of that very enterprise's plans, programs, assumptions, etc. It is this aspect of deliberate challenge that distinguishes red teaming from other management tools.

All plans are based on assumptions, all assumptions are based on understanding, and that understanding is frequently limited and often flawed. By challenging your assumptions, red teaming makes your plan stronger. But there is a lot more to red teaming than just challenging assumptions. There are red teaming techniques that will help you solve complex problems and identify the unintended consequences of your actions. There are red teaming techniques that will show you how your plans could fail and how the future might unfold in unexpected ways. And there are red teaming techniques that will help you do what you do better. These game-changing tools can help your company avoid costly mistakes and take advantage of opportunities you did not even know were there. But before you learn how to use them, you must first understand what red teaming is—and what it is *not*.

What Red Teaming Is

Red teaming is both a science and an art. The science of red teaming lies in using these tools and techniques to overcome the limitations of human decision making. As I will discuss in the next chapter, red teaming is rooted in cognitive science and the psychology of decision making. For centuries, we assumed that human beings generally made the best decisions possible with the information they had available. But in the past few decades, researchers have found that is simply not the case. They have discovered an uncomfortable truth: Each of us, no matter how smart, or well educated, or well intentioned we may be, is unduly influenced by a dizzying array of cognitive biases and logical fallacies that skew our decision making and lead us in unintended directions without us even being aware of it. Red teaming not only makes us aware of these biases and limitations, but also offers us a means of overcoming them.

The art of red teaming lies in deciding which tools and techniques to use under which circumstances. Some of these methods are designed to analyze a particular type of problem. Others are more generic and can aid in any analysis. Some require significant commitments of time, personnel, and other resources. Others can be done on the fly with little preparation and no overhead. Some are best employed early in the planning process. Others can help you make snap decisions at the last minute. It is not enough to know *how* to use these tools and techniques; you must also know *where* and *when* to use them.

A comprehensive red teaming analysis is typically divided into three phases. It starts by using analytical tools to question the arguments and assumptions that too often go unquestioned during the regular planning process. The next step is to use imaginative techniques to figure out what could go wrong—and what could go right—with the plan, in order to expose hidden threats and missed opportunities. Finally, it uses contrarian thinking to challenge the plan and force the organization to consider alternative perspectives.

The art of red teaming also lies in knowing when to stop red teaming and *act*. You can overthink any decision. The military calls this "analysis paralysis." But a good red team leader knows how to red team just enough, and no more.

Red teaming is both a mind-set and a set of tools. The tools used by red teamers are drawn from the tradecraft of intelligence analysts and the research of cognitive psychologists. These methods are designed to dissect and challenge existing assumptions and established ways of thinking. They are an arsenal of weapons aimed squarely at the heart of two of the biggest banes of business: groupthink and complacency. By incorporating red teaming into your planning process, you can banish both from your organization.

Adopting a red teaming mind-set means taking *nothing* for granted. It means questioning the unquestionable, thinking the unthinkable, and challenging everything. It means looking at the future, and not getting mired in the past. It means examining problems from the point of view of your competitors, your suppliers, your employees, and other key stakeholders. Red teaming helps you see your company's products and services as your customers see them—or, even better, as your future customers *will* see them. Red teaming is not just about thinking "outside the box." It is about examining the box itself and understanding how it shapes your thinking.

Red teaming is independent. Think about your organization. Each division, each group, each individual has vested interests that they are eager to promote and protect. That makes it very difficult for those people, those groups, and those divisions to think critically and objectively about any aspect of a plan or strategy that they own, or are responsible for, or that impacts something near and dear to them. Red teams, on the other hand, own nothing. They have no turf or vested interests to protect. They have no dog in the fight. They are beholden only to the truth. And that gives them the ability to see the truth through an undistorted lens, to objectively analyze a strategy or plan, to identify its problems and shortcomings, and to suggest ways in which it could be improved.

That is the ideal, at least. There are a number of different ways of incorporating red teaming into your organization, ranging from standing, in-house red teams to outside red team facilitators. Each model has its advantages and disadvantages. But whichever approach you choose, to be effective, your red team needs to be given the intellectual freedom to ask the tough questions and answer them honestly.

Red teaming is universal. As I discussed in the previous chapter, countries around the world have made red teaming part of their military and intelligence planning, and each of these nations has made important contributions to its methodology. Foreign businesses have also begun experimenting with red teaming. One of the first organizations I shared red teaming with was the DBJ Investment Advisory Company, which was established by the Development Bank of Japan in 2009 to help Japanese companies through value-added equity investment. President Harry Murakami was quick to see how red teaming could add real value in a country that had seen so many once-great companies become trapped by their past success.

"In Japan, we had decades of success that fostered conformity," Murakami told me in our first discussion about red teaming. "Since the 1990s, we have not been able to take that success for granted. However, too many Japanese companies still have not begun questioning what they do and how they do it."

Murakami saw how red teaming could help those companies take a hard look at the things they have taken for granted for too long. It can help your company do that, too.

Red teaming is about embracing change. Red teaming in a business environment is predicated on the knowledge that there is no end state for any company and no equilibrium in the marketplace. Change is the only constant. No matter how dominant or great your company is today, the only way it can stay great is to continue to evolve. If you doubt that, grab a copy of Jim Collins's business classic *Good to Great*, which was published in 2002, and see how many of the companies he holds up as models are still great—or even still in business—today. As Collins himself wrote in his later book, *How the Mighty Fall*:

> When institutions fail to distinguish between current practices and the enduring principles of their success, and mistakenly fossilize around their practices, they've set themselves up for decline.

Or, as MIT management guru Peter Senge put it in his seminal work *The Fifth Discipline*:

> A corporation cannot be "excellent" in the sense of having arrived at a permanent excellence; it is always in the state of practicing the disciplines of learning, of getting better or worse.

The most innovative companies not only understand the need for change, they embrace it. Just look at Page's memo. He and Google co-founder Sergei Brin understood the inevitability of change when they started their company in 1998, and they made it part of Google's DNA. That is why so many other companies—large and small—live in fear of waking up one morning and discovering Google has decided to enter their space. Even if change is not part of your founding DNA, you can still make it part of your company's culture through red teaming.

Few business leaders have embraced change the way Steve Jobs did. In many ways, Jobs was a one-man red team. His 1997 advertising slogan for Apple, "Think Different," sums up the spirit of red teaming perfectly (if not grammatically). The story of Apple's resurrection is filled with examples of how Jobs used critical, contrarian analysis to cut through the confusion that was holding his company back and to show Apple the way forward with laser-like clarity. One of the most poignant examples of this came during a product review shortly after Jobs returned to Apple as acting CEO in 1997. As Walter Isaacson describes in his 2011 biography:

> The product review revealed how unfocused Apple had become. The company was churning out multiple versions of each product because of bureaucratic momentum and to satisfy the whims of retailers. "It was insanity," [Apple marketing chief Phil] Schiller recalled. "Tons of products, most of them crap, done by deluded teams." Apple had a dozen versions of the Macintosh, each with a different confusing number, ranging from 1400 to 9600. "I had people explaining this to me for three weeks," Jobs said. "I couldn't figure it out." He finally began asking simple questions, like, "Which ones do I tell my friends to buy?" . . .
>
> After a few weeks Jobs finally had enough. "Stop!" he shouted at one big product strategy session. "This is crazy." He grabbed a magic marker, padded to a whiteboard, and drew a horizontal and vertical line to make a four-squared chart. "Here's what we need," he continued. Atop the two columns he wrote "Consumer" and "Pro"; he labeled the two rows "Desktop" and "Portable." Their job, he said, was to make four great products, one for each quadrant. "The room was in dumb silence," Schiller recalled.

Apple had been wandering in the wilderness for years and was nearly bankrupt when Jobs returned. In that one moment, he put the company back on the right track. He did it by thinking critically about Apple's product offerings. He did it by challenging the assumptions that had led the company to approve all these different machines in the first place. He did it by understanding who Apple's customers were and what they really wanted. In other words, he did it by thinking like a red teamer.

When analyzing a strategy, red teams begin by identifying and assessing the key assumptions that underlie it, rather than considering the arguments used to justify it in the first place. That is what Jobs was doing as he sat there listening to Apple's product program leaders describe their offerings. Presumably, there had been logical reasons for bringing each of these dozen different computers to market. No doubt the men and women who championed these products made compelling cases for them before winning approval from Apple's senior management. But Jobs had not listened to those arguments because Jobs had been forced out of the company twelve years earlier. So he was able to look at each of these offerings objectively, and when he did, he could see that most of them were superfluous. Because he was approaching the problem as an outsider, albeit one with a deep understanding of Apple's original brand promise, Jobs could see that Apple was trying to be too many different things to too many different people. Jobs knew that because he had looked at the same marketplace and seen not dozens of little segments, but rather four big ones: consumer and professional, desktop and laptop. And he saw the way to make Apple great again was by offering the best machine possible in each of those four segments.

As Brent Schlender and Rick Tetzeli point out in *Becoming Steve Jobs:*

> *The quadrants put Apple on the exact opposite course of the Windows PC manufacturers, who were busy churning out all manner of unremarkable, albeit faster and more powerful boxes. The quadrants returned Apple to its historic mission—to serve the high end of the consumer and professional markets with leading-edge products.*

Alan Mulally is another CEO who turned out to be a natural red teamer. In 2006, Mulally was hired by Bill Ford to save his struggling car company. Ford was on the brink of bankruptcy, and no one in the automobile industry thought it could be saved. Ford's problems ran too deep. Its products were boring, its labor contracts were uncompetitive, and its corporate culture was downright caustic. Ford's executives spent more time fighting with one another than they did competing with Toyota or General Motors. Ford was a lost cause, and everyone in Detroit knew it. But Mulally was not from Detroit. He was an aerospace engineer from Seattle, the president of Boeing's commercial aviation division. News of his hiring was met with guffaws by Ford's crosstown rivals. At GM and Chrysler, executives scoffed at the idea of someone who knew nothing about the way Detroit operated trying to save Ford.

"They were right. I didn't know how they did things in Detroit," Mulally later told me. "But I knew it wasn't working."

And that was all he needed to know. Mulally looked at the same problems that seemed so insurmountable to everyone else and figured out how to solve them. He streamlined Ford's product lineup just as Jobs had done at Apple and used the money he saved to give Ford's remaining products class-leading features and jaw-dropping styling. Mulally gave the United Auto Workers the choice of changing their contract so that the company could profitably produce those new vehicles in the United States or see them outsourced to Mexico, and as a result, won more concessions from the union than anyone in the industry had thought possible. And he helped Ford shed its caustic, careerist culture by showing the company's executives how they could be more successful working together as a team than they could ever be as rivals. In just over three years, from the end of 2006 to the beginning of 2010, Mulally not only saved Ford, but also made it one of the most profitable automakers in the world—and he did it against the backdrop of the worst economic crisis since the Great Depression, and without taking a government bailout.

Mulally had never heard of red teaming and had no formal training in its tools or techniques. But like Jobs at Apple, Mulally approached Ford's problems the same way a red teamer would. He examined the assumptions underlying the company's business strategy and popped them like so many soap bubbles. He asked tough questions and refused to take *because that's the way we've always done it* as an answer. He thought about Ford's problems not just from the perspective of the automaker itself, but also from the point of view of dealers, suppliers, and labor unions, and he crafted solutions that met their needs as well as Ford's. Most important of all, when the global economy collapsed and took the automobile market down with it, he figured out how to turn that calamity to Ford's advantage by doing the opposite of what Ford's competitors did. When General Motors and Chrysler cut investment in new products to conserve cash, Mulally ordered Ford to keep its foot on the gas. When those companies asked the federal government to save them, he passed on a taxpayer bailout and promised the American people that Ford would fix the problems it had created itself by itself. And when GM and Chrysler went bankrupt, Ford posted record profits.

That is the power of red teaming. Your company may not have a Steve Jobs or an Alan Mulally, but you can build a red team that provides the same sort of critical analysis and contrarian thinking that Jobs and Mulally brought to Apple and Ford.

Two centuries ago, the Prussian army used a similar approach to beat Napoleon.

In 1806, Napoleon defeated the Prussian army at Jena and pushed the Prussian state to the brink of collapse. The Prussian generals took a hard look at themselves and realized that none of them were Napoleon's equal. But they also realized that, if they worked together as a team, they might be able to beat him. They persuaded their king to entrust the reformation of his army not to one general, but to a team of his best and brightest officers. They called this team the *General Staff*. Together, that General Staff rebuilt the Prussian army and, six years later, helped defeat Napoleon at the Battle of Leipzig. When the wily emperor escaped from Elba two years later, the Prussians—along with their British-led allies—did it again at Waterloo. And the Prussians kept right on winning throughout the rest of the century,* prompting many other nations, including the United States, to adopt their general staff system.

---

*The Prussian General Staff became the German General Staff after the unification of Germany in 1871. Germany's defeats in World War I and World War II resulted in part from Kaiser Wilhelm II and Adolf Hitler overruling the General Staff on key issues.

Think of Amazon or Uber as modern incarnations of Napoleon, rampaging through the business world the same way he once tore through Europe, overturning the established order and toppling dynasties. Just as the Prussians assembled a team of generals that was able to turn the tables on Napoleon, companies that find themselves in the crosshairs of corporate conquistadors can create red teams to not only counter such threats, but perhaps even become one of the disruptors themselves.

What Red Teaming Is Not

Red teaming is not a challenge to leadership. The role of the red team is not to make decisions or weaken the authority of leaders or managers. The red team's role is to empower leaders and managers to make *better* decisions by providing them with a more objective analysis, a more comprehensive picture of the business environment, and alternative options to consider.

"It is important for leaders to know that, when they embrace red teaming, they are not giving up any power," explains retired Colonel Steve Rotkoff. "The red team never forces a leader's hand. The red team never says, 'Do this' or 'Don't do this.' Leaders who employ red teams still have the ability to make whatever decision they want. What red teaming does is allow those leaders to make that decision based on a more informed understanding of the problem."

Red teaming can even act as a sort of insurance policy for leaders. In this era of close regulatory and board scrutiny, conducting a thorough red teaming analysis of a new plan or a change in strategy provides proof that all risks and reasonable alternatives have been duly weighed and considered.

Red teaming is not a substitute for planning. "The red team doesn't make the plan; it makes the plan *better*," explains retired Colonel Ray Damm, head of the red team training program at the Marine Corps

University in Quantico, Virginia. A red team does that by challenging the assumptions upon which an organization's strategies and plans are based, by exposing logical fallacies inherent in them, and by cutting through the groupthink that too often clouds decision making.

A red team can do this most effectively when it is not directly involved in developing those plans and strategies. Having a red team develop the plan itself defeats the purpose of having a red team in the first place. That said, there may be times and circumstances where it may make sense to include members of the original planning group in the red teaming process. But even then, they need to approach the problem with a fresh set of eyes.

Red teaming is not an excuse for inaction. As General George S. Patton famously said, "A good plan, violently executed now, is better than a perfect plan next week." But an unexamined plan will never be as good as one that has been subjected to independent scrutiny and critical analysis.

Some red teaming techniques require a significant investment of time to be used effectively, and some decisions require that sort of careful approach. But red teaming can also be done quickly and effectively under extreme time constraints. Some of the tools I will describe in this book can be used effectively even if you have only a few minutes to spare before making a decision.

If you do not have a few minutes to spare, you should not be red teaming. One of the most important rules the army teaches red team leaders is: *Don't red team if the enemy is in the wire.*

Red teaming is not fortune-telling. The red team's job is not to predict the future but rather to ensure an organization's strategy accounts for all reasonable possibilities the future may hold. For this reason—and this is a crucial point—red teams do not need to be *right* to be *effective*. In fact, for red teaming to work, it must take place in an environment in which it is okay to be wrong.

Remember, the red team's job is not to come up with a better plan; it is to make the existing plan better by offering alternative explanations, challenging its assumptions, and anticipating issues that could derail it during execution. To really think outside the box, red team members need to have the freedom of thought that comes only from not having to be right. A red team that makes an organization think more deeply and more critically about its strategies and plans has done its job. You may find that your original plan was the right one all along. But you can never be sure until you subject it to the careful, critical scrutiny red teaming provides.

Red teaming is not cynical. There is a big difference between being critical and being negative, and there is a big difference between being skeptical and being cynical. In both cases, red teams should always be the former, and they should always be on guard against becoming the latter.

The feedback red teams provide should always be positive, collegial, and constructive. The red team's job is not to expose the faults or shortcomings of employees—or management. Its job is to support both by helping the organization think more deeply about its strategies and plans.

"The way red teams fail is by acting like the Inspector General's Office or the internal affairs division of a police department," Colonel Damm cautions. "You don't want to get to the point where people groan when you show up."

At the same time, the rest of the organization needs to take the red team's feedback in the constructive and collegial spirit in which it is intended. If others take the red team's criticisms personally or get defensive, that can make it difficult for the organization to take advantage of the insights and analysis the red team provides.

Red teaming is not just about reducing mistakes or mitigating risks. Over the years, many different systems have been proposed to help companies reduce errors and manage risks. While red teaming can help with both of these important objectives, it goes far beyond that. Red teaming is also about identifying new options and new opportunities.

Dr. Gary Klein helped me appreciate just how important that can be to companies. An influential researcher in the field of decision making, Klein is responsible for developing one of the most powerful tools in the red teaming arsenal: *Pre-Mortem Analysis* (which will be described in chapter 7). As I was explaining red teaming to him one day over lunch, he took out a piece of a paper and wrote out a simple formula:

$$P = \uparrow + \downarrow$$

Klein explained that *P* stands for "performance improvements," the up arrow represents "insights," and the down arrow represents "errors."

"The problem with most systems, such as Six Sigma,* is that they only focus on identifying and reducing errors," he told me. "For a system to really boost an organization's performance, it needs to not just reduce errors, but also offer new insights. If red teaming can do both, then it has the potential to make a real difference."**

It can, and it does.

Red teaming helps identify opportunities planners may have overlooked by looking at problems from different perspectives and exploring alternative solutions. Moreover, red teams use contrarian analysis to figure out how to take advantage of downturns and other market volatility by charting a course through these uncertain waters that is different from the ones their competitors are likely to take.

Red teaming is not just for leaders. While red teaming is most effective when it is embraced by an entire organization, it can still make a big

---

*Six Sigma is a data-driven approach to improving quality and reducing errors developed by Motorola in the 1980s. It has since been adopted by many companies, especially in manufacturing.

**For a more detailed discussion of Klein's formula, see his book *Seeing What Others Don't: The Remarkable Ways We Gain Insights* (New York: PublicAffairs, 2013).

difference even when it is only used by a single division, department, project team, factory, retail location, or any group that is still responsible for developing and executing its own strategies and plans. Even if your group's strategy is set by people above your pay grade, you can use red teaming to figure out the best way to execute that strategy, identify the ways in which it could fail, and determine how to proactively address those challenges. By using the methods described in this book, you may be able to discern opportunities others have missed and adjust your plan to take advantage of them. If nothing else, you can use red teaming to get to the root of problems your group is struggling with and identify solutions.

Even if you are in charge of no one besides yourself, you can use these same tools and techniques to better evaluate your own decisions and think more critically about your work—and your life.

Red teaming is not just for running armies or corporations. Businesses of all sizes can benefit from red teaming. So can nonprofits and charities. One of the army's most effective applications of red teaming involved working with the Bill & Melinda Gates Foundation on polio eradication. Other charities have begun exploring ways to use red teaming to help them vet candidates for funding. Venture capital firms have used similar techniques to assess potential investment targets, while investment firms have successfully used red teaming tools to pick stocks.

Red teaming is ideal for any organization that wants to stress-test its strategies, fine-tune its plans, consider alternative perspectives, and make better decisions. That means it is just as valuable to nonprofit organizations and private investors as it is to publicly traded companies and hedge funds.

Red teaming is not a panacea. Each year, new systems are advanced that promise to cure all the ills of business and guarantee the future success of any company wise enough to embrace them. Red teaming is not another one of those systems.

Red teaming is not a replacement for a good product or a compelling service, but it can help to make your products and services better. Red teaming cannot overcome the business cycle, but it can help your company better weather its ups and downs. Red teaming cannot prevent new competitors from entering the marketplace and doing what you do better, but it can make you aware of your vulnerabilities beforehand so that you can deal with your shortcomings proactively. Red teaming cannot change an organization that does not want to evolve, but it can provide powerful insights and guidance to those that do. Finally, red teaming cannot overcome bad leadership, because red teams need the support of an engaged leader to be effective. However, with that support, red teaming *can* make a good leader into a great one.

Change or Die

In August 2004, Toyota Motor Corporation chairman Fujio Cho was asked to give a presentation at the annual automobile industry conference organized by the University of Michigan's Center for Automotive Research. The Japanese automaker still considered Michigan hostile territory back then. The company had a modest research-and-development facility not far from the university in Ann Arbor and had just opened a new design studio there, but Toyota was so concerned about the backlash from its seemingly unstoppable march into the market space once dominated by Detroit's Big Three that it kept its name and logo off the buildings. For the past decade, Toyota's share of the U.S. car market had increased year after year, while the share controlled by General Motors, Ford, and Chrysler steadily declined. That was the reason for the low profile in a state that was home to thousands of unemployed autoworkers. It was also the reason why Cho had been asked to deliver the keynote address.

There was lukewarm applause as he took the stage. The auditorium was filled with executives from all the world's major automakers, but the crowd was dominated by suits from the three home teams. Cho began with a detailed slide presentation showing how Toyota was exceeding each of its strategic goals in every market around the world. It was impressive stuff, and many of the American automobile executives in the auditorium were scowling jealously by the time he was finished. Then Cho stopped, looked up from his notes, and declared that the time had come for Toyota to rethink its strategy.

"Any company not willing to take the risk of reinventing itself is doomed," he said.

For Toyota, the time to do that was now, while it was at the top of its game.

"The world today is changing much too fast," Cho warned as he began detailing the steps Toyota was taking to reevaluate and refine its core business strategy. "Our industry has never been more competitive."

There was dead silence in the room when Cho finished his remarks. Nobody seemed to know what to make of them. Half the executives there were smugly confident they could keep Toyota at bay, despite its impressive gains. As one GM executive told me over coffee that afternoon, GM would stay number one because, well, it was GM. The other half were dismayed by Cho's declaration. They were working overtime trying to match what Toyota was *already* doing, and here was Toyota's boss talking about how worried *he* was about the future and vowing to make his company work that much *harder* to figure out how to confront the challenges that lay ahead.

What Cho was calling for that day in Michigan was red teaming. Although he did not know it by that name, he was advocating the same sort of rigorous, self-critical analysis that red teaming provides. And red teaming is exactly what Toyota did. Instead of taking its success for granted, instead of waiting for its competitors to catch up, Toyota figured out how to do what it was already doing well even better. The next five years would see Toyota catapult to the top of the global automobile industry. It would stumble along the way, but it would take an unflinching look at the reasons for those missteps and move decisively to correct them. GM would also stumble, but it would respond only with more excuses as Toyota gobbled up its market share, snatched its crown, and became the largest automaker in the world. That is what can happen when you bring red team thinking into your organization—and when you do not.

Companies like Toyota realize they will never have all the answers. That is why they continue to ask questions, the same sort of questions red teams are designed to answer. Done right, red teaming can pay huge dividends to any organization, not just by testing its plans and assumptions and making sure they are sound, but also by making everyone who learns about it more aware of potential problems, pitfalls, and opportunities. The process of red teaming makes managers better planners and deeper thinkers. In the companies where I have been a consultant, red teaming discussions do not end in the conference room but continue outside in the hallway and in the next staff meeting. Red teaming rapidly becomes part of a company's lexicon, and the phrase "Let's take a minute and red team this" becomes a common refrain.

You do not have to be in charge to benefit from red teaming. The tools and techniques taught in this book can and should be used by anyone who wants to plan better, think more critically, and make better decisions for themselves or their organizations. Yet if you are in charge, let me be clear about one thing: If you are just looking for validation of your existing strategies and plans, red teaming is not for you. But remember that the best companies and the most effective leaders know there is always room for improvement. If your red team fails to find it, then it is not doing its job. So only use red teaming when you are willing to make changes—changes that will make your organization more competitive and more successful. If you are happy with where you are and do not want to change, then don't red team. Just sit back and wait for one of your competitors to do it for you.

CHAPTER 3

The Psychology of Red Teaming

A great many people think they are thinking when
they are merely rearranging their prejudices.

—William James

From the time Adam Smith first caught sight of the invisible hand moving markets and distributing the necessaries of life back in 1759, it was widely believed that people generally made the best decisions possible with the information available to them. Yes, there were exceptions, but these were chalked up to strong emotions like anger, fear, or an unhealthy obsession with tulips. By the 1970s, however, cognitive psychologists and behavioral economists had begun to prove this *rational choice theory* wrong. In experiment after experiment, researchers such as Dr. Daniel Kahneman and Dr. Amos Tversky demonstrated that human beings were, in fact, predictably *irrational*.* They found our

---

*Kahneman was awarded the Nobel Prize in Economics in 2002 for these efforts. Tversky would likely have shared the Nobel Prize with Kahneman, but he had passed away in 1996.

brains take many shortcuts and cut corners. That allows us to think quickly, which is a helpful trait if one is trying to survive on the savanna, where there is little benefit in thinking deeply about the motives of a lion licking its chops. But these same mental shortcuts can cause real trouble when we try to make complicated decisions about complex problems, like whether or not to double down on subprime mortgages.

Most cognitive psychologists now believe that we rely on two mental processes to make decisions. System 1 is instinctive and associative. It knows fire is hot, ice is cold, and the person with brown eyes, gray hair, and apple cheeks is your mother. It knows these things without having to think about them, which is helpful if you are confronted by an open flame, a Popsicle, or your mother. System 2 is much more sophisticated. It can tell you today's date, the number of letters in the word *serendipity*, and whether to double down on subprime mortgages. It does not know these things intuitively, but it can figure them out. As a result, System 2 thinking is a lot slower than System 1, and it also requires a great deal more effort and attention in order to function properly. But the results it provides are usually worth it.*

Unfortunately, there is one big problem with System 2: Our brains are lazy, and because they are lazy, they often turn to System 1 for answers.

"The attentive System 2 is who we think we are. System 2 articulates judgments and makes choices, but it often endorses or rationalizes ideas and feelings that were generated by System 1," Kahneman explains in his acclaimed book, *Thinking, Fast and Slow*. "You believe you know what goes on in your mind, which often consists of one conscious thought leading in an orderly way to another. But that is not the only way the mind works, nor indeed is that the typical way. Most impressions and thoughts arise in your conscious experience without your knowing how they got there."

---

*While the philosopher and psychologist William James was probably the first to suggest this dual-process theory, the terms *System 1* and *System 2* were first used by Keith Stanovich and Richard West in a piece titled "Individual Difference in Reasoning: Implications for the Rationality Debate?" which was published in the journal *Behavioral and Brain Sciences* in 2000.

Kahneman describes System 1 as "a machine for jumping to conclusions." Those conclusions are often correct, as in the case of fire, ice, or your mother. But they can also be skewed by a dizzying array of cognitive biases and heuristics. Cognitive biases are inherent, systematic errors in our thinking that follow predictable patterns. Heuristics are mental shortcuts that help us make quick decisions—though not necessarily correct ones. As Tversky and Kahneman wrote in their groundbreaking 1974 article on the subject in the journal *Science,* "These heuristics are quite useful, but sometimes they lead to severe and systematic errors."

Fortunately, red teaming can help us avoid these errors. But before we can start red teaming, we need to know what these biases and heuristics are so that we can understand how they influence the thinking of others and guard against them in ourselves. There is a lot to digest in this chapter, but the information here is an essential prerequisite for effective red teaming. A number of recent bestselling and critically acclaimed books, such as *Thinking, Fast and Slow; Predictably Irrational; Switch;* and *Nudge,* have described in detail these tricks our minds play. If you are already familiar with these concepts, you can skim through this section. But in my work with executives in the United States and abroad, I have found that many are not. For that reason, I offer the following overview of the cognitive biases and heuristics that pose the most significant threat to business planning. (For those interested in learning more about these and other threats to sound decision making, I have included a list of recommended readings in the appendix.)

Cognitive Biases and Heuristics

Affect heuristic. Sometimes, we make decisions based on strong emotions, rather than on objective data. Positive emotions can blind us to troubling statistics, which explains the success of cigarette advertising. Negative emotions can skew our perceptions even more strongly. Psychologist Gerd Gigerenzer, for example, found that in the months following the September 11, 2001, terrorist attacks on Washington and New York, Americans were less likely to travel by plane and more likely to travel by car than they had been before the attacks. As a result, highway deaths increased substantially in the United States, because even with the threat of terrorism factored in, the odds of dying in a car crash were substantially higher than the odds of dying in a plane crash. In fact, Gigerenzer's analysis showed that *more* people were killed because they chose not to fly in the months following 9/11 than were killed in those terrorist attacks. Business decisions can be similarly swayed by strong emotions. Just think about all of the companies that overpaid for tech acquisitions in the late 1990s when business leaders were high on the irrational exuberance of the dot-com boom. One of the most costly examples was the 2000 acquisition of Lycos by the Spanish telecommunications company Terra Networks, which paid a whopping $12.5 billion for the Internet search engine. Already an also-ran, Lycos soon faded into oblivion and was sold four years later to Korean Internet firm Daum for just $95.4 million.*

Red teaming guards against the affect heuristic by considering strategies and plans objectively, rather than emotionally. It can also help identify ways in which this same tendency can affect the behavior of consumers and competitors.

Anchoring bias. The first piece of data we are given can sometimes set the baseline for an entire discussion. Cognitive psychologists have shown that, in negotiations involving money, the first offer tends to establish the range of expectations for both parties. A higher number will tend to create higher expectations; a lower number will tend to create lower expectations. The first number *anchors* the discussion in both parties' minds. Skillful negotiators can use this to their advantage, using anchoring to shape everything from union negotiations to pricing agreements with suppliers. But anchoring can also distort decisions in less obvious ways.

---

*Daum sold Lycos six years after that to India's Ybrant Digital for $36 million.

For example, two groups of German judges were asked to roll a pair of loaded dice before reviewing a hypothetical criminal case and deciding on the sentence. One group was given dice that always rolled a three, while the other group was given dice that always came up nine. The average sentence of the group that rolled nines was 50 percent higher than the average sentence of the group that rolled threes. Those judges' decisions were affected by a number that had absolutely nothing to do with the case they were considering—or any criminal case, for that matter.

Red teaming helps mitigate the anchoring bias by making sure relevant numbers are reviewed objectively—and by people who were not part of the original discussions, and therefore not unconsciously influenced by other anchors.

Automation bias. One way organizations attempt to mitigate these biases and mental shortcuts is by creating automated systems or formulaic processes to eliminate the possibility of human error. While such systems can help reduce errors and speed up decision making, they can also ignore vital information, leading to erroneous recommendations. The problem is that once we begin relying on automated systems, we tend to stop questioning them. Studies of professional pilots in cockpit simulators found more than half of them either disregarded important information when automated systems failed to alert them to it or, worse, made dangerous mistakes when such systems gave them erroneous information. Automation bias has been cited as a factor in real-world crashes, too, including the tragic losses of Eastern Airlines 401 in 1972 and Air France 447 in 2009. Problems with automated trading algorithms show just how costly this can be in business. In 2012, Knight Capital almost went bankrupt after its new program made $440 million in bad trades in just forty-five minutes. Automation bias will become increasingly problematical as companies delegate more responsibility for planning to artificial intelligences and expert systems.

Red teaming prevents automation bias by subjecting recommendations generated by automated systems to an independent, critical review.

Availability heuristic. We tend to give more credence to information we are already aware of—even if that awareness is subconscious. This is particularly true when that information is dramatic or emotionally charged. The twenty-four-hour news cycle has magnified this effect to a troubling degree, which helps explain why terrorism has become such an effective tactic for groups that want to sway public opinion. Major news events can also disproportionately influence our thinking about financial matters. In Franklin Templeton's 2012 Global Investor Sentiment Survey, 66 percent of those polled believed the S&P 500 Index had been down or flat in 2009, with about half of the respondents expressing the same bearish belief about 2010 and 2011 as well. In fact, the S&P 500 Index was up in all three of those years. Why the disconnect? Investors were still reeling from the shock of the 2008 global economic crisis, an event so traumatic it continued to color their view of financial markets long after the recovery had begun. Positive information also can unduly influence our decisions, as it did during the real estate boom of the mid-2000s when the money friends and neighbors were making selling their houses convinced legions of Americans to stake their life savings on risky property investments.

Red teaming overcomes the availability heuristic by considering potential risks and rewards objectively and ensuring a variety of options are considered, not just those that are top of mind.

Bandwagon effect. We are more likely to believe something is true if others around us already believe it to be true. Conversely, we are more likely to believe something is not true if others in our organization already believe it to be false. This is a classic example of groupthink. It helps to explain the waves of well-intentioned, but often ill-conceived, initiatives that sweep through corporations with disturbing regularity. The bandwagon effect also helps explain the subprime mortgage crisis that precipitated the collapse of the U.S. housing market in 2008. While most lenders were initially apprehensive about offering financing to people with low credit scores or no documentation, those reservations began to disappear as they saw more and more of their peers offering riskier and riskier loans. The bandwagon effect makes individuals and organizations go against their better judgment. It can turn otherwise rational thinkers into lemmings.

Red teaming counteracts the bandwagon effect by judging proposals on their merits, rather than their popularity.

Base rate fallacy. We have an innate tendency to ignore general information and focus instead on data that is more specific, but less meaningful—particularly when that data says what we want it to say. Businesses fall victim to this all the time. In 2012, for example, a Chrysler executive boasted to me about the "tremendous progress" his company had made in overcoming its long-standing quality problems. As proof, he produced the results of an internal audit that showed several key vehicles had a double-digit decrease year-over-year in the number of things gone wrong, a standard metric used by the automobile industry to measure quality. It certainly looked impressive, at least until I checked the overall quality rankings and found those cars still scored near the bottom of their class in reliability. Chrysler had overvalued the progress it was making by ignoring the base rate for the industry. Companies fall victim to this fallacy in other ways as well. They assume the reaction of existing customers to a new product or service is a good gauge of how the market as a whole will react. They trumpet their success with a single client, while ignoring that company's declining market share. Or they become so enamored with a promising start-up that they overlook the high rate of failure in its sector and decide to acquire it.

Red teaming challenges the base rate fallacy by fully considering the context of all statistics.

Clustering illusion. Human beings are hardwired to look for patterns, so much so that we often discern them where no pattern actually exists. We see geometric shapes in our freckles, faces on Martian rocks, and religious icons in burned toast. During World War II, London newspapers regularly published maps showing recent rocket strikes on the British capital, leading to elaborate theories about just who the Germans were—or were not—targeting. The most popular of these held that, because more missiles seemed to be striking working-class neighborhoods, the Germans must be aiming at them deliberately and sparing better-off Britons in the hope of inflaming class tensions. After the war, German rocketeers laughed at the idea that these early missiles were capable of such precision. They had simply pointed them at London and hoped they hit something. Businesses fall victim to these sort of illusions just as readily as war-weary Londoners. They see patterns in sequences of numbers that are entirely random and draw important conclusions from data samples that are too small to be meaningful. The clustering illusion is a particular threat to entrepreneurs, who too often misinterpret initial high demand for a new product or service as a meaningful baseline. They boost production, hire more staff, open another office, or add manufacturing capacity, only to find themselves overextended and headed for bankruptcy.

Red teaming helps guard against the clustering illusion by considering alternative interpretations of data and challenging perceived patterns.

Confirmation bias. We tend to give more credence to information that supports what we already believe, or that validates decisions we have already made. We also tend to be more aware of such information, and more likely to skip over information that calls into question what we have already determined to be true. Scientists proved this to be true by examining how people's brains react to information that confirms or challenges their strongly held beliefs. During the 2004 U.S. presidential election, researchers at Emory University had partisan voters read seemingly contradictory statements from Republican candidate George W. Bush, democratic candidate John Kerry, and a politically neutral male celebrity while their brains were being monitored by an MRI machine. It revealed the subjects not only were far more likely to identify the contradictions in the statements made by the candidate they opposed, but also showed that their brains processed the contradictory statements made by *their* candidate differently. This explains why it is so hard for us to challenge our own assumptions. It also explains the persistence of discredited beliefs. If an organization has long believed something to be true, it is going to have a hard time considering new information that suggests it is wrong—no matter how compelling that information may be. This is why it is so much easier for new entrants to disrupt existing market segments and beat older, established players at their own game.

Red teaming offsets confirmation bias by forcing organizations to consider contrarian points of view and alternative perspectives.

Curse of knowledge. Better-informed people often find it difficult to think about an issue from the perspective of those who are less informed. This can be a major problem for companies when it comes to predicting how consumers will react to a product. Panasonic knew its plasma television technology was vastly superior to the LCD technology being peddled by its competitors. So did most videophiles. Plasma televisions produce deeper blacks, truer colors, higher contrast ratios, less motion blur, and a wider viewing angle. But there is one area in which LCD televisions were noticeably superior: They look better under bright, fluorescent light—the sort of lighting found in big-box retail stores. Unfortunately for Panasonic, most consumers decided what television to buy not by considering its technical merits or even how good it would look in their den, but by walking into an electronics store and pointing to the one that looked the best on the shelf. Panasonic was forced to pull the plug on its plasma televisions in 2014, even though they were consistently rated number one by experts. The curse of knowledge also helps explain why engineers get so frustrated with marketing people, and vice versa.

Red teaming overcomes the curse of knowledge by offering tools to analyze issues from a variety of perspectives that are often overlooked in the regular planning process.

Framing effect. We tend to draw different conclusions from the same information, depending upon how that information is presented. Advertisers and political spin doctors use this to their advantage every day, exploiting our inherent aversion to loss and desire for gain to peddle products and build support. But framing can also have a big impact on business decisions. A presentation that emphasizes the potential benefits of a proposed deal is almost certain to be received more favorably than one that emphasizes its risks. Framing can impact business decisions in less obvious ways, as well. Xerox developed many of the technologies behind the personal computer revolution; its Star workstation was the first commercially available computer to offer a bit-mapped display, windows-based graphical user interface, icons, folders, Ethernet networking, e-mail, and a mouse. But Xerox saw itself as a copier company, and because it could not see beyond that frame, it marketed the Star as a document management machine—one that it only sold as part of a "personal office system" that cost between $50,000 and $100,000 when it was launched in 1981. Xerox sold few of these workstations and never became a player in the computer business. Companies such as Apple and Microsoft looked at the technologies Xerox pioneered through a different frame, and used them to dominate the computer industry.

Red teaming offsets the framing effect by considering options objectively, without regard to how they are presented. It also helps reframe problems in ways that generate new insights and perspectives.

Gambler's fallacy/hot-hand fallacy. These biases stem from the mistaken belief that future probabilities are altered by past events. The gambler's fallacy refers to the misperception that, because something is occurring more frequently than normal now, it will happen less frequently in the future. A famous example of this occurred on August 18, 1913, at the Casino de Monte-Carlo when black came up twenty-six times in a row on a roulette wheel. As word of this amazing streak spread through the casino, gamblers flocked to the table. They lost millions of francs betting on red in the mistaken belief that the streak *must* end.

Actually, the odds of each spin coming up black remained the same each time, just as the odds of a tossed coin coming up "heads" are still 50:50, even if the last one hundred tosses came up "tails."* The hot-hand fallacy refers to the opposite, but equally erroneous, belief that a perceived streak is bound to continue. The name comes from basketball, where players who score repeatedly are often said to have "a hot hand." Both of these biases can lead companies to make bad decisions by mistaking luck for skill. In 1973, Princeton University economist Burton Malkiel declared that "a blindfolded monkey throwing darts at a newspaper's financial pages could select a portfolio that would do just as well as one carefully selected by the experts." In 1988, the *Wall Street Journal* decided to put that claim to the test. Over the next ten years, the *Journal* conducted a hundred stock-picking contests pitting professional portfolio managers against blindfolded journalists (who stood in for the monkeys for insurance reasons). They proved Malkiel wrong, but not by much. The pros won, but only 61 percent of the time. So just because the last three acquisitions a CEO made were home runs does not mean the next one is bound to be as well. This fallacy can lead companies to expect more of people than they are capable of delivering—and lead them to credit competitors with more skill than they actually possess.

Red teaming keeps both of these fallacies in check by objectively analyzing the chances of success and failure, identifying the real reasons for success and failure, and separating random events from those resulting from skill.

Hindsight bias. After an event has occurred, we often erroneously believe it could have been predicted and therefore avoided—or taken advantage of, in the case of, say, a surge in the price of a company's stock. Researchers have found this to be a significant problem in the health care arena, where morbidity studies and autopsies can exaggerate the

---

*Actually, scientists have proven the odds are 51:49 in favor of whatever side was up when the coin was flipped by a human. If tossed by a machine, the odds are indeed 50:50.

likelihood of spotting a medical problem sooner than doctors did. In business, this bias leads to unrealistic demands being placed on employees, and unreasonable expectations by investors. In postmortem analyses, it can lead people to focus on a single cause rather than exploring all the different causes that contributed to the failure. On the other hand, it can make successful planners overconfident.

Red teaming cuts through the distortions caused by hindsight bias by fully exploring the reasons why events occurred.

Illusions of control. We have a tendency to exaggerate our ability to influence external events, and that can create big problems in business. A 2003 study of financial traders working at four City of London investment banks found those "with a high propensity to illusion of control exhibit a lower profit performance and earn less than those with low illusion of control." The same study also found a strong correlation "between illusion of control and poor risk management and analysis." Illusions of control can lead executives to exaggerate their ability to find and recruit top talent, design winning products, or secure needed financing. This fallacy can also lead managers to spend too little time questioning their plans beforehand or doing the grunt work necessary to guarantee their success. Ironically, researchers also have found that, in situations in which people do have a great deal of control, they tend to *underestimate* the amount of control they actually exert. That can blind companies to their own contributions to a competitor's success.

Red teaming dispels illusions of control by seeking out the actual causes for every effect.

Loss aversion. Given the choice, most of us would rather avoid a loss than reap a reward. This can help us avoid making expensive mistakes, but it can also make us risk averse and prevent us from taking advantage of lucrative opportunities. Loss aversion played a big role in the downfall of Polaroid. Though Polaroid was a leader in digital photography in the late 1990s, its senior leadership was reluctant to commit to that new technology and abandon its traditional film business. Why? Because the margins for Polaroid's instant film were in excess of 65 percent—far higher than the margins for digital cameras. The company, which could easily have remained a leader in the digital space, went bankrupt in 2001 as its traditional film business declined and ultimately disappeared. Loss aversion helps drive the sort of short-term thinking that so often proves costly to companies in the long run. It helps explain why repairs are deferred and machinery is kept in operation until it breaks down, and why problems with high-performing employees are ignored until it is too late.

Red teaming helps overcome loss aversion by objectively assessing the risk and rewards of the different options available.

Negativity bias. Because we are hardwired to recall unpleasant memories more vividly than positive memories, we tend to overweight bad experiences, sometimes giving them more credence in our calculus than they deserve. Researchers have shown that when evaluating outcomes with both positive and negative consequences, we tend to view the whole situation in a negative light. As with loss aversion, this can be a desirable trait when it protects us from making the same mistake twice, but it can also lead us to undervalue positive experiences. A single significant failure can sour a company on an approach that has been successful many times before. The negativity bias can also affect consumer perception. Customers are more likely to recall a company's mistakes than its successes. This bias also comes into play when evaluating a person or group that we dislike. We tend to attribute their positive behaviors to external factors and their negative behaviors to their intrinsic character (while ascribing our own positive behaviors to our intrinsic character, and our mistakes to external factors). This can be a problem when selecting the right person to lead a key initiative or business unit, and it can blind an organization to the strengths of a competitor.

Red teaming counters the negativity bias by considering experience dispassionately, and evaluating individuals and organizations objectively.

Normalcy bias. We have a hard time planning for and reacting to disasters that have yet to occur. That leads us to underestimate the odds of a worst-case scenario and minimize its potential impact. This helps explain why some people refuse evacuation orders during emergencies and why there were not enough lifeboats on the *Titanic*. It also helps explain why companies fail to develop robust contingency plans, and why their worst-case forecasts prove too rosy in hindsight. In January 2006, for example, Ford launched a sweeping restructuring plan for its North American business that it dubbed the "Way Forward." It anticipated ten years of low gasoline prices and a modest decline in demand for the company's big trucks and sport utility vehicles. However, by April of that year, the average price of gasoline in the United States had soared to three dollars a gallon and that gradual decline in truck sales had become a full-scale rout. Nassim Nicholas Taleb discusses the dangers of the normalcy bias in his bestselling book, *The Black Swan*. Black swans are events that lie outside the realm of expectations, yet have a major impact when they occur. The breakdown of markets following the September 11, 2001, terrorist attacks was a black swan event, as was the financial meltdown of 2008. Black swan events seem to occur with disturbing regularity in today's fast-changing world, which makes this bias an even greater liability now than it was in the past.

Red teaming combats the normalcy bias by helping organizations learn from others' experiences, and by using counterfactual reasoning to help evaluate risk—precisely the sort of action Taleb recommends for mitigating black swan events.

Optimism bias. Too often, we underestimate our shortcomings, overestimate our abilities, and exaggerate our chances of accurately predicting the future. Psychologists suggest most of us suffer from *illusory superiority,* the belief that we are better than others. A 1977 survey of professors at the University of Nebraska found that 94 percent rated themselves above average relative to their peers. A 2000 survey of M.B.A. students at Stanford University found that 87 percent rated their own academic performance in the top 50 percent, while only 10 percent rated themselves below average in quantitative skills. A stunning 93 percent of all Americans believe they are above average drivers. While these are all statistically impossible, such undeserved optimism is not without its merits. It encourages us to take risks, the sort of risks that move companies, societies, and even civilization forward. It also helps us to persevere in the face of adversity. Kahneman even refers to the optimism bias as "the engine of capitalism." But he also points out that it helps explain why so many businesses—particularly small ones—fail. While only 35 percent of American small businesses survive five years, studies show the average American entrepreneur believes his or her business has a 60 percent chance of success—and fully 33 percent put their chances of failure at zero.

Red teaming balances the optimism bias with objective assessments of success that accurately factor in the true abilities of the organization and the true risks of the strategy or plan.

Ostrich effect. Nobody likes bad news, which is why so many of us actively—and often unconsciously—avoid it. Researchers have shown we will often go to great lengths to ignore negative information or data that is likely to contradict or challenge our assumptions. A 2009 study of investors in Sweden and the United States found they were significantly less likely to check the value of their investments during bear markets. This is a dangerous tendency because it can lead us to omit negative or contradictory data from our analyses, which can skew the results and lead us to make poor decisions.

Red teaming prevents the ostrich effect by actively seeking out data that challenges the underlying assumptions of a strategy or plan, ensuring that all facets of an issue are thoroughly examined, even if they are not pretty.

Outcome bias. Everybody loves a winner, so we naturally assume a decision was correct if the outcome was positive. But what if we just got lucky? No intelligent person would argue that drinking and driving is a good idea simply because they managed to make it home from a bar without killing themselves or anyone else in the process. Yet, in business, we often stop asking questions about a plan or strategy that is initially successful. We also tend to give more credence to people with a track record of success without analyzing the reasons for their success. Remember, past performance is no guarantee of future profitability.

Red teaming cuts through outcome bias by subjecting even successful strategies to critical analysis to test whether they can continue to be successful in the future. And it actively seeks out alternatives that may be even more *successful.*

Overconfidence. Success can also lead us to place too much faith in our own expertise. Nothing demonstrates this more dramatically than the results of an ongoing study led by Philip E. Tetlock, which has pitted top forecasters from Wall Street, the intelligence community, and academia against some twenty thousand amateurs with no forecasting expertise. Tetlock first assembled his group of "intellectually curious laypeople" in 2011. Each year, they are asked a number of questions: Will the Nikkei close above 9,500 by a certain date? Will the price of gold exceed $1,850? Will the Israelis launch an attack on an Iranian nuclear facility? Will OPEC cut production? Will Greece leave the Eurozone? The same questions are also posed to four other groups made up of top experts in these fields and professional prognosticators. The results have been stunning. The amateurs have consistently outperformed the experts by a wide margin. The top 2 percent even outperformed intelligence analysts with access to classified information. How were they able to do this? Tetlock found that his nonexperts approached these questions with a more open mind, were less sure of their initial conclusions, and were more likely to consider a range of views on the topic before submitting their answer. As he explains in his 2015 book, *Superforecasting,* "Foresight isn't a mysterious gift bestowed at birth. It is the product of particular ways of thinking, of gathering information, of updating beliefs." Tetlock discovered experts were more likely to consult only themselves and make their decisions based on their existing views. This helps explain why three-quarters of all U.S. stock mutual funds have failed to beat the market over the past decade.

Red teaming deals with overconfidence by requiring experts to rely on more than just their own expertise to prove their recommendations are valid. Red teams function a lot like Tetlock's superforecasters: They approach problems with an open mind, gather as much information as possible, and challenge their own biases and assumptions before drawing a conclusion.

Planning fallacy. This refers to the tendency to create forecasts and plans that, in the words of Kahneman and Tversky, are "unrealistically close to best-case scenarios." Kahneman cites a 2005 study that examined rail projects built around the world between 1969 and 1998. Planners overestimated the number of passengers that would take advantage of these improvements over 90 percent of the time. While the shortfalls were widely reported and the data was easily accessible, it appears to have done nothing to moderate the expectations of later planners, who continued to overestimate the number of riders on new rail projects by an average of 106 percent—contributing to an average cost overrun of 45 percent. In these days of big data, there is no excuse for business planners not to ground their estimates on the bedrock of statistical evidence. Too often, however, people still prefer to close their eyes and hope for the best.

Red teaming combats the planning fallacy by comparing forecasts to similar cases and seeking out relevant data that puts goals and targets in their proper perspective.

Regression fallacy. This is not so much a bias or heuristic as it is the failure to account for a hard, statistical reality: *regression to the mean.* This refers to the statistical likelihood that a variable that is extreme in its first measurement will tend to be closer to average on subsequent measurements. Our failure to grasp this fact leads us to draw all sorts of erroneous conclusions about the way the world works. To prove that, Kahneman makes the following claim: "Depressed children treated with an energy drink improve significantly over a three-month period," then explains the rationale behind it:

> *I made up this newspaper headline, but the fact it reports is true: if you treated a group of depressed children for some time with an energy drink, they would show a clinically significant improvement. It is also the case that depressed children who spend some time standing on their head or hug a cat for twenty minutes a day will also show improvement. Most readers of such headlines will automatically infer that the energy drink or the cat hugging caused an improvement, but this conclusion is completely unjustified. Depressed children are an extreme group, they are more depressed than most other children—and extreme groups regress to the mean over time. The correlation between depression scores on successive occasions of testing is less than perfect, so there will be regression to the mean: depressed children will get somewhat better over time even if they hug no cats and drink no Red Bull.*

The implications for business are significant. How many theories of management are nothing more than rationalizations of statistical aberrations or dumb luck? Kahneman himself points out that, on average, the gap in corporate profitability and stock returns between the outstanding firms and the less successful firms examined in *Built to Last* (1994) shrank to almost nothing in the period following the study. The average profitability of the companies identified in the book *In Search of Excellence* (1982) dropped sharply as well. A study of *Fortune*'s "Most Admired Companies" finds that, over a twenty-year period, the firms with the worst ratings went on to earn much higher stock returns than the most admired firms. Of course, given the cyclical nature of markets, it is unfair to expect any company to stay on top forever. I and others who study business believe valuable insights can still be gleaned from companies that achieve even temporary success. But it is important to remember that sometimes companies, and the men and women who lead them, just get lucky. Or unlucky.

Red teaming helps mitigate the regression fallacy by ensuring regression to the mean is considered as a possible cause when assessing past performance and planning for the future.

Status quo bias. We tend to prefer things as they already are, and that can have a big impact on our choices. A study of American equity mutual fund investors found they had a strong preference for maintaining their current fund choices even if those choices were no longer the best ones. Researchers also found this preference increased the more choices those investors were given. In other words, given the choice, many people would prefer not to choose at all. Related biases include *existence bias*, which refers to the tendency to perceive something as good simply because it already exists, and *longevity bias*, which refers to the tendency for that positive view to increase the longer something has been in existence. Status quo bias helps explain why some companies persist in following ineffective processes—and why they make the same mistakes over and over again.

Red teaming counters the status quo bias by forcing organizations to review their strategies and plans and ensure that they are still the best options available.

Sunk-cost fallacy. Most of us have a hard time cutting our losses, even in the face of overwhelming evidence that the current course of action will lead to even greater losses. This helps explain why manufacturers keep factories running even though they are losing money, why failed products are kept on the shelf, and why ineffective CEOs get their contracts renewed. The cost that is sunk does not have to be monetary; it can also be time, political capital, or any other finite resource. The sunk-cost fallacy can also lead to *irrational escalation*, in which we incrementally up our investment to reach a desired outcome to the point that we end up paying far more for something than it is actually worth, as anyone who has won a bidding war can attest.

Red teaming prevents organizations from falling victim to the sunk-cost fallacy by objectively analyzing the future risks of a failing strategy or plan without regard to the cost already incurred in pursuing it.

Temporal discounting. This refers to a spectrum of biases connected to our desire for instant gratification. Most of us would rather have a smaller reward today than a bigger reward tomorrow. Most of us prefer to defer solving problems now even though that will make them more expensive to deal with in the future. And most of us have a hard time understanding compound interest. Temporal discounting leads us to downplay the future negative consequences of decisions that have positive consequences right now, and it helps explain why we tend to focus on the immediate consequences of an action without fully considering its long-term effects. All of these have huge ramifications for business. They are why so many companies avoid fixing problems until they are forced to, and why so many companies, and investors, emphasize near-term success over long-term profitability.

Red teaming addresses temporal discounting by forcing organizations to consider the long-term impact of their decisions, as well as the short-term ones.

* * *

Not all cognitive psychologists are convinced that these biases and heuristics play such a central—and detrimental—role in our thought processes. Gary Klein is one of the skeptics. He believes people do a better job of making decisions than Kahneman lets on, and he has conducted several impressive studies that demonstrate the ways in which we unconsciously draw on the power of experience to make good, intuitive decisions. But Klein, too, is worried about our limitations.

"I am more troubled by the difficulty of learning from experience. We cannot often see a clear link between cause and effect. Too many variables intervene, and time delays create their own complications," he writes in his fascinating treatise on naturalistic decision making, *Sources of Power: How People Make Decisions*. "If managers find themselves having success—getting projects completed on schedule and under budget—does that success stem from their own skills, the skills of their subordinates, temporary good luck, interventions of higher-level administrators, a blend of these factors, or some other causes altogether? There is no easy way to tell. We can learn the wrong lessons from experience. Each time we compile a story about an experience, we run the risk of getting it wrong and stamping in the wrong strategy."

Mental Models

Our decision-making process is also affected—often unconsciously—by mental models, which management expert Peter Senge defined as "deeply ingrained assumptions, generalizations, or even pictures or images that influence how we understand the world and how we take action." Mental models are related to, and are often shaped by, our biases and heuristics. Like them, mental models serve a useful function—at least up to a point. They help us make sense of a complex reality. But they can also make it difficult for us to change our view of that reality. We are often unaware we are relying on these mental models, so we allow them to go unchallenged, even in the face of new evidence and insights. Senge offers an example of this in his 1990 classic, *The Fifth Discipline*:

> *I will never forget visiting with a group of Detroit auto
> executives after their first factory visits to Japan over twenty
> years ago. This was right around the time that US automakers
> were finally waking up to the fact that Japan was steadily
> gaining market and profit share in their industry—and it might
> be attributed to how they managed, not just because they had
> "cheap" labor or protected home markets. A little way into
> the conversation, it was clear that the Detroit executives were*

unimpressed. I asked why and one said, "They didn't show us real plants." When I inquired as to what he meant by this, he responded, "There were no inventories in any of the plants. I've been in manufacturing operations for almost thirty years and I can tell you those were not real plants. They had clearly been staged for our tour." Today we all know that they were indeed real plants, examples of the "Just-in-time" inventory systems that the Japanese had been working on for many years that dramatically reduced the need for in-process inventories throughout the manufacturing system.

Because our mental models tend to remain unexamined, the gap between them and the evolving reality of the wider world increases over time. Not only do we fail to take advantage of new innovations, but our actions can also become increasingly counterproductive.

Red teaming challenges our mental models with contrarian thinking and forces us to reexamine them. By doing so, red teaming gives us an opportunity to modify our mental models and ensure that they are better aligned with the current reality.

Groupthink and Other Organizational Faults

Organizations are also prone to irrationality in their decision-making processes. These tendencies often become deeply ingrained in a company's culture, making them difficult to isolate and stamp out. Once again, red teaming can help.

Groupthink. Irving Janis famously defined *groupthink* as "a psychological drive for consensus at any cost that suppresses dissent and appraisal of alternatives in cohesive decision making groups." At its most benign, groupthink makes it hard for organizations to question their own assumptions. It also makes it difficult for them to embrace new mental models. But groupthink is often much more virulent, and when it is, it can lead groups to make irrational decisions. In the political arena, groupthink has been blamed for everything from America's ill-conceived Bay of Pigs Invasion in 1961 to the erroneous belief that Saddam Hussein had amassed an arsenal of weapons of mass destruction in Iraq in 2003. Groupthink also has been blamed for many high-profile business failures, such as the collapse of Swissair and the Enron debacle.

Janis identified eight symptoms of groupthink:

1. Illusions of invulnerability: the belief that the group cannot fail.

2. Morality: the belief that the group's motives are inherently good and correct.

3. Rationalizing: the tendency to "explain away" contradictory information or data.

4. Stereotyping: the tendency to portray others who are opposed to the group as evil or stupid.

5. Self-censorship: the tendency of group members to keep their doubts to themselves.

6. Illusions of unanimity: the belief that silence is the same as agreement.

7. Mindguards: the emergence of self-appointed thought police who actively shield the group from information that might challenge its assumptions.

8. Conformity: the tendency to view dissent as disloyalty.

Later researchers have added to our understanding of the nature and pathology of groupthink, but these original observations are probably all too familiar to those of us who have worked for large corporations or government bureaucracies.

Red teaming counteracts groupthink by directly challenging an organization's assumptions and actively encouraging contrarian views.

Abilene paradox. This phenomenon is similar to groupthink, but while groupthink occurs unconsciously, the Abilene paradox refers to situations in which members of a group *consciously* act against their own wishes or beliefs in order to preserve group harmony and cohesion. This is what happens when we say *yes,* but we really mean *no.* The term was coined by management expert Jerry B. Harvey, who used the example of an unpleasant family trip to Abilene, Texas, that no one actually wanted to take to illustrate what he saw as a major source of organizational dysfunction: the inability to manage agreement. Abilene paradoxes occur when no one in a group is willing to talk about the proverbial elephant in the room—and that elephant can be anything from a belief that Abilene is not a particularly pleasant destination for a family outing to the recognition that a plan that once seemed so promising is clearly not going to work.

Red teaming helps resolve the Abilene paradox by asking if the trip an organization is taking is really necessary.

Conformity. Our desire for conformity is so powerful it can distort our view of reality at the most basic level, as the psychologist Solomon Asch famously demonstrated in a series of experiments that began in 1951. Asch told his subjects they were participating in a study of perception and gave them a pair of cards. The first (Fig. 1) had a straight line drawn on it. The second (Fig. 2) had three lines on it. Line A was clearly shorter than the line on the first card, while Line B was clearly longer. Line C was exactly the same length as the line on the first card.

Sample cards from the Asch experiments

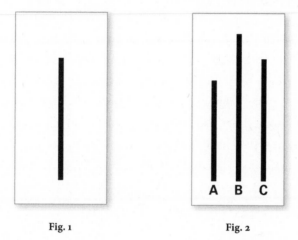

Fig. 1   Fig. 2

Asch next asked the participants to identify which of these three lines matched the line on the first card. It was a simple task, and in control groups, the error rate was less than 1 percent. But Asch was not actually studying perception, and most of his subjects were not put in control groups. Instead, they were assigned to a group with seven other students, all of whom were actors. The group was shown a pair of cards, and each person in the group was asked to say which line on the second card matched the line on the first card. The actors were always called on first, and each of them gave the exact same answer. In the first two rounds, they all gave the correct answer. In the next sixteen rounds, they unanimously gave the wrong answer twelve times. Amazingly, 75 percent of the actual test subjects gave the wrong answer, too, in at least one of these rounds.

Asch also found that having just one of the actors give a different answer from the majority in each round dramatically reduced the chances the test subject would echo the majority's incorrect answers. The lone dissenting voice did not even have to give the correct answer; by simply offering a different perspective, they gave the test subjects permission to think for themselves.

Red teaming provides that lone dissenting voice in an organization that allows others to think for themselves.

Satisficing. This is the practice of making a decision by choosing the first available option that works—even if it is not the best one. First identified by Herbert A. Simon, satisficing can be quite valuable, particularly when making a decision under time constraints. The problem is that organizations sometimes use satisficing as their default decision-making method, even if they have the time and resources necessary for a more thorough analysis of their options.

Where time and resources permit, red teaming challenges organizations to probe deeper and look for optimal solutions.

Swallowing the Red Pill

Reading about these biases and heuristics may make you feel a little bit like you've just popped the red pill and opened your eyes to the Matrix. Thinking about them will keep you up at night. They will make you question choices you've made in the past and hesitate when called upon to make decisions in the future. After spending several days studying the science and psychology of human decision making as part of the red team training course at Fort Leavenworth, my classmates and I found it hard even to order a pizza. After all, do you *really* want mushrooms, or is that just the bandwagon effect talking?

But just because our brains are prone to these biases and like to take these shortcuts does not mean we are condemned to making poor judgments or bad decisions. By being aware of these threats to rational thought, we can guard against them in ourselves. Through red teaming, we can help our organizations avoid them as well.

While it may be true that we really don't know what we don't know, we can use red teaming to find out.

CHAPTER 4

How to Start
Red Teaming

*The general who wins a battle makes many calculations in
his temple ere the battle is fought. The general who loses a
battle makes but few calculations beforehand. Thus do many
calculations lead to victory, and few calculations to defeat.*

—Sun Tzu

On a rainy London afternoon in October 2014, I splashed across
Horse Guards Road, dashed into a rather unassuming door-
way cut into a quiet corner of Her Majesty's Treasury at the foot of the
Clive Steps, and shook my umbrella out in the foyer of the bunker that
served as Winston Churchill's headquarters during the dark days of
World War II. Recognizing the historic significance of what were officially known as the Cabinet War Rooms, the British government had
the presence of mind to preserve these claustrophobic chambers exactly
as they were at the war's end—right down to the half-smoked cigar in
the ashtray on Churchill's desk. What struck me as I wandered through

the narrow, dimly lit hallways was the sheer amount of information crammed into this small, heavily fortified space. The walls, including those of Churchill's bedchamber, were covered with maps and reports. They showed everything from the current position of Allied forces in every theater of the war to the number of V-2 rockets striking London each week. Those missiles and the Luftwaffe bombers that preceded them may have forced the prime minister underground, but the reams of data that covered the walls of his bunker and the tangled telephone and telegraph lines snaking through the labyrinthine structure made it clear he never stopped scanning the horizon for new insights and information.

No place in the bunker demonstrates this more poignantly than the secret room concealed behind door number 63. Emblazoned with the warning KEEP LOCKED, most of the bunker's staff were fed the lie that it contained Churchill's private loo—a cover story that helped explain why the prime minister would often disappear into it only to emerge sometime later in a cloud of pungent cigar smoke. In fact, the tiny room contained a direct telephone line to the White House. Thanks to this secure connection and the privacy afforded by his secret phone booth, Churchill could converse at his leisure with President Franklin Roosevelt. The two men would often spend the better part of an hour discussing the progress of the war, bouncing ideas off each other and dissecting the weightiest problems then confronting humanity.

Churchill's bunker may have been sealed behind stout blast doors, but it was hardly a vacuum. Rather, it was a nerve center that sucked in information and ideas from around the world, giving the prime minister the intellectual ammunition he needed to help save the world from fascism.

If you study the few photographs taken inside Adolf Hitler's *Führerbunker*, the contrast is striking. Yes, there were a few maps on display in the conference room. But most of the walls, including those of Hitler's private chamber, were bare concrete—unadorned except for the odd piece of looted artwork. Hitler surrounded himself not with charts and statistics, but with icons of Germany's glorious past captured in oil paint like insects in amber. When Hitler's generals intruded with the increasingly dismal news of the outside world, he would rail against them, denouncing them as incompetent, and ridiculing them in one of his infamous tirades. Churchill also argued with his generals, but he never overruled them.

"You can't red team in the *Führerbunker,*" Colonel Steve Rotkoff once told me when I asked him what was required for successful red teaming. "You need top cover. You need buy-in from the senior leadership of your organization. And you need them to be open to new ideas and insights. They have to at least be willing to consider that there *may* be room for improvement in their strategies and plans. If they are not, there's not much point in red teaming."

Assuming your organization has the sort of buy-in from the top that red teaming requires, and is ready to embrace red teaming as part of its planning process, the next step is to decide what sort of red team you want to create—or if you want to establish a standing red team at all.

Choosing the Right Model

Red teaming can be conducted formally or informally. It can be done by members of a company's senior leadership team, an ad hoc committee made up of staff members selected for their critical thinking skills, or by a dedicated red team whose only job is to provide a fresh set of eyes to examine the organization's strategies and plans. It can be led by an in-house expert or an outside facilitator. There are several different models for red teaming. Each approach has its advantages and disadvantages; choosing the right model depends on what your company, organization, division, or group hopes to gain from red teaming, as well as the resources it is willing and able to devote to it.

Informal red teaming. Instead of setting up an actual red team, or even conducting a red teaming exercise, your senior leadership team or planning staff can simply use one or more of the red teaming techniques described in the book to take a deeper look at a plan or strategy before implementing it. This is not something I recommend, because it lacks the analytical rigor and objectivity of a more formal red teaming exercise. The people who participate in this sort of informal analysis will likely already have an opinion about the strategy or plan being examined, making it easier for them to fall victim to bias, not to mention groupthink and other organizational pressures. That said, using the tools and techniques in this book will help you plan better and think more clearly about the challenges and opportunities facing your business. Just recognize that this is not the same thing as formal red teaming.

Outside red teaming. Rather than go to the expense of building and maintaining a standing, in-house red team, your organization can hire a red team consulting firm to conduct an analysis of your strategy or plan. The advantages of this approach are the costs are known up front, the investment in time is minimal, and it can make red teaming as simple as picking up the telephone and calling the right consultant. An independent red team will be inoculated against your organization's biases, immune to its internal politics, and can offer an honest assessment to senior leadership. But there are significant disadvantages to this model as well. An outside red team may miss important nuances because of its lack of familiarity with your company, your industry, or the competitive environment. This can be a big concern in and of itself, but it also makes it easy for senior management to dismiss the findings of the red team. Moreover, the decision to bring in an outside red team is bound to create an adversarial relationship with the organization's staff. As Daniel Kahneman told me, "It's the same problem you have whenever you bring in consultants. You already have people in the company whose job it is to solve the problem [that is being analyzed by the red team]. Every effort will be made within the organization to sabotage the red team, to paralyze them, to deny them the information that they need, and to make them look stupid."

Facilitated red teaming. This approach employs one or more outside red team leaders as facilitators. These trained experts work with your organization's leadership team to conduct a rigorous analysis of a specific strategy or plan. Using an outside red teaming expert can mitigate groupthink and force team members to challenge their assumptions and examine their biases. And having a company's leaders participate in the analysis, and draw their own conclusions, helps to ensure that the red team's findings are taken seriously and not ignored. It also allows the team to benefit from the red teaming expert's experience and insights. Another advantage of this model is it does not require your organization to pay for red team training, nor does it require you to dedicate staff to a standing red team. As with outside red teaming, the cost is known up front, and it makes it easy for a company to get started with red teaming. The downside of this approach is that it does not give you in-house, on-demand red teaming capability, which can be valuable—particularly for large organizations. This approach also may do less to transform the culture of your organization, which can be an important side benefit of red teaming.

Ad hoc red teaming. This model relies on a trained, in-house red teaming leader to pull together a team from within the organization to analyze strategies, plans, and problems on an as-needed basis. There are many advantages to this approach, as well as a couple of significant disadvantages. This model ensures all the red team participants are familiar with your company and your industry, but it also means they will be prone to the same biases and groupthink that affect the rest of your organization. Ad hoc red teaming is hard to ignore because its work is often done by senior members of the company, but that also makes these red teams vulnerable to internal politics. This approach gives a business an in-house, on-demand red teaming capability, but other work responsibilities can make it hard for members to dedicate sufficient time and energy to red teaming. The main expense is training one of your employees to be a red team leader, but that can also be a valuable investment in leadership development. In fact, this approach can allow a company to spread red teaming throughout the organization, and make its entire culture more thoughtful and analytical—particularly if the position of red team leader is a rotating one that becomes a required stop on the corporate ladder for high-potential executives. Over time, a business that takes this approach will end up with a senior leadership team that is well versed in the techniques of red teaming, which will make them better planners, better strategists, and more agile thinkers.

Dedicated red teaming. The original model for red teaming, this approach involves establishing a permanent, standing team of dedicated analysts trained in the full panoply of red teaming tools and techniques. This team's entire purpose is to provide alternative analysis and critical review of the organization's strategies and plans. It is also available to analyze individual problems and to war-game competitors. The advantage of this approach is it gives you an in-house, on-demand red teaming capability that—if organized correctly and led effectively—is also insulated from your company's internal politics and less susceptible to groupthink and other organizational biases. Moreover, dedicated red teams have the time and space necessary to generate comprehensive analysis and explore a wide array of alternatives and possibilities. These standing red teams can also monitor a strategy or plan as it unfolds, and continue to provide input and support to your staff as it executes. This allows your organization to more rapidly adapt to the changing business environment and take advantage of new opportunities as they arise. Ideally, the red team's performance will be judged by the depth of its analysis and its ability to challenge your organization's assumptions, giving it the freedom to think differently and offer unvarnished assessments, and making it a powerful tool for driving long-term success. The main disadvantage of this model is its cost, in terms of both money and talent. For a red team to function at its best, it needs to be staffed by some of the best and brightest minds in your organization. Assigning those talented individuals to a standing red team means they are unavailable for other work. As a result, this approach is probably a better option for large corporations, which can offset this by rotating staff in and out of the red team. Dedicated red teams also run the risk of developing an adversarial relationship with the rest of the organization. A skilled red team leader will prevent that, but it is important to make certain neither the red team nor the regular planning staff adopts an us-versus-them mentality.

The Evolution of Red Teaming

The U.S. Army's original concept for red teaming called for the creation of permanent, standing red teams at the theater, corps, division, and brigade level—each staffed by a cadre of trained red teamers and led by a certified red team leader. This approach usually proved quite effective. But not always.

Army red teams have worked well when they molded themselves to fit into the organizations they were assigned to, and were quick to demonstrate their value to the leaders they served. But teams ran into problems when they insisted on remaining aloof from the rest of the organization's staff and went out of their way to prove they were smarter than everyone else. This mixed experience, combined with harsh fiscal realities imposed by the drawdown of forces in the Middle East and the budget battles back in Washington, have forced the army to rethink its approach to red teaming. While the army maintains dedicated red teams at the combat theater level,* it is making greater use of ad hoc red teams.

"We are training staff officers to serve as red team leaders and red team members in addition to their other responsibilities. They all have other day jobs, but their commander can pull them together when necessary to look at a problem or analyze a plan," Rotkoff explains. "That

---

*Even red teams at this level are due to be phased out by the end of the 2017 fiscal year.

has proven very successful, and it's why our program continues to grow even in this time of budget cuts and austerity."

NATO's alternative analysis group often provides this sort of facilitation, with trained analysts leading red teaming exercises for different organizations within the alliance, rather than giving each of those groups its own standing red team.

"We don't have standing red teams, because the culture of NATO is to be polite. When you have Europeans working with Americans, that critical way of looking at things wouldn't necessarily be helpful. We created a middle ground because of necessity," says Johannes de Nijs, head of the NATO alternative analysis program. "We are not stakeholders. We are always supporting someone else. That helps us remain disconnected from a particular option or outcome."

The U.S. Marine Corps has taken a slightly different approach to red teaming.

"We have both standing red teams and ad hoc red teams," says Colonel Ray Damm. "Red teaming is probably more institutionalized in the army than it is in the Marine Corps. Our approach is less formal."

Kristy Hill, who heads up the New Zealand Defence Force's red teaming program, says her country decided to model its program after the Marines'.

"Kiwis are quite practical and independent thinkers," she says. "Because we have a small military, everybody has to wear more than one hat. Our intent is to create a cadre of red team leaders that we can call upon on an ad hoc basis."

At the other end of the spectrum, the British Ministry of Defence has created an elaborate, highly structured approach to red teaming that relies on two teams of dedicated analysts augmented by outside red team members selected for their diverse perspectives. One of these groups, known as *frackers,* is tasked with breaking a plan down into its constituent parts and extracting all of the stated and unstated assumptions upon which it is based. The second group, known as *mappers,* takes this raw data and turns it into a chart that shows the correlations and dependencies connecting each of these assumptions. It analyzes this map, identifies weak links and inconsistencies, then goes over its findings with the *frackers* before preparing a final report. The point is to separate the ideas behind the plan from the way in which those ideas are presented by the plan's author. The MoD has developed its own three-dimensional mapping software to display this data, both for the benefit of the red team and for briefing senior officers.

"The advantage of that, if I am brutally rude, is that most senior military officers get bored with briefings," says the group's leader, Brigadier Tom Longland. "If you give them a long, verbal briefing, their eyes glaze over and the moment is lost after about thirty minutes. But if you show them a map of a problem, they are onto it. They are interested and they are asking all of the right questions. So that's what we do. We end up with a map of the concept, which will show quite clearly if there is a logic that runs through the whole, or if there are ideas that seem very attractive and sound wonderful but actually are not really related to what we are talking about."

While red teaming is most effective when it is carried out by an independent team of trained experts whose only job is to provide decision support and alternative analysis, that is not always practical—or even desirable.

"After the recent global economic crisis, there has been tremendous pressure on corporations all over the world to cut costs and keep them low, particularly at the top. That will make it difficult for many companies to create a dedicated red team," points out Harry Murakami, president of the Development Bank of Japan's Investment Advisory Company. "But that does not mean they cannot find other ways to use red teaming."

Businesses have only just begun to experiment with red teaming. I am not aware of any that have established the sort of full-time, in-house red teams used by the U.S. Army. Most have taken a less formal approach. Yet even that has paid big dividends, according to companies such as Vaughan Nelson, an investment management firm based in Houston.

Vaughan Nelson, which works primarily with large, institutional clients, started red teaming as a way of differentiating itself in a very crowded field of competitors. Instead of the formal investment committee model employed by most firms, Vaughan Nelson portfolio managers are encouraged to develop an investment plan, pitch it to their colleagues, and then defend it as they try to discover the ways in which it could fail.

"Our process culminates in what we call a 'hall brawl'—which literally takes place in the hallway outside my office," explains senior portfolio manager Scott Weber. "The idea is not to make a thirty-minute meeting out of this. It's just to take a step back and create a bit of a red teaming environment—not to be adversarial, but to challenge each other and make sure we've really thought of everything. I call it a *council of devil's advocacy*."

A major insurance company that was one of the first in the United States to embrace formal red teaming says the ad hoc approach is the only one that made sense to it, though its red team meets regularly regardless of whether it has a specific plan to study.

"We could never afford a permanent, standing red team," says the team's leader, speaking on the condition that I not identify him or his company for competitive reasons. "We have to limit the amount of time we dedicate to red teaming, because we all still have day jobs that need to get done. At the same time, we think it is important to meet regularly so that we do not lose cohesion as a team. There is always something worth looking at."

How do they keep company politics out of their red team?

"We don't. It's better to embrace it right from the word *go*. What we do is make sure that the politics get identified and called out in our results and in our reports," says the team leader, who also advocates a cautious approach when tipping sacred cows. He and his team rarely tell senior leadership their favorite ideas are wrong. Instead, the red teamers acknowledge the value of those ideas, then point out the shortcomings.

"It's like judo. I use the organization's expectations to get them leaning in the right direction. Then it's much easier to put them on my hip and turn them over."

Most of my own experience has involved working with companies as an outside red team facilitator. In a typical engagement, a company will hire me to guide its senior leadership team through a red teaming exercise, focusing on the organization's general strategy or a particular plan. My role in these exercises is to explain how the different red teaming tools and techniques work, choose the ones that are most suitable for the issue under review, and then lead the executives through those exercises. The actual analysis is done by the executives themselves, which, as I said earlier, makes it hard for them to dispute or ignore.

In the summer of 2015, Dale Carnegie and Associates was preparing a comprehensive plan aimed at reviving its once preeminent professional development program. CEO Joe Hart asked me to work with his team to make sure that plan fully addressed all the challenges and opportunities facing the Dale Carnegie company before he submitted it to the board of directors. To do that, we broke the plan down into its major components, using the *Liberating Structures* I will discuss in chapter 5 to identify the aspects of the plan most likely to fail. Then we employed a number of different red teaming techniques, including *Four Ways of Seeing* and *Pre-Mortem Analysis* (both of which will be described in chapter 7), to figure out how to improve those areas of the plan to better ensure success.

"As a team, we had put together what we thought was really a solid plan, and we were very excited about it. Then we went through this process of red teaming it, and we started to see all of the hidden weaknesses in the plan," says Hart. "In the absence of red teaming, we more than likely would have missed some pretty significant areas, and there's no question that the plan we executed would not have been as effective. As it happened, we had extraordinarily positive results that would not have been possible without the red teaming exercise."

My advice is to adopt the most aggressive model for red teaming that your organization can readily accommodate, both in terms of cost and complexity. But be honest about this. If you stretch too far in setting up your red team, it can become a cumbersome burden that sours your entire organization on this worthwhile endeavor. You can always start small and build out your red teaming capabilities over time. The important thing is to *start* red teaming. And there is no better time than *now*.

Justifying the Cost of Red Teaming

Ask anyone in the field to name the most challenging aspect of red teaming and you are certain to get the same answer: justifying the investment.

"What is the sound of no dogs barking?" asks Colonel Greg Fontenot. "That's the question you're constantly trying to answer when you're pitching red teaming."

It is easy to view red teaming as an expensive luxury, because it is hard to put a price on avoiding a catastrophe that never happens. How do you put a price on not making a bad investment? How do you calculate the cost of new a competitor never emerging because your company figured out how to disrupt your industry before they did? How do you tally the return on investment for a team that saves you from yourself?

These are questions every organization must answer for itself. Because red teaming is not essential to the day-to-day operations of a company, it can be hard to get going, and easy to cut in times of austerity. Yet the value red teaming can bring to your organization is immense—and the costs of *not* red teaming can be enormous.

One way to make it easier to account for the cost of a standing red team is to make it part of a broader functional group. Kahneman suggested this approach when I told him that, as much as the companies I had been working with liked the idea of a dedicated red team and saw the value of having one, most could not figure out how to afford such a permanent luxury. He said a red team could earn its keep by also managing things such as data mining.

"My inclination would be to have one piece of the organization that reports directly to the very top that is in charge of many things: it's in charge of decision making, it's in charge of leadership training, and it's in charge of data. That's a very valuable function, and that's a very powerful person. You give that job to an executive who is a candidate for CEO," he said. "Don't call it a red team. Call it a *decision support group.*"

While even that approach might be too expensive for many businesses to justify, my experience has shown me that most companies of any size spend a good deal of money on consulting services each year, and too often walk away with little to show for it. Instead of giving a big consulting firm a boatload of cash to tell you something you already know, why not use that money to pay for a red team that can show you what you are missing?

Making Space for Red Teaming

Regardless of which model you choose, your red team needs to be plugged into your organization chart as near to the top as possible. Red teams have the greatest impact when they are as close to decision makers as possible while still maintaining a degree of separation from senior leadership. By keeping the red team close, those managers can ensure that their concerns are fully addressed in the red team's analysis; by keeping it separate, the red team has the space and independence it needs to think differently. That separation is vital if you want to make sure your red team is not infected by groupthink, or unduly influenced by other organizational pressures. This proximity also will help ensure the red team's work is not forgotten or ignored.

Ideally, a red team should report directly to the CEO. At the very least, the red team should report to the head of the division or group responsible for the strategy or plan under review. At the insurance company I mentioned, the red team reports to the chief financial officer, but includes representatives from other departments as well. And the team leaders share their findings directly with that company's entire executive team. Whatever you do, make sure the red team's reporting chain excludes individuals or groups whose status, influence, or resources could be affected by those recommendations. Such conflicts of interest are a sure way to guarantee a red team's findings are distorted, or even buried.

Whoever your red team reports to, it should be someone with the authority to act upon the red team's recommendations, or at least the ability to present those recommendations to someone who can. Otherwise, the red team runs the risk of becoming a modern-day Cassandra—able to see where the danger lies, but unable to get anyone to heed its warnings.

Since red teaming can be costly in terms of time and resources, it is important to ensure your red team is set up in such a way that it can actually make a difference in your organization. To do that, your red team must have the freedom to speak truth to power.

Red teaming is most effective when the red team has permission to question the unquestionable, think the unthinkable, and challenge everything. If you ask a red team to review a plan, you need to be willing to listen to the team's findings—even if they are critical—and not take it personally. The moment you punish someone in your organization for red teaming is the moment red teaming becomes impossible in your company. For the red team to do its job effectively, those who serve on it need to know they are not only free, but expected, to challenge the organization's assumptions. You do not have to go along with the red team's recommendations, but you need to allow the red team to make them.

Your red team also needs to know its work is taken seriously. If the red team is routinely ignored, it will not take long for the people on the team to realize your organization is only paying lip service to red teaming. In that case, red teaming will become just another bureaucratic chore—one more box to check in the planning process. On the other hand, if you use the red team's findings to improve your plans and strategies, that sends a powerful message to your whole organization. It tells all your employees that you are not afraid of the truth, even when that truth is painful. Over time, that unflinching honesty will change the culture of your company for the better, making it more self-critical, more innovative, and better able to handle the challenges and opportunities of today's rapidly changing world.

Creating a Red Team

If you decide to create an in-house red team, selecting the right people to serve on it will be critical to its success.

The optimum size for a red team is between five and eleven people. A group can red team with fewer people, but the diversity of perspectives will be more limited. A group can red team with more people, but it becomes harder to remain focused and on task. That said, it can sometimes be useful to include more people when tackling a particularly complicated problem. This allows you to divide the team into subgroups and give each one a different facet of the problem to analyze. Regardless of how many people you assign to your red team, I recommend you allow the red team leader to help select them, so that he or she can assemble the right mix of talent, personality, and experience.

Whether you create an independent, standing red team or pull together a red team as needed, it is essential to include men and women with good analytical and critical thinking skills, close attention to detail, and the ability to think outside the box. They need the confidence and assurance to challenge the status quo, as well as the self-awareness required to recognize their own biases and limitations. They also should be intellectually honest and able to resist the pressures of organizational politics.

A good candidate for a red team is:

1. Intelligent

2. Imaginative

3. Inquisitive

4. Analytical

5. Strategic

6. Logical

7. Self-aware

8. Self-confident

9. Open-minded

Dr. Mark Mateski, founder and editor of *Red Team Journal,* says, "The superior red teamer understands that no truly objective view of the world exists. This includes the red teamer's own view. The ability to perceive, understand, and empathize with other worldviews and perceptions characterizes a good red teamer more so than any other characteristic. The superior red teamer also is self-aware. In practice, this means that he or she constantly runs a self-check routine. This routine is especially sensitive to bias and ego. In practice, this should yield a red teamer who listens to both the spoken and the unspoken."

A strong red team member also needs good communication skills.

"Being a good red teamer is about asking good questions," says Susan Craig, a graduate of the first red team leader course at Fort Leavenworth in 2006. "Effective communication is vital. This means knowing how and when to ask questions, knowing your audience and the personalities with which you are dealing and for whom you are crafting your message, and using and demanding precise language."

Another important factor to consider when putting together a red team is diversity. Whenever possible, make sure your red team includes a mix of men and women, veteran employees and recent hires—even different generations. The point of this diversity is not to meet some affirmative action test, but to ensure your red team can leverage a myriad of different perspectives, and take advantage of as broad a range of insights as possible. The British go out of their way to include at least one young intern on their red teams. Brigadier Longland learned how valuable this could be when his red team was analyzing an overhaul of the Ministry of Defence's human resources policies.

"We had one young girl on the team with a mind like a razor. As we were going through the proposed changes, she said, 'What worries me is there is absolutely nothing in this policy that takes care of unmarried mothers.' When we raised that issue during the briefing, one of the very senior officers was heard saying to another senior officer, 'Do we have unmarried mothers in Her Majesty's armed forces?'" Longland recalls with a chuckle. "She knew nothing about the military, but she came and she listened. She then applied her brain and said this is part of the problem. And I thought, *well done!* It was something that would never have occurred to any of the other team members."

Diversity should not just be limited to gender, age, or race. You should also strive to create a diversity of experience on your red team. Look for people who have an unusual educational background, an unconventional career path, or distinctive personality traits. Find people who have lived and worked abroad. Include people who have firsthand experience with a key competitor or other outside stakeholder—anyone whose background suggests they may have different perspectives to offer. Include people from different functional areas, different departments, different divisions. The more diverse your red team is, the better able it will be to look at your strategy, plan, or problem from different angles, offer different insights, and find things others in your organization may have missed.

One corporate red team leader says putting people from different departments on the same ad hoc red team can even help dilute the influence of company politics. He says including people with a natural red teaming bent can also help in this regard: "If you can find people who are contrarian by nature, they are often willing to argue against their own cause as reflex."

Whatever you do, make sure you populate your red team with some of your best and brightest employees. Do not allow it to become a ghetto or dumping ground for people who do not fit in elsewhere in your organization. When this has been allowed to happen in military red teams, those red teams have proven ineffective at best.

Because top talent is at a premium in most organizations, managers can be understandably resistant to giving up a high-potential executive or star employee. One way to overcome that resistance is by rotating people in and out of your red team on a regular basis. I believe that is something you should do as a matter of course. Otherwise, your red team will develop its own blind spots and fall victim to its own group-think over time.

"A large, robust, bureaucratic institution probably needs some stand-alone red teaming capability. But the people in it should not be tenured," says Fontenot. "You should task-organize the red team so that you bring in different skill sets. For something like the army, I thought it made sense to have a core group of two or three red teamers that would be rotated and supplement that with subject matter experts on a case-by-case basis."

The use of subject matter experts is perhaps the biggest area of disagreement in the global red teaming community. A subject matter expert is someone with direct, firsthand experience relevant to the topic under consideration. If you were red teaming a plan to expand into India, for example, a subject matter expert might be an executive with prior experience working on the subcontinent or a marketing consultant specializing in the region.

The U.S. military believes it is valuable to have at least one person on the team who has intimate knowledge of the issue being analyzed, because that person's expertise will enable the other team members to dispense with a lot of easy questions quickly. In addition, a subject matter expert's knowledge can help the team avoid the sort of "rookie mistakes" we all make when tackling topics that are unfamiliar to us.

The British, on the other hand, believe having an expert on a red team can skew results in favor of the status quo. Longland describes an early red teaming exercise his group conducted involving submarine operations. That red team included a submariner in the group, who initially seemed to be a real asset. He was able to answer many of the questions that occurred to the other red team members—questions it could have taken them days to research on their own. But as the analysis proceeded, it became clear that the submariner's answers were based on his subjective experience, not on objective facts. For example, he told the group that submarines could not operate below a certain depth. That was true in normal operations, but the team later discovered exceptions were possible. This ended up being a critical piece of information they would have missed if they had continued to rely solely on his experience.

"Even with that knowledge, it proved difficult for the rest of the team to challenge him because of his vast expertise," Longland said. "You can use subject matter experts. You can use their expertise. But because of the intellectual baggage they carry, you cannot use their analytical skills."

The MoD now asks red team members to recuse themselves from analyses that involve their area of expertise. For example, the standing team at the Development, Concepts and Doctrine Centre in Shrivenham includes a lawyer—they often make excellent red team members—but she was excluded from a recent review of proposed changes to British military law.

NATO takes a middle path. It includes experts on red teams that are working on plans that require technical understanding, but it takes steps to ensure those experts do not unduly influence the red team's thinking.

"If you have an expert participate on your red team, you need to prep them beforehand so that they do not dominate the discussion," de Nijs offers. "An expert can warn you if the recommendations you are putting together are totally unworkable, and that can help you have a good outcome."

When they do not include experts on the actual red team, NATO makes sure relevant subject matter experts do review the red team's findings and proposals before they are submitted to senior leadership.

The CIA, too, struggled with this issue when it established its Red Cell back in 2001.

"By design, the initial Red Cell did not include any terrorism experts and only had one Middle East specialist. Members were individually selected for their analytical capabilities, creativity, and unique mind-sets," reported Micah Zenko, adding that these traits remain in demand today. "Directors seek people who are analytically fearless, excellent writers, and deeply knowledgeable about history and world affairs. Harder to find, but nevertheless necessary, are individuals with the characteristics of 'playing well in the sandbox with others,' checking their rank and ego at the door, being bureaucratically savvy, and having the ability to laugh at themselves daily. Red Cell analysts contend that such traits are meaningful because—when compared to other intelligence community offices—the development of ideas and final products is done through a much more collaborative process of constant dialogue and feedback."

According to Zenko, such analysts can be assigned to the CIA Red Cell for anywhere from three months to two years. But they are never allowed to remain on the red team indefinitely. The agency wants to ensure that fresh ideas and perspectives are constantly being added to the mix. It also wants to make sure as many of its analysts as possible are exposed to the contrarian techniques and alternative perspectives of the Red Cell.

Moving people in and out of your red team offers opportunities for leadership development. Over time, this approach will yield a whole cadre of people who have the skills and the experience to be phenomenal planners and strategic thinkers. By ensuring that red teaming assignments are never permanent, you will also ensure that your red team continues to provide your organization with fresh perspectives and innovative thinking.

Choosing a Red Team Leader

Picking the right person to serve as the team leader is critical when assembling a red team. The red team leader will be the conduit between the red team and senior leadership, so that person must possess excellent management and communications skills. The red team leader needs to be someone who is strong enough, confident enough, and secure enough in his or her position to speak truth to power, to demand the data the red team needs to function, and to keep its members on track, on point, and on schedule.

"Good red teamers are a little bit prickly," says former U.S. undersecretary of defense James Miller. He says managing people with a contrarian bent and unorthodox views can be challenging. It requires patience, an open mind, and a willingness to challenge one's own assumptions. A red team leader not only needs to give team members the latitude and leeway to explore a problem from a variety of different perspectives, but also needs to keep them from going too far down a rabbit hole. He or she needs to know how to promote divergent thinking and when to shift the team's focus to convergent thinking. And a red team leader needs to have a solid grasp of the science and psychology behind red teaming so that he or she can help the team guard against the biases I discussed in chapter 3.

"You also have to live and breathe the methods, to be able to adapt the techniques and combine them as needed," says Andy Williams, section head in charge of solutions analysis at NATO Allied Command Transformation headquarters.

Red teamers can learn these tools and techniques from this book, and through more in-depth red team training, but real mastery only comes with experience and practice. For that reason, I advise red teams to start with smaller problems and plans and work their way up to red teaming broader business strategies. As they gain experience and understanding, red team leaders will be better able to decide which tools to use and when to use them. A red team leader should also be able to teach these techniques to others.

Finally, an effective red team leader must be able to communicate the red team's findings and recommendations at the right time and in the right way to be able to help shape the organization's planning and guide its decision making. To do that, he or she needs to cultivate a strong relationship with whomever the red team reports to in senior management. But the red team leader must also take care to not allow that relationship to distort their results.

Joseph Pulitzer famously said newspapers should have no friends; the same is true of red teams. But neither should they make enemies.

"You have to be empathetic and legitimately want to help people solve their problem," says NATO's de Nijs.

The first step in doing that is figuring out what the problem actually is.

CHAPTER 5

The Problem and the Solution

One thing a person cannot do, no matter how rigorous
his analysis or heroic his imagination, is to draw up
a list of things that would never occur to him.

—Thomas Schelling

Coca-Cola had a problem. In the mid-1970s, archrival Pepsi discovered Americans preferred its brand of cola to Coke's in blind taste tests and began trumpeting that fact to consumers through a high-profile advertising campaign that invited people to "Take the Pepsi Challenge." People did, and by 1977, Pepsi had passed Coke in food store sales and was undermining Coke's century-long dominance of the soft drink market. Coca-Cola could do little to counter the Pepsi Challenge; its own research found the same preference for its competitor's product. So, in the early 1980s, Coca-Cola's chemists secretly began working on a new formula.

The company began testing the new concoction in 1984, and those tests showed consumers liked this new formula better than either Pepsi or Coke. Still, Coca-Cola executives knew changing their formula was a risky move, so they kept testing. In one of the biggest and most expensive market research studies ever, Coca-Cola surveyed nearly 200,000 consumers across the United States. Given the choice between "new Coke" and "old Coke," 61 percent of those surveyed said they preferred the new formula. Coca-Cola chairman Roberto Goizueta would later call the decision to reformulate the company's flagship beverage "one of the easiest we have ever made."

Initially, it seemed to be the right one, too. After being launched with great fanfare on April 23, 1985, sales of new Coke proved even stronger than expected, at least for the first few weeks. Then came the telephone calls and letters—tens of thousands of them. After that came the protests. Coke loyalists held rallies across America. They carried signs saying, OUR CHILDREN WILL NEVER KNOW REFRESHMENT and wore T-shirts emblazoned with motto COKE WAS IT! They smashed cases of new Coke and poured the contents into gutters.

"How can they do this?" raged Gay Mullins, who was so mad he founded the group Old Coke Drinkers of America with the aim of forcing Coca-Cola to bring back its original formula. "They were guarding a sacred trust! Coca-Cola has tied this drink to the very fabric of America—apple pie, baseball, the Statue of Liberty. And now they replace it with a new formula, and they tell us just to forget it. They have taken away my freedom of choice. It's un-American!"

On July 10, just seventy-eight days after the launch of new Coke, Mullins got his wish. News anchors broke into afternoon soap operas to inform the people of the United States that Coca-Cola was bringing back the old formula. And there was much rejoicing. America's short national nightmare was over.

Coca-Cola survived this embarrassment, but it cost the company millions and made it the laughingstock of the beverage industry. The new Coke debacle became the subject of countless business school case studies and marketing articles, while Coca-Cola itself became the poster child for what happened when companies failed to ask the right questions. Over the next several years, marketing experts would excoriate Coca-Cola, faulting the corporation for asking consumers only which version of Coke tasted better, rather than asking them how they felt about its plan to dump a beverage that was as much a part of the American psyche as Guinness was to the Irish. But the truth was Coca-Cola *did* ask the right question. It just decided to ignore half the answer.

In addition to asking survey participants which version of Coke tasted better, the company also asked people if they would be upset if Coca-Cola changed its formula. Based on those interviews, the company estimated that between 10 percent and 12 percent of Coke drinkers would be upset, but half of them would get over it. At the same time, Coca-Cola conducted a series of focus groups around the same question. The results were surprisingly different. Once consumers started talking among themselves about the proposed reformulation, some of them started to get really upset. And when they did, many of the other focus group participants started to get upset as well. Coca-Cola executives who observed these groups were stunned by the passion they had unleashed. One later said, "It was like saying you were going to make the flag prettier."

Faced with such wildly conflicting results, Coca-Cola decided to go with the results of the individual surveys, because they reflected the views of hundreds of thousands of representative individuals from across the nation, and ignore the results from the focus groups, which after all captured the feelings of only a few hundred people in key regions.

"With the benefit of hindsight, the locus of their research mistake becomes clear. It was to respond to the conflict between the results of the focus groups and the survey of individuals by trusting only the survey. As it turned out, one can see that both procedures had provided important information," wrote Rutgers University marketing professor Robert M. Schindler in 1992. "When new Coke was first introduced, people made individual decisions on it, and most at least acquiesced to the change. . . . [But] individuals have no means of predicting how their own feelings will change after being exposed to the responses of others."

Schindler concluded that Coca-Cola's real error was in failing to understand the complicated ways in which social dynamics could influence consumer reaction to its decision to alter an iconic product. It was a complex problem, one any company would have struggled with. It was also precisely the sort of problem that red teaming was created to address.

The Cynefin Framework

All red teaming begins with a problem, but not all problems require red teaming.

Webster's defines a *problem* as: "a question raised for inquiry, consideration, or solution." Some questions are easy to solve because the answer is readily available. Does your company want to know how to reduce manufacturing defects? Ask a Six Sigma expert. Are you interested in knowing how much to bid for commercial real estate in downtown Chicago? Ask a real estate agent. Are you concerned about whether you are going to hit your numbers for the next quarter, or for the year? Ask your CFO. You could red team these problems, but that would be like using a sledgehammer to drive a nail: It would work, but it might cause more harm than good.

Other problems, however, like those involving the reformulation of an iconic soft drink, are not so easy to answer. They involve many different variables, and those variables may affect one another in ways that are not readily apparent. Problems such as these not only benefit from red teaming, they demand it.

Before you begin red teaming a problem, you first need to understand what sort of problem it is. Sometimes this is obvious, but sometimes a problem that seems simple actually turns out to be quite complex—and that is where organizations can get into trouble. That was what happened to Coca-Cola. To avoid making those sorts of mistakes, the U.S. military classifies problems using a matrix called the Cynefin Framework. It is a powerful model that can help businesses, too, figure out what to red team and how to red team it.

The Cynefin* Framework was developed by David Snowden, a Welsh researcher in the areas of knowledge management and complexity theory. He describes it as "a *sense-making* framework" because it helps decision makers make sense of complicated problems. It divides the universe of problems into two domains, *Unordered* and *Ordered*, and into four quadrants—*Complex, Complicated, Chaotic,* and *Simple*—with an amorphous area of *Disordered* ambiguity in the middle:

Unordered   Ordered

Complex	**Complicated**

Cause/Effect:
    only seen in retrospect
Answers:
    emerge over time
Leader:
    probe-sense–
    respond
	Cause/Effect:
	    may need experts
	Answers:
	    many good
	Leader:
	    sense-analyze–
	    respond

Disordered

Chaotic	**Simple**

Cause/Effect:
    none
Answers:
    none
Leader:
    act-sense–respond
	Cause/Effect:
	    easily seen by all
	Answers:
	    one best
	Leader:
	    sense-categorize–
	    respond

*As David Snowden has explained, "The name Cynefin (pronounced *kun-ev'in*) is a Welsh word whose literal translation into English as 'habitat' or 'place' fails to do it justice. It is more properly understood as the place of our multiple affiliations, the sense that we all, individually and collectively, have many roots, cultural, religious, geographic, tribal, and so forth. We can never be fully aware of the nature of those affiliations, but they profoundly influence what we are. The name seeks to remind us that all human interactions are strongly influenced and frequently determined by the patterns of our multiple experiences, both through the direct influence of personal experience and through collective experience expressed as stories."

At first glance, this may look like a typical business school quad chart, but it is not. While those tend to imply that one of the quadrants—usually the upper right—is more desirable than the others, there are no value judgments in the Cynefin Framework. Things are what they are, and the matrix is there to help us understand how best to deal with them as they are. If they are in the *Ordered* domain, we can address them through a straightforward, reductionist approach to problem solving because, as Snowden says, "The whole is the sum of the parts, and we achieve optimization of the system by optimization of the parts." If they are in the *Unordered* domain, "the whole is never the sum of the parts," and we must get more creative.

In the *Chaotic* quadrant, cause and effect are irrelevant because the situation is fluid and changing too rapidly to analyze in any meaningful way. Problems here are in your face and require immediate attention. An airline that loses one of its planes, a power utility trying to control a meltdown at one of its nuclear plants, or an investment firm trying to cope with a stock market crash are dealing with *Chaotic* problems. In the *Chaotic* quadrant, there is no time for red teaming. Remember the army's rule: *Don't red team when the enemy is in the wire.*[*]

Problems in the *Simple* quadrant may not actually be that simple to solve, but they do have a solution that is easy to find. Resolving such problems is simply a matter of applying that solution. The *Simple* quadrant is the realm of best practices, process engineering, and standard operating procedures. You may not know the answers to questions posed here, but someone in your organization does, or can find them in a straightforward way. Figuring out how to reduce defects on the assembly line, how much to charge for a new service, or how to deal with the countless minor issues of day-to-day business operations are examples of problems that fall in the *Simple* quadrant. Such problems are well defined, governed by well-established rules, and have a finite number

---

[*]Problems in the *Chaotic* quadrant are ideally suited to the sort of naturalistic decision making studied by Dr. Gary Klein.

of right answers. You could red team them, but why bother? Not only would that be a waste of time and resources, but trying to reinvent the proverbial wheel might also create new problems.

The *Complicated* and *Complex* quadrants are where red teaming becomes not just valuable, but essential. These are areas where traditional decision-making approaches start to show their limitations. Knowing which of these two quadrants your problem lies within will help you decide which red teaming tools to use to solve it.

Complicated problems are those where the answer is knowable, but not immediately apparent. While you must track down the solution, you can rely on established analytical methods to find it. Figuring out how to leverage a new technology, the best way to increase employee engagement, and whether it makes sense to build another factory are examples of *Complicated* problems. While you will often find it valuable to bring an array of different red teaming tools to bear on a problem, those in the *Complicated* realm are best addressed with the analytical techniques described in chapter 6. But you must take care to apply those tools with the critical eye red teaming demands, for as Snowden warns, "This is the domain in which entrained patterns are at their most dangerous, as a simple error in an assumption can lead to a false conclusion that is difficult to isolate and may not be seen."

Complex problems are much more open-ended and have more than one right answer, as well as plenty of wrong ones. In this quadrant, cause and effect are not readily discernible and not always consistent over time. There are many variables, and changing one often alters several others. Retired U.S. Marine Corps Lieutenant General Paul Van Riper says working on these sorts of problems is "kind of like playing a game of chess in which all the pieces are connected with rubber bands." For Coca-Cola, the Pepsi Challenge presented precisely this sort of problem. Other examples of *Complex* problems include how to maintain your competitive edge in a rapidly changing industry, whether you should expand into a new market, and whether you should buy out your biggest competitor. Problems such as these can certainly benefit from an analytical approach, but they also benefit from the imaginative and contrarian red teaming techniques described in chapters 7 and 8. As Snowden notes, "Narrative techniques are particularly powerful in this space."

Of course, red teaming need not be limited to a particular problem or plan. While red teaming cannot predict the future, it can reveal the universe of *possible* futures. That is why it can be useful to periodically red team your company's strategy, or use red teaming to explore white space areas before you begin developing a plan for addressing them. However, while a red team can often offer valuable insights to help inform your planning process, that is not its primary purpose. As I said before, red teaming should never be allowed to become a substitute for planning. The red team's job is not to develop the plan, but to make the plan better.

When to Start Red Teaming

Ideally, red teaming should begin after a plan has been created but before it has been approved, while there is still time to modify it. If you begin red teaming too early, you will interfere with the regular planning process and run the risk of ending up with no plan at all. If you start red teaming after your organization's senior leadership has already signed off on a plan, it may be difficult, or even impossible, to revise it.

"This idea of delaying closure is I think the key, because once the leader had made up his mind, and the subordinates have an idea where things are going, it becomes very difficult to change that direction," advises Daniel Kahneman.

In some cases, changing course like this can also be counterproductive, as I learned the hard way with one of my clients, San Diego–based technology start-up CoachLogix.

When I told CoachLogix CEO Alex Pascal about red teaming, he was excited about making it part of his company's strategic planning process. I began teaching him how to use the different tools and encouraged him to try them out with his staff. We started with *Four Ways of Seeing* (see chapter 7), which worked well. Pascal was eager to learn more, so next I taught him the *Five Whys* (see chapter 7). He was intrigued by the technique but was not sure what problem to try it out on.

"What is the fundamental question your company is trying to answer?" I asked Pascal without giving the matter sufficient thought. He told me, and I suggested he try it out on that. He promised me he would.

The next time we talked, I sensed that Pascal's enthusiasm was a little diminished.

"How did the *Five Whys* go?" I asked.

"To be honest, we didn't find it particularly helpful," he admitted.

That surprised me, so I asked Pascal to walk me through his work with the *Five Whys*. He shared the diagrams he and his team had developed using this technique, and the problem quickly became clear: I had asked Pascal to red team the very problem his company had been set up to solve. He and his team had already answered this question, and they were working around the clock to launch a product that represented their solution to it.

It reminded me of another important lesson they taught us at Fort Leavenworth: You cannot red team the decision to take out a suspected terrorist training camp after a pilot has already squeezed his trigger and shouted, "Missile away!" Asking a start-up to red team a plan it is in the middle of executing is kind of like that. Once a decision has been made, the time for red teaming it is over.

That does not mean that there is not a role for the red team to play during the execution phase. If you have an in-house red team, either a standing team or an ad hoc team, it can continue to provide valuable support and offer new insights as your plan is being implemented. It can scan the horizon for emerging threats and new opportunities, watch for developments that could signal potential problems with the plan, and provide alternative assessments of developments in your business environment. This is one of the benefits of investing in the development of an in-house red teaming capability.

How long should you allow for red teaming? That depends on the complexity of the problem, and the amount of time you have available to examine it. But red teaming should never be an open-ended exercise.

In cases where red teamers are analyzing a specific plan or course of action, the deadline for a decision will necessarily limit the length of the red teaming exercise. In cases when there is no set time for a decision, or when a red team is doing a white space analysis, it should impose its own deadlines. In the army, red teams will often establish what they refer to as a GICOT, or good idea cut-off time. Without such a hard stop, there is a danger the analysis will continue indefinitely. There is always one more question to ask, one more rabbit hole to plunge down. But endless red teaming hinders decision making, prevents action, and reduces the red team to a group of navel-gazers. That may prove to be an entertaining diversion for analytically minded employees, but it will never have a meaningful impact on your organization. Remember, red teaming must never stand in the way of action when action is required.

Your red team needs to produce a product. What that product looks like will be determined by the nature of the problem itself; there is no standard template. *And it needs to deliver that product in a timely manner in order for it to be actionable.* If there is no time left to modify a plan, then there is little point in second-guessing it.

Red Teaming the Problem

Because of the importance of understanding the sort of problem you are dealing with, every red teaming exercise should begin with a technique called *Problem Restatement.*

Human beings are natural-born problem solvers. While that bodes well for our red teaming ability, it is also a liability. When we are presented with a problem, we are usually so eager to solve it that we do not take the time to examine it and make sure the problem, as it is stated, actually makes sense. Analyzing the wrong problem or a poorly framed one not only wastes time and resources, but also can yield solutions that fail to address the underlying issues.

"You can make a well-considered, well-thought-out decision, but if you've started from the wrong place—with the wrong decision problem—you won't have made the smart choice," write John S. Hammond, Ralph L. Keeney, and Howard Raiffa in their book *Smart Choices*. "The way you state your problem frames your decision. It determines the alternatives you consider and the way you evaluate them. Posing the right problem drives everything else."

Poorly articulated problems include those that:

- Are stated too broadly. (e.g., *How do we grow our business?*)

- Are stated too narrowly. (e.g., *How do we grow our business by 12 percent next year without adding additional products, hiring new staff, or expanding into new territories?*)

- Contain inherent assumptions. (e.g., *How can we ensure our patented process remains the industry's first choice?*)

- Contain a presumed solution. (e.g., *How can we use Six Sigma to improve our quality while boosting productivity?*)

To make sure problems are framed correctly, the U.S. Army teaches red teamers to start by examining the issue under review from a variety of different angles. This can be as simple as paraphrasing the problem, because using different words to describe the problem can often yield valuable new perspectives. For example, if you were asked, *How can we ensure our patented process remains the industry's first choice?* you might restate the problem more bluntly: *We believe there is no better process possible than ours, but we're worried someone will invent one.* If you did, it would reveal the assumption inherent in the original question—that the company cannot improve its process. Hopefully, it would also lead your red team to answer the more important question: *Is there any way to do what we do better, faster, or cheaper?* Because if you answer that question first, not only will you not have to worry about your competitors, but you will also strengthen your fundamental business.

Other ways of restating a problem include broadening its focus to place it in a bigger context (e.g., instead of: *How do we grow our business by expanding in China?* framing the problem as: *How do we grow our business in Asia?*) or shifting the focus entirely (e.g., rather than asking, *How can we increase sales?* ask, *How can we reduce costs, and thereby increase profits?*). Turning a problem on its head can also yield valuable insights and new perspectives. For example, instead of asking, *How can we use Six Sigma to improve our quality while boosting productivity?* you might ask, *How can we* reduce *our quality and* lower *our productivity using Six Sigma?* If you did, you might discover that the original question was not really about improving quality and boosting productivity, but about how to employ Six Sigma.

Examining problems in this way requires healthy discussion and a free flow of ideas. The best way to encourage that is to begin with *divergent thinking* and work toward *convergent thinking.*

Getting at the Truth

Successful red teaming depends on the ability of the team to look at an issue or problem from as many different perspectives as possible. That is not how most organizations typically approach problem solving.

"In the army, people generally try to come together around a solution as quickly as possible and then try to figure out how to implement it. Our doctrines require us to consider three different options, but the truth is that we quickly converge on a course of action and pay little attention to the other two," says Colonel Steve Rotkoff, offering a textbook example of the *satisficing* approach I discussed in chapter 3. "Satisficing is a good strategy if you are dealing with simple problems. But the problems we deal with in the military are rarely simple."

In my experience, many companies approach decision making in much the same way. Red teaming requires a different approach. To the degree time allows, the goal of the red team should be to consider as many different ideas, explanations, and alternatives as possible before attempting to decide which one is the most desirable or correct. The U.S. Army has come up with a number of different ways of doing that, but they all begin with a simple concept: *Think-Write-Share.*

Think-Write-Share

Think-Write-Share is a way of ensuring that the red team begins with *divergent* thinking and moves to *convergent* thinking. The technique works like this: Start by asking team members to think about a problem or question, then write down their thoughts and share them with the group (lined five-by-eight index cards work well for this and many of the other tools and techniques that I will introduce in the coming chapters). This sequence is important because, too often, people working together in groups are in a rush to share their ideas. They are eager to demonstrate how smart they are or establish their expertise with the topic under consideration. Red teaming is not about intellectual grandstanding; it is about taking the time to consider ideas fully. By requiring a short amount of time for silent reflection at the beginning, team members have a chance to consider their responses before sharing them with the group. Writing those responses down is important, too, because it forces people to "own" their answers. It is far easier to equivocate when people are just blurting out the first thing that comes to mind. This method also forces people to precommit to an idea and not modify their thinking based on what they hear from the rest of the group.

I was taught *Think-Write-Share* by U.S. Marine Corps Lieutenant Colonel William Rasgorshek, who was serving as a guest instructor at the army's University of Foreign Military and Cultural Studies. A former Osprey pilot, he went by his call sign, "Razz." When I met Razz in 2015, he had just come back to Fort Leavenworth from a stint doing red teaming for Strategic Command, or STRATCOM, the part of the military responsible for the United States' strategic nuclear arsenal. Razz had been teaching *Think-Write-Share* to the folks who, as he put it, "spend their days planning unscheduled sunrises."

"*Think-Write-Share* is based on the science of how people work in groups," he told our class. "It is by far the best way to get a group to collaborate effectively."

Razz is also a big believer in the concept of *active listening*. When we listen to someone else speaking, he explained, we immediately start to jump to conclusions about what they are saying. These conclusions may be right or they may be wrong. *Active listening* requires everyone who is not speaking to hold these conclusions at bay until the speaker has finished talking. They do not react—neither verbally nor nonverbally—to what is being said. That means no frowns, scowls, or guffaws. It also means no nods, smiles, or thumbs-up.

"Try to avoid that and keep your head clear," Razz advised. "You're going to find that you start to frame and understand things differently than you did before."

The final rule of *Think-Write-Share* is: *No one speaks twice until everyone speaks once.* This is important, because it prevents the people with the strongest personalities or biggest egos from dominating the conversation and ensures that red teaming remains a group activity.

This collective approach is essential.

"The world is going from *complicated*, where you could solve problems with a math equation, to *complex*, where you have to work with others, and cooperate and collaborate," says General Robert Brown, head of the Combined Arms Center at Fort Leavenworth, during my time at the school.* "You have to be able to not just be comfortable, but *thrive*, in conditions of uncertainty and chaos. To do that, you must work as teams."

While individuals can use the techniques in the red teaming tool kit

---

*General Brown is now commander of the U.S. Army Pacific.

to plan and strategize better, the process of red teaming is predicated on a recognition of the limits of our individual analytical abilities, and the desirability of having as many eyes as possible look at a problem. As a Japanese proverb states: "None of us is as smart as all of us."

How to Tell the Truth

For red teams to function effectively, each member's voice must be heard in a meaningful way. That can be challenging—particularly in a rigidly hierarchical organization like the military. Or most large corporations. Which is why the U.S. Army's training program teaches red team leaders how to use a series of collaborative communications tools called *Liberating Structures* to ensure each team member's observations and insights are given due consideration.

While the term *Liberating Structures* may seem better suited to college quads than military headquarters, the army has found these techniques to be extremely effective ways of getting people to talk frankly about difficult issues or controversial ideas. Many of these approaches were developed by Keith McCandless and Henri Lipmanowicz of the Plexus Institute, who first used them in the health care arena. Rotkoff was introduced to *Liberating Structures* through his work with the author Ori Brafman, who cowrote *The Starfish and the Spider: The Unstoppable Power of Leaderless Organizations.* In 2009, the army hired Brafman to teach its leaders to become less hierarchical and more receptive to information and insights from their subordinates. Rotkoff took a hiatus from the red team training program to head up that effort, and he was impressed with many of the unconventional approaches Brafman taught him.

"In the military, if you are a senior leader and you go down and visit your subordinate organizations, people want to do two things: They want to impress you, and they want you to go away without learning anything—because if you learn something, you're going to create more work for them. So, something I always struggled with when I was a senior officer was how to get people to give me honest feedback. You can present yourself as the Dalai Lama; it doesn't matter. They know who you are in the organization and they are going to self-censor," Rotkoff told me. "*Liberating Structures* can get people to open up and get at that truth by taking them out of their comfort zones, suspending rank, and encouraging input from folks with differing perspectives. These are great ways of getting people to talk."

I have found them to be very effective in my work with corporate clients, too—and not just for red teaming. Some of the companies I have taught these techniques to have found they can be quite effective in stimulating discussions and soliciting opinions from employees at all levels of their organization. Many of these *Liberating Structures* are designed to create anonymity, not only to protect people from any negative consequences that might come from sharing their observations and insights, but also to keep other members of the group from allowing their view of the person sharing them from coloring their perception of what he or she has to say.

"This approach allowed me to express something I would not normally have shared with our team," one Japanese executive told me. "Our business culture is extremely hierarchical, and we often have a hard time speaking frankly about difficult issues. These techniques made it easier for me to voice my concerns about the deal we were analyzing. I think they can be very effective—not just for red teaming, but for our organization in general."

While McCandless and Lipmanowicz have developed thirty-three different *Liberating Structures,* the army has identified a handful that are particularly helpful in red teaming, and modified them to meet the needs of alternative analysis. These include:

1-2-4-All

Start by giving each member of your red team a pencil, a piece of paper, and the same simple question to answer, such as:

How could this plan fail?

Why have we been unable to achieve this goal?

Where is the weakest link in our supply chain?

Who has a vested interest in killing this initiative?

What is the biggest threat to the success of our strategy?

Ask each person to ponder this question silently, and then write down their answer in as few words as possible. Next, pair people up and have them share their answers with each other and discuss them. They can refine their answers based on this feedback, or come up with something entirely new together. Next, double up each of those pairs to create groups of four. Have first one pair, then the other, share what they have come up with so far. Then have each foursome discuss these responses and decide which points are the strongest. Finally, reconvene the entire team and have each foursome present their best answer to the group at large. Repeat this last step as often as time permits or until the full range of ideas has been discussed by the team collectively.

Colonel Kevin Benson, my instructor at Fort Leavenworth, says this approach is particularly useful at the beginning of a red teaming exercise.

"You restrain your impulse to do a deep-dive immediately, and you create a universe of potential answers or solutions," he says. "It also allows you to get everyone's input right at the start. You're going to hear everybody's voice. I guarantee that you are going to get better results, and it's only going to cost you a little bit of time."

This exercise can be completed in as little as fifteen minutes, but you can spend more time with it if circumstances allow. If you are working with a larger team, you can break a complex problem down and have different groups look at different aspects of the problem. For example, if you were red teaming a potential acquisition, one group might look at the financial aspects of the deal, while other groups tackled integration and the impact on customers and other stakeholders.

*Weighted Anonymous Feedback**

This is a great technique for tapping into the collective wisdom of the group. It allows people to share their real concerns about an issue without having to worry about the repercussions. It encourages the sort of radical candor most leaders never hear, but which can help them avoid making a catastrophic blunder. (Because this technique is designed to encourage *divergent thinking* rather than *convergent thinking*, I do not recommend using it to actually make decisions.)

Start by passing out index cards and identical pens to each member of the group and posing a single question, such as:

What is the biggest threat to our strategy?

Which goal are we most likely to miss?

Which of our business units are you most concerned about?

Ask each participant to write down their answer as succinctly as possible on the card in block letters. This is important, because it keeps people from trying to guess whose handwriting they are reading. If you are working with a small group and want to generate more ideas, ask each person to write down the top three answers that come to mind—each on a separate card.

When everyone is finished, collect their cards, shuffle them, and deal

---

*This is my variation of the *Liberating Structures* known as 5 *Will Get You 25*.

them back to the group, giving each person one card. It does not matter if someone ends up with his or her own card, because each person will have an opportunity to read and rate each response.

Once everyone has been dealt a card, have each person read the answer silently and consider that response. Then, on the *back* of the card, have them rate that response from 1 to 5, with 5 being an excellent answer they wholeheartedly agree with and 1 being a response they categorically reject. It is important to ask people to rank the card before looking at the numbers on the back so that they are not influenced by others' ratings. Repeat the process until everyone has had a chance to read and grade each card once (when someone ends up with a card they have already graded, have them swap it for a new card).* Once the group is finished, tally the numbers on the back of each card and write the responses that receive the highest scores on the board—generally, the top three to five. You can discuss these issues further or make them the focus of the rest of your red teaming exercise.

Weighted Anonymous Feedback is a great way to make sure everyone's input gets the same consideration. For example, in 2012, red team facilitators from the army were asked to lead a review of the Department of Defense's new Capstone Concept for Joint Operations, the high-order vision of how the American military will fight future wars and respond to future threats. They pulled together an ad hoc red team that included representatives from each of the four military branches, a retired general, an expert on national security from the Massachusetts Institute of Technology, and experts in anthropology and cyber warfare. Together, this team reviewed a draft of the document. Then the facilitators asked the red team members to write down the three areas of the plan that most needed to be reconsidered.

"All three of the ideas proposed by the most junior member of the group, a major, made the cut. None of the ideas from the general sur-

---

*If you are working with a large group or have limited time, you may want to limit the exchange to five rounds.

vived," said Rotkoff, who was one of the facilitators. "This would likely not have happened in the normal operational planning team process. The ideas of the retired general or the Ph.D.s would immediately have credence, while the ideas of the junior members would have been drowned out, or at least received far less attention."

Weighted Anonymous Feedback helps you zero in on the areas of greatest concern when red teaming a complex strategy or plan. If you have limited time, it can quickly reveal the areas you should focus on in your red team analysis.

Dot Voting

This is another effective method for anonymously determining a group's priorities. Start by using one of the methods discussed above to develop a list of issues or concerns to consider, or simply break the strategy or plan down into discrete elements. Make sure there is no overlap between the items on your list. If there is, find a way to combine them.

Have each person copy the list onto a note card, putting each item on the list on its own line. Alternatively, you may want to have someone type up the list on a computer and print out a copy for each team member. Next, add up the number of items on your list, divide that number in half, and add one to it. This is how many votes each team member gets (for example, if there are twelve issues on your list, each person would have seven votes; if there were five issues, each person would have three votes). Give each member of the team a quantity of dot stickers equal to the number of votes they get.

Tell the group to decide which issues they feel are most important and ask them to distribute their dots accordingly. People cast their votes by placing one or more stickers next to one or more of the items on the list until they have used up all their stickers. Those who feel strongly about one particular issue can cast most, or even all, of their votes for it. Or they can spread their votes among several different issues they believe merit further consideration.* Once everybody has placed all their dots, collect the cards and tally the votes to find out which issues people feel are most important, then let the results guide your red teaming effort.

Dot Voting is effective because it forces people to prioritize, which can be important when you have limited time for red teaming. It also weights the results so you can see how concerned people are about one issue relative to another. Finally, it allows people to flag more than one issue that they feel needs to be addressed. Because of this, *Dot Voting* can also be used as part of your organization's regular planning process to help establish priorities.

Fishbowl

This is a powerful technique that red teamers can use to gain insights and understanding from people with firsthand experience relating to the strategy or issue they are analyzing. It is a way of getting at the sort of knowledge and perspectives that are too often missed in the regular planning process.

Invite three to seven people who have direct knowledge of the issue being considered to participate. Prepare the room ahead of time by creating an inner circle of chairs facing one another in the center, one for each of the invitees. If possible, seat them around a small round table and give them a hot or cold beverage and some snacks to make them comfortable. If not, try placing them on barstools. If a large group will be observing, you might even want to put the subjects on a raised platform in the center of the room.

Whatever layout you choose, have the members of the red team sit in a wider circle around this imaginary fishbowl. Once everyone is seated, ask those in the center to ignore the rest of the room and imagine that

---

*If you do not have stickers, you can simply ask people to draw their dots with a pen—just make sure they do not cast more votes than they are entitled to.

they are in a café or bar with a group of friends or coworkers. Then, ask them to talk about the issue, inviting them to share their personal stories and insights with one another. The red team's job is just to sit back, listen, and take notes. Let the discussion continue without interruption. Those in the center should talk to themselves, not to the audience. Once the conversation starts to ebb, or after a predetermined time limit (say, thirty minutes) has been reached, have them turn their chairs to face the outer circle and invite the members of the red team to ask questions about what they have just heard—or what they have *not* heard.

The army has used the *Fishbowl* method as an alternative approach to debriefing officers returning from Afghanistan, to make sure the knowledge and experience they gained there was passed on to the officers taking their places. Among the questions that were raised was how the officers established trust and developed relationships with Afghan village elders and women in the communities they were responsible for patrolling. Instead of red teamers, those sitting in the outer circle were officers about to deploy to the same region.

"[The officers were] sitting on the edge of their chairs because they felt they were getting important firsthand, unfiltered information," said Lisa Kimball, who taught *Fishbowl* to the army. "In the space of a couple hours, there was a huge amount of understanding and progress made."

If your red team is analyzing a plan to improve customer service, you might invite a couple of frontline retail employees, a couple of call center employees, a retail manager, and a call center manager to be the subjects of your *Fishbowl* exercise. If you are studying a plan to boost factory output, you might bring in some production employees representing the different jobs on your assembly line, as well as a quality inspector and a supervisor. If you are red teaming a plan to expand into Latin America, you might fly in consumers from the region who match your target demographic. Whatever you do, the important thing is to spend time listening before asking questions.

TRIZ

TRIZ is an abbreviation of the Russian phrase *Teoriya Resheniya Izobretatelskikh Zadach*, or "the theory of inventive problem solving." It was developed by Soviet inventor and science fiction writer Genrikh Saulovich Altshuller as "a problem-solving, analysis and forecasting tool derived from the study of patterns of invention in the global patent literature." Some may have already encountered *TRIZ* as part of the Six Sigma process, where it is used to help solve problems without creating new ones. However, its use in red teaming is a little different. In red teaming, we are only interested in one part of the *TRIZ* methodology: identifying those things the organization is currently doing that are standing in the way of the successful execution of the plan under consideration.

To do this, work together as a group to figure out everything the organization *could* do to ensure its plan *will* fail. Have fun with this. Pretend your team has been sent to sabotage the effort by a rival company, has successfully infiltrated the organization, and is now trying to come up with all the possible ways to ensure the plan ends in disaster. You can use one of the other *Liberating Structures* to develop your list, or just work together informally. Be as detailed as possible and as exhaustive as time permits.

When you are finished, examine your list item by item, and ask this question: *Is there anything the organization is currently doing or thinking about doing that remotely resembles this in any way, shape, or form?* The results can be shocking.

TRIZ is an excellent way to challenge a company's conventions and encourage a critical discussion of "the way we do things around here," which is often at the root of a company's problems. Altshuller used it a little too effectively and wound up in a Soviet gulag. But used constructively as part of a broader red teaming process, *TRIZ* can be a powerful tool for identifying the real barriers to success that exist inside your organization.

Yes, and . . . or Circular Response

This is not officially part of the *Liberating Structures* tool kit, but the army has found it to be an effective complement to those exercises. It was developed by Cort Worthington, a lecturer at the University of California, Berkeley's Haas School of Business, who was brought in by the army as part of the Starfish program to teach officers about a set of leadership tools he had developed based on the techniques of improvisational comedy.

"Most of them were a little too 'California' for the army," Rotkoff says. "But *Yes, and . . .* was easy to teach and very powerful."

So powerful Rotkoff made it part of the red teaming curriculum.

The concept is simple: Someone makes a statement about the issue being analyzed and the person to his or her right says, "Yes, and . . ." followed by another statement that builds upon the original statement. Then the person to the right of the person who just spoke says, "Yes, and . . ." followed by another statement that builds upon the second statement, and so on until each person on the team has contributed to the conversation. The key is that each person has to say something that expands on or complements the statement made by the previous speaker; they cannot contradict them, at least not directly.

Circular Response is similar, but does not require subsequent speakers to agree with the original statement. The first person to speak has one minute to share his or her thoughts. When they are finished, the next person must use some or all of what the first speaker said as a springboard for his or her own comments, but they are free to contradict the previous speaker or take issue with something he or she said. This process continues until each person in the group has had a chance to speak.

The value of both methods is that they ensure everybody's voice is heard. Moreover, the last person to speak has no advantage over the second person to speak, because neither one knows what the person to their left is going to say beforehand.

Putting It All Together

You can use these *Liberating Structures* individually, or in mash-ups that combine two or more techniques, as circumstances dictate. I encourage you to try different combinations and see what works best for you, and your red team.

These methods—combined with basic critical thinking skills and an awareness of our cognitive biases, heuristics, and logical fallacies—will help leaders and managers plan better and think more effectively. They will also provide an organization with the foundation necessary for successful red teaming.

In the following chapters, I will show you how to use these tools to transform even the most hidebound company into a learning organization that is more reflective, more innovative, and better able to respond to emerging threats and new opportunities. As I said before, a comprehensive red teaming analysis is typically divided into three phases: analyzing your strategy or plan, imagining how it could fail and how it could succeed, and using contrarian thinking to reveal alternatives and ensure that your plan or strategy is really the best.

It all starts by checking your assumptions.

CHAPTER 6

Questioning the Unquestionable: Analytical Techniques

It is vital to analyze everything down to its basic elements, to incontrovertible truth. One must not stop halfway, as is so often done, at some arbitrary assumption or hypothesis.

—Carl von Clausewitz

On July 2, 1863, a thirty-four-year-old colonel named Joshua Chamberlain stood with what was left of his 20th Maine Volunteer Infantry Regiment atop a small hill overlooking the blood-soaked battlefield at Gettysburg, Pennsylvania, and watched as the Confederate forces at the base of the hill regrouped and formed up for their third assault. He was wounded and his men were greatly outnumbered, but that was the least of Chamberlain's worries. They were also out of ammunition. The 20th Maine was the left flank of the Union's defensive line, and the Confederates knew it. Chamberlain had been ordered to hold his position at all costs. If the 20th Maine fell back, the Union line would begin to collapse, and there were few Federal troops left between Gettysburg and Washington, D.C. But he had nothing left to spend.

Like his men, Chamberlain was not a professional soldier. A year earlier, he had been a professor of modern languages and rhetoric at a small liberal arts college. Unlike many of the generals on both sides of the battlefield that day, he had not been trained at West Point or the Citadel. While those men were being blooded in battles in Mexico or upon the Great Plains, Chamberlain was reading the classics and studying logic. So, though he did not know much about the art of war, he did know how to think. And what Chamberlain thought as he looked down at the Rebel troops beginning their grim march up the hill for the third time was that the one thing he and his men still had going for them was gravity.

"Bayonet!" Chamberlain shouted, ignoring his instructions to hold his position atop the hill. Instead, he ordered his men to charge down the hill as the Confederates began their charge up it. As Chamberlain's troops tore down the hill, he ordered part of his force to swing to the right like a door slamming shut, simultaneously enveloping the advancing Rebels and falling upon them like a blue avalanche. The Confederate assault was shattered before it could even begin. Many of the Rebels surrendered or were impaled upon the bayonets of the 20th Maine. Those who escaped fell back in disarray.

Many historians would later credit Chamberlain's unorthodox counterattack with turning the battle in the North's favor. Some would even credit him with saving the Union. General Robert Brown credits Chamberlain with exemplifying the sort of applied critical thinking that future army officers will need to lead their men—and now women—to victory in an increasingly complex world.

"We need red teaming, but we also need critical and creative thinking all the way across our ranks from Specialist Brown to General Brown," the general told me. "People are always looking for the technology that is the silver bullet. But today, it's easy to copy technology. When we introduce a new weapons system, it only takes a short time for our adversaries to produce their own version. In World War II, we won by outproducing our enemies. Today, our enemies have figured out how to fight in ways that make that sort of advantage irrelevant. But if we can consistently *think* better than our enemies and achieve *cognitive dominance,* that is a strategic offset that would prove very difficult to overcome."

Businesses face similar challenges today, and have the same opportunity. As Jim Collins demonstrated in *Good to Great,* coming up with a novel product or service only gets you so far. It is only a matter of time before one of your competitors or a new entrant in your space figures out how to do what you do better. Companies such as Gateway and Yahoo! failed to understand that and paid the price. Companies such as Apple and Google understood that and reaped the rewards by outthinking their opponents. That is why all red teaming begins by thinking critically about the problem.

Thinking Critically

The notion that knowing how to think critically is a prerequisite for effective red teaming might seem obvious. But it also poses a challenge at a time when almost 40 percent of college seniors are "unable to distinguish the quality of evidence in building an argument or express the appropriate level of conviction in their conclusion," according to the results of a nationwide survey released in 2015 by the Council for Aid to Education. Companies already know this. That same year, the American Association of Colleges and Universities released the results of a survey that found nine out of ten employers "judge recent college graduates as poorly prepared for the workforce in such areas as critical thinking, communication and problem solving." In other words, they lack the very skills red teamers rely on to conduct their analyses.*

For those who view critical thinking as the exclusive purview of

---

*Teaching basic critical thinking is beyond the scope of this book. However, I have included a list of books in the appendix that I believe will prove invaluable if you want to hone your critical thinking skills.

philosophy majors, consider how Billy Beane turned Major League Baseball on its head by thinking critically about the sport after becoming general manager of the Oakland Athletics in the late 1990s. As Michael Lewis describes in his memorable book *Moneyball,* Beane ignored the largely meaningless statistics and stereotypes that had guided baseball scouts for the better part of a century. To analyze and select players for his team, Beane used instead a new set of metrics that were empirically proven to translate directly into on-field performance. Armed with this data, he built one of the most successful teams in baseball—and he did it with a budget that was a fraction of what other top teams were spending. The Athletics made it to the playoffs four times in a row, from 2000 to 2004, and in 2002 became the first team in a hundred years to post twenty consecutive wins.

"Reason, even science, was what Billy Beane was intent on bringing to baseball," Lewis wrote. "At the bottom of the Oakland experiment was a willingness to rethink baseball: how it is managed, how it is played, who is best suited to play it, and why."

As Beane told Lewis:

> *I start with the game, with the things that I see there and the things that people say there. And I ask: Is it true? Can you validate it? Can you measure it? How does it fit with the rest of the machinery?*

This is a textbook example of critical thinking in action—the sort of critical thinking that can give your business an edge over its competitors. As you can see, it starts with asking the right questions. Here are some that a red team should always ask when given a problem to analyze:

> *What are the issues and the conclusions?*
>
> *What are the reasons?*
>
> *Which words or phrases are ambiguous?*
>
> *What are the value conflicts and assumptions?*

What are the descriptive assumptions?

Are there any fallacies in the reasoning?

How strong is the evidence?

Are there rival causes?

Are the statistics deceptive?

What significant information is omitted?

What reasonable conclusions are possible?

Adapted from *Asking the Right Questions: A Guide to Critical Thinking,* by M. Neil Browne and Stuart M. Keeley.

But critical thinking is not just a matter of asking the right questions; it also requires taking a hard look at the answers. Thinking critically means guarding against not only the biases I discussed in chapter 3, but also the logical fallacies that creep into so many of our conversations, arguments, and plans. Unlike those mental shortcuts that seem to be hardwired into the human brain, this faulty logic is the product of sloppy thinking or, in some cases, deliberate intellectual dishonesty designed to make a weak argument appear stronger. These logical fallacies are like microscopic fractures in the structure of a strategy or plan: They may not be visible at first, but they could ultimately cause it to fail. You are probably already familiar with some of these, but here are the more common ones to keep in mind as you are red teaming:

Common Logical Fallacies

Ad hominem attack: Criticizing the person making the argument rather than the argument itself (e.g., *"That's ridiculous. What do the factory guys know about engineering?"*)*

---

*This applies only to arguments, not to information. Knowing the source of information can be crucial to assessing its value and accuracy. See *appeal to questionable authority*.

Appeal to age or tradition: Basing an argument on the assumption that previous generations were wiser or knew more than the current generation (e.g., *"James has been here since the Old Man was running the show, so I think we should do as he suggests."*)

Appeal to emotion or fear: Playing on people's heartstrings or anxieties instead of arguing the merits of a position (e.g., *"If we don't approve this plan, we'll all be looking for jobs next month."*)

Appeal to popularity: Asserting that something is inherently good or right because others believe it to be so (e.g., *"All of our competitors are doing it."*)

Appeal to novelty: Asserting that something is inherently good or desirable because it is new (e.g., *"There's a new version of that software out; we need to upgrade immediately."*)

Appeal to questionable authority: Supporting an argument with weak sources or spurious information (e.g., *"I read it on the Internet."*)

Appeal to ridicule: Rejecting an idea on the grounds that it will subject the organization to mockery (e.g., *"If we introduce a small pickup, we'll be the laughingstock of the automobile industry!"*)

Begging the question: A type of circular reasoning in which the conclusion of the argument is predicated on its premise (e.g., *"It would be good to open a branch in Spain, because Spain is a really important market."*)

Biased sample: Using weak statistical evidence to support an argument (e.g., *"Based on a survey of our customers, people really like the current design."*)

Confusion of cause and effect: The mistaken belief that correlation implies causation (e.g., *"Our marketing department is weak; that's why our products aren't selling."*)

Explaining by naming: To imply that you have resolved an issue simply because you have identified it (e.g., *"We figured out what was causing the production slowdown: absenteeism."*)

False dichotomy: Oversimplifying the argument by reducing it to black-and-white choices (e.g., *"It's up to you: We can either approve the plan or go out of business."*)

Faulty analogy: Using a comparison that does not support the conclusion that is being drawn from it (e.g., *"Ford saved itself by bringing in an outside CEO, so we should hire an outside CEO."*)*

Glittering generality: Justifying an argument by wrapping it in an appealing phrase or statement that allows the argument itself to go unquestioned (e.g., *"Well, that's the Six Sigma approach."*)

Hasty generalization: To make assumptions based on insufficient evidence (e.g., *"The focus group didn't like our prototype, so there's clearly no market for that product."*)

Loaded question: Posing a query that cannot be answered without appearing to advocate something negative or undesirable (e.g., *"So you'll sleep better tonight knowing that we decided to can 300 of our workers?"*)

Middle ground: Assuming a compromise between two extreme points of view is the best option (e.g., *"Rick wants us to double down in China, and Terry wants us to pull out, so why don't we just maintain our current investment?"*)

Neglect of a common cause: Assuming one thing causes another thing because they are regularly associated with each other (e.g.,

---

*The most glaring example of this logical fallacy is *Reductio ad Hitlerum,* comparing somebody to Hitler, or the related Godwin's Law, which holds that "as an online discussion grows longer, the probability of a comparison involving Nazis or Hitler approaches 1."

"It's not the discharge from the plant that's causing that smell; it's all those dead fish.")

Oversimplification: Ascribing a single cause to something that is complex and has different, interrelated causes (e.g., *"We'd be hitting our production goals if it weren't for the union."*)

Post hoc, ergo propter hoc: Literally, "After this, therefore because of this." To assume that one thing caused another thing simply because it occurred before it (e.g., *"People don't like the new color; sales started to go down right after we introduced it."*)*

Red herring: Introducing an irrelevant topic in an attempt to shift the argument away from the original issue (e.g., *"Forget the design problems; what we really should be talking about is how marketing screwed up."*)

Slippery slope: Assuming a proposed action will set off a series of undesirable events, even though the means of preventing that exist (e.g., *"If we can't meet this deadline, our new product line is dead in the water!"*)

Straw man: Distorting or exaggerating an argument in order to make it easier to attack (e.g., *"Nancy wants to hire a new compliance officer. She couldn't care less about payroll; all she wants to do is keep adding positions."*)

Wishful thinking: Assuming a premise is true simply because you want or need it to be true (e.g., *"If we open a new office in St. Louis, sales in the region are bound to go up!"*)

Often, just being aware of these logical fallacies is enough to identify them. But when red teaming a particularly complicated—or

---

*Most superstitions are examples of this sort of logical fallacy.

controversial—strategy or plan, it may be helpful to conduct a more formal analysis using *Argument Dissection*.

Argument Dissection*

This technique involves asking the following questions of any argument that is used to justify a particular course of action, or that is offered as an explanation for a problem:

1. Does this argument address the real problem?

2. What is the point of view of the person or group making this argument?

3. Does the argument include any vague or ambiguous words or loaded language?

4. Does the argument include any value conflicts?

5. Does the argument include any *descriptive assumptions* (i.e., statements about the way things are)?

6. Does the argument include any *prescriptive assumptions* (i.e., statements about the way things *should* be)?

7. Are there hints of bias? If so, what is that bias?

8. Does the argument include any logical fallacies?

9. How good is the evidence used to support the argument?

10. If statistics are provided, how good are they? Are they presented with the proper context?

*This is often referred to as the *Argument Deconstruction Framework*.

11. What information is missing from the argument?

12. Is the argument based on intuition or a "gut feeling"?

13. If the argument relies on analogies, are they appropriate to the situation?

14. Are there any rival causes or other plausible hypotheses?

15. Could a different conclusion be drawn from the same evidence?

16. What are the implications of accepting the argument as stated?

There is not necessarily a right answer to any of these questions. But by answering them, the red team will gain a deeper understanding of the argument being presented, as well as useful fodder for further analysis using the more robust red teaming techniques described below.

Some of these techniques were developed by the U.S. Central Intelligence Agency during the Cold War. Others, by the U.S. Army. They may not be as innovative or sexy as the imaginative and contrarian techniques that I will detail in the coming chapters, but they provide an excellent starting point for any red teaming exercise. Even if your company already uses similar approaches as part of its planning process, these techniques are worth studying because they offer a more formal, structured approach—and that is essential if you really want to stress-test your strategies and plans.

Key Assumptions Check

In red teaming, it is essential to differentiate between *facts* and *assumptions*. *Facts* are things that are objectively true right now. They are not matters of opinion, open to debate, or things we believe will be true in the future. *Assumptions* are things that may be true but cannot be proven to be true at this time. Ideally, *assumptions* are simply facts that are not yet true, but will become true in the future. Too often, however, *assumptions* are nothing more than wishful thinking. If your company earned $3.6 billion last quarter, that is a *fact* (unless your accounting team has been cooking the books). If you tell Wall Street you will earn $3.6 billion next quarter, that is an *assumption*. If you say your new product tested well in focus groups, that is a *fact*. If you say your new product will be a hit with consumers, that is an *assumption*. If you say your plant has the capacity to produce 25,000 more widgets each month, that is a *fact*. If you say your plant can easily accommodate demand for your new widgets, that is an *assumption*.

There is nothing inherently wrong with assumptions. Every strategy, every plan, every decision an organization makes is based on them. Assumptions have to be made as part of any planning process. The challenge is making the right assumptions, because the better your assumptions are, the stronger your plan will be—and the more likely it will be to succeed. The danger lies in making the wrong assumptions, or worse still, failing to recognize them as assumptions at all. Most plans fail because they rely on unstated or unexamined assumptions. To make sure that does not happen to your plan, it is vital that you identify and examine all the assumptions it is based on before approving it.

A *Key Assumptions Check* is designed to help you do just that. Start by having the red team take a careful look at the plan and list all the stated and unstated assumptions that must be true for the plan to work. You can do this informally or with the help of one of the *Liberating Structures* I described in chapter 5. If your plan is complex, it may be better to break it down into its constituent parts and examine each of those separately.

If you were red teaming a plan to launch a new line of running shoes, your list of assumptions might include the following:

- There is room in the market for a new line of running shoes.

- Demand for running shoes will remain constant or grow at the pace anticipated by the plan.

- The new line will be perceived as desirable by consumers.

- The new line will not cannibalize demand for the company's existing running shoe lines beyond what is anticipated in the plan.

- The company has the production capacity necessary to meet demand for the new shoe line.

- The company has the right marketing plan for the new line.

- Retailers will understand the rationale behind the new line and stock it.

- The price the company has set for the new line will be sufficient to cover costs and make an adequate profit.

This is not an exhaustive list, but it gives a sense of the sort of assumptions that are often left unstated.

After completing your list, the next step is to examine each of the assumptions and make sure they are necessary to the planning process. If there are stated assumptions in the plan that are unnecessary, then they should be identified and eliminated. At best, unnecessary assumptions needlessly complicate the analysis; at worst, they open doors to new problems that could have just as easily been left shut. In our example, an unnecessary assumption might be that running will remain a popular activity for health-minded consumers. That *is* an assumption, and while you may well want to examine it as part of a broader strategic review, there is unlikely to be much value in questioning it as part of this product plan.

Once any unnecessary assumptions have been removed from the list, the next step is to challenge each of the assumptions that remain by posing the following questions:

1. *Is this logical?*

2. *Is this accurate?*

3. *Is this based on preconceived notions or biases?*

4. *Is this based on historical analogies, and if so, are they relevant?*

5. *What has to happen for this to become true?*

6. *How much confidence do the planners have that this will happen?*

7. *If this becomes true, will it remain true under all conditions?*

8. *If this proves to be untrue, how would that alter the plan?*

Any assumptions that prove weak or that threaten the outcome of the plan need to be flagged. If possible, the red team should come up with recommendations for strengthening those assumptions or even propose contingency plans in case they prove false. If neither of these is possible, then the entire plan may need to be reevaluated.

However, when it comes to dealing with assumptions, it is important to understand that they are not all created equal. Some assumptions may have such a low probability of failure that they are not worth worrying about, unless they are critical to the plan's success. Our plan to introduce a new line of running shoes assumes that the company will continue to have access to the raw materials necessary to produce the shoes. That *is* an assumption, but if the company is already making running shoes, it is probably already true and likely to remain true, barring a major global catastrophe. Other assumptions may have a high potential for failure but are not vital to the success of the plan. These are probably not worth spending too much time on as a red team. Our shoe strategy has implicit assumptions about currency exchange rates, for example. Those rates can fluctuate wildly and could impact how much money we make from the new shoes, but they are unlikely to jeopardize the plan—unless our margins are thin, in which case exchange rates would be worth taking a hard look at.

The red team should focus its efforts on those assumptions that have a high potential for failure and would have major impact on the outcome plan if they prove false. This is particularly true when the red team has limited time to complete its work. These same assumptions should help inform the metrics the organization uses to monitor its progress against the plan as it is being executed. That way, you can be sure you are making *real* progress, not just getting lucky.

To identify these critical metrics, the red team can use a technique I call a *Probability Analysis*.

Probability Analysis

This tool is designed to identify the assumptions in a strategy or plan that merit special attention. *Probability Analysis* is based on a method I learned from the army,* but I have modified it to better suit the needs of businesses, with help from executives at the Development Bank of Japan's Investment Advisory subsidiary.

Start by printing out a list of all the assumptions you have identified. Give a copy to each member of the red team. Ask them to study each assumption on their own and estimate the chances, expressed as a percentage, of it proving true. Remember, the chance of any assumption being true must be less than 100 percent; otherwise it is not an assumption, but a fact. Once all the team members have completed their estimates, tally the totals for each assumption, and divide the sum by the number of people on your red team. The result is the confidence the red team has, expressed as a percentage, that each of these assumptions will prove true.

For example, if you have eight people on your red team and they return the following results . . .

75%, 80%, 55%, 90%, 80%, 65%, 70%, 75%

---

*That method is known as the *Assumption Sensitivity Analysis*.

... that would mean the team is 73.75 percent confident that the assumption in question will end up being a fact, because:*

$$75 + 80 + 55 + 90 + 80 + 65 + 70 + 75 = 590$$

$$590 \div 8 = 73.75$$

Once you have those numbers, you can calculate the probability that *all* of the plan's assumptions will prove true by multiplying these averages together. For example, if you have identified five assumptions with probabilities of . . .

73.75%, 94.5%, 80.25%, 70.5%, and 50.5%

. . . there is about a 20 percent chance that your plan will be executed flawlessly, because:

$$.7375 \times .945 \times .8025 \times .705 \times .505 = .1991220567$$

You can then subtract that number from 1 to find out the chances that at least one of the plan's assumptions will not hold:

$$1 - .1991220567 = 0.8008779433$$

In other words, there is about an 80 percent chance that at least one of the plan's assumptions will prove erroneous.

You can now create a short list of those assumptions that have a high probability of proving to be false, and concentrate on those. Or you can

---

*This method is used extensively by intelligence analysts to determine the likelihood that information that cannot be absolutely verified is true. I am told it was used to assess the odds that the individual being protected in a fortified compound in Abbottabad, Pakistan, was in fact Osama bin Laden before President Barack Obama authorized the raid that took out the al-Qaeda leader. This is alluded to in the 2012 film *Zero Dark Thirty*.

narrow that list even further by using *Dot Voting* to develop a short list of those assumptions your red team members believe are most critical to the plan's success, tallying the results, taking the assumptions that receive the most votes, and reordering them according to the percentages attached to them. This will yield a list of assumptions that have a high probability of failure *and* the potential to impact the plan in a big way, and you can focus your red teaming exercise on these.

It is important to understand that this technique evaluates each assumption independently and does not account for the fact that the failure of one assumption could lead to the failure of other assumptions that depend on it. Accounting for that level of interdependency requires a more robust—and time-consuming—approach, such as *String of Pearls Analysis*.

String of Pearls Analysis

If time and resources permit, you can extend your analysis to look not only at the assumptions a plan is based on, but also at all the things that have to happen for it to work and the cascading effects it may trigger. Unintended consequences are the consequence of insufficient planning. By identifying these unintended consequences beforehand, you can take steps to avoid them. *A String of Pearls Analysis* can help you do that. It can also expose hidden vulnerabilities, weaknesses, and gaps in the plan. This technique is not designed to help you decide between different courses of action or assess the probability of different outcomes. Rather, it is designed to dissect completed plans and concepts while there is still time to improve them. Developed by the U.S. Army's Directed Studies Office, *String of Pearls Analysis* is one of the most powerful tools in the red teaming arsenal.* I have modified it slightly to better meet

---

*The British Ministry of Defence's *Concept Testing* approach is a more elaborate version of this technique.

the needs of businesses. The result is a structured, five-step process that yields a detailed, graphical analysis that can be useful in explaining the red team's findings to senior leadership:

Step 1: Analyze the planning document and identify all the major tasks, both stated and implied, that must be completed for the plan to reach fruition. Number these tasks sequentially to create your "string of pearls." It may be helpful to color-code these to differentiate among different phases of the plan (e.g., construction, preproduction, production, etc.) or areas of responsibility (e.g., production, marketing, distribution, sales, etc.):

Step 1: Graphically Represent All of the Individual Tasks

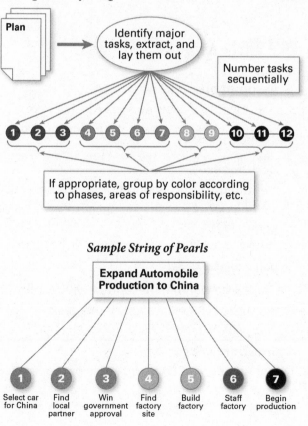

157

Step 2: Create a "spiderweb" chart for each task that maps out each of its assumptions, dependencies, and cascading effects:

Step 2: Create a "Spiderweb" Chart for Each Task

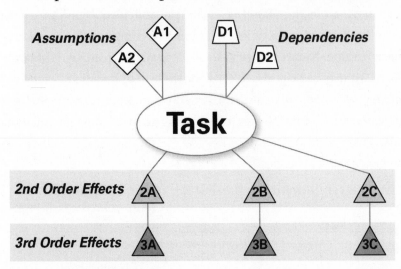

Assumptions
List the stated assumptions for this task
List the unstated assumptions for this task

Dependencies
Identify the critical conditions and precursor actions necessary for the successful execution of this task

2nd Order Effects
List the cascading effects that will result from the successful execution of this task

3rd Order Effects
List the indirect consequences of those effects using *If/Then Analysis*

It is easiest to do this on a whiteboard, but you can also use presentation software such as PowerPoint or Pages. Look at each task independently and identify all the stated and unstated assumptions behind it, just as you would in a *Key Assumptions Check*. For example, if you were red teaming a plan to expand automobile production in China, one of those tasks might be winning approval from the Chinese government. That single task is predicated on several assumptions. It assumes the Chinese government is willing to allow an expansion of local automobile production by a foreign manufacturer, that it is willing to work with your company on such a project, and that your company is willing to abide by whatever conditions Beijing might impose. All of these assumptions should be identified on the chart.

Next, identify each task's dependencies. These are conditions or events that are necessary for the successful completion of the task. Dependencies can include other tasks already identified as part of your analysis of the plan, or subsidiary requirements. Key dependencies of winning approval from the Chinese government might include establishing the necessary connections with the Chinese, finding a suitable local production partner, and negotiating an agreement that meets the needs of both the company and Beijing. All of these need to be added to the chart as well.

Finally, identify each task's second- and third-order effects. These are the direct and indirect consequences of the task being completed. Second-order effects of winning approval from the Chinese government might include problems with trade unions back home and negative reaction from consumers opposed to moving production to China. Third-order effects stem from second-order effects, and that relationship should be reflected on the chart. In our example, the increased tensions with unions might make upcoming labor negotiations more challenging, while the negative impact on consumer sentiment back home might require the company to launch a new advertising campaign touting its domestic investments and ongoing commitment to producing cars there as well.

If you think about it long enough, you will realize there are an infinite number of cascading effects for any action. The point is not to capture them all but rather to identify the most significant ones that could lead to negative consequences not anticipated by the plan.

Sample Spiderweb Chart

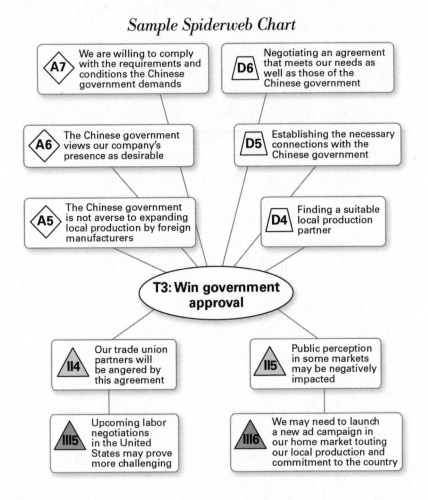

Step 3: Once you have completed a spiderweb chart for each task, create a spreadsheet listing each task, along with its assumptions, dependencies, and effects:

Step 3: Create a Spreadsheet

Task	1 Select Car for China	2 Find Local Partner	3 Win Government Approval	4 Find Factory Site	5 Build Factory	6 Staff Factory	7 Begin Production
Assumptions	A1: One of our existing vehicles would be well-suited for production in China	A2: A Chinese automaker exists with the skills and expertise we require	A5: The Chinese government is not averse to expanding local production by foreign manufacturers	A8: A suitable location for our factory exists in China	A9: We will be able to secure the necessary approvals from local government	A11: We will be able to find sufficiently skilled workers locally	A13: We will have the necessary components on hand
		A3: That automaker is not already allied with one of our competitors	A6: The Chinese government views our company's presence as desirable		A10: We will be able to secure the funding necessary to build the new plant	A12: We will be able to negotiate acceptable labor agreements	A14: The plant will be supplied with power, water, and other production necessities
		A4: That automaker views us as a desirable partner	A7: We are willing to comply with the requirements and conditions the Chinese government demands				
Dependencies	D1: Having the design for that vehicle completed	D2: Negotiating mutually acceptable terms with that automaker	D4: Finding a suitable local production partner (See Task 2)	D7: That site also meets the needs of our local partner	D10: Completing a design for the new factory	D13: Successfully completing labor negotiations with state-run unions	D16: Having the necessary agreements in place with suppliers

Task	1 Select Car for China	2 Find Local Partner	3 Win Government Approval	4 Find Factory Site	5 Build Factory	6 Staff Factory	7 Begin Production
		D3: Having a vehicle design that matches that automaker's needs and abilities	D5: Establishing the necessary connections with the Chinese government	D8: That site also meets the requirements set forth by the Chinese government	D11: Finding a construction company to build the plant	D14: Hiring the necessary workers with the necessary skills	D17: Having the necessary agreements in place with local utilities
			D6: Negotiating an agreement that meets our needs as well as those of the Chinese government	D9: We can secure that site for favorable terms	D12: Securing the necessary permits and approvals	D15: Training those workers	
2nd Order Effects	I1: Moving production of an existing vehicle to China will create excess capacity in the plant where it is currently produced	I2: Our production capacity and product plans will now be dependent on this automaker	I4: Our trade union partners will be angered by this agreement	I6: Securing the factory site will increase our real estate expenses	I8: Our capex budget will increase by the cost of the new factory	I9: Our labor costs will increase	I11: Finished vehicles will need to be shipped to dealers
		I3: We will have to share IP with our Chinese partner	I5: Public perception in some markets may be negatively impacted	I7: It may be more difficult to fund future expansion		I10: We may incur new obligations to state-run unions in China	I12: Supplier stocks will be diminished

Task	1 Select Car for China	2 Find Local Partner	3 Win Government Approval	4 Find Factory Site	5 Build Factory	6 Staff Factory	7 Begin Production
3rd Order Effects	III1: We will need to find another product to produce in that facility	III3: If our Chinese partner is unable to honor its commitments to us, production plans and global capacity will be negatively impacted	III5: Upcoming labor negotiations in the United States may prove more challenging		See II7	III7: Our production in the country could be negatively impacted by local labor unrest or workplace actions	III8: We will need to ensure that sufficient transport capacity is in place to get our vehicles to dealers
	III2: If not, we will have to reduce staffing at that factory	III4: Our Chinese partner may use our IP without our permission or share it with other Chinese companies	III6: We may need to launch a new ad campaign in our home market touting our local production and commitment to the country				III9: We may need to find additional sources for key components to cope with increased demand

As you create this spreadsheet, consider how critical each of these items is to the plan's success. If the failure of an assumption would put the plan *at risk,* mark it with an *R*. If it would cause the plan to *fail,* mark it with an *F*. Challenge each assumption, and flag those that are weak or unlikely to prove true.

Next, move on to the dependencies and effects. Assign a different color to each of them and, as you go through the list, take note of any risky dependencies, as well as any undesirable cascading effects.

When you have completed the spreadsheet, count how many times each assumption, dependency, and effect occurs over the course of the plan. It may become obvious that certain events occur repeatedly across multiple tasks. These merit special attention. Take the time to stress-test these assumptions, because the success or failure of the entire plan could well hinge on them. If these dependencies are not already identified as tasks, add them to your task list, and do a spiderweb chart for them as well. Finally, determine whether the organization is prepared to deal with these second- and third-order effects and note any that might require additional planning.

Step 4: Create a graphic representation that aggregates and displays these results and identifies any gaps or weaknesses in the plan. Begin by laying out your string of pearls. Note any at-risk or weak assumptions that they depend on above them:

Step 4a: Add the Assumptions

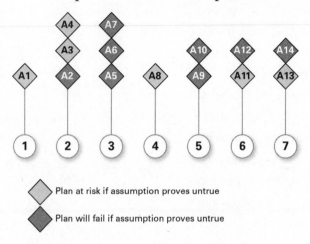

Next, add the key dependencies above each task using a different shape keyed to the colors in your spreadsheet:

Step 4b: Add Dependencies

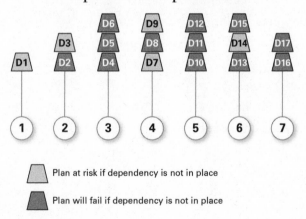

Then add the second- and third-order effects beneath each task, again using colored shapes:

Step 4c: Add 2nd- and 3rd-Order Effects

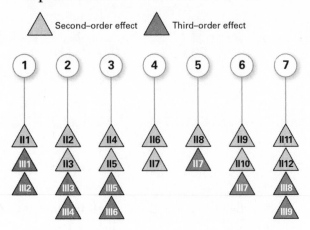

Now, combine all of these elements into one chart:

Step 4d: Combine All Elements

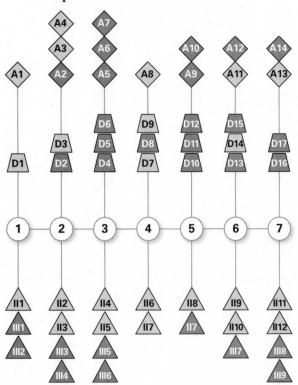

Step 5: Analyze this chart and highlight any tasks that are at high risk for failure—tasks that rely on weak or invalid assumptions, have significant dependencies, or will create undesirable cascading effects.

Share the final chart with your organization's decision makers, noting any gaps and weaknesses the red team has identified. I also recommend sharing these findings with the people who developed the original plan. This will give them the opportunity to reevaluate these tasks or develop contingency plans to deal with these potential points of failure.

String of Pearls Analysis is not perfect. The different factors it examines are not weighted against one another. But I have found no other method that is as effective at mapping out all the interconnected elements that have to come together for a strategic plan to be executed flawlessly. A *String of Pearls Analysis* can take several days, or even weeks, to complete. Because of the time and effort involved, I recommend that you reserve it for plans that could have far-reaching consequences for your company. If the plan you are analyzing is critical to your company's success, the time will be time well spent.

Stakeholder Mapping

At the beginning of a red teaming exercise, in addition to identifying assumptions, it can also be helpful to look at all of the groups that have a stake in the strategy or plan you are evaluating. This is particularly true if you know of groups that could oppose or derail the plan, such as trade unions, government regulators, or competitors. The simplest way to identify these constituencies is through a technique called *Stakeholder Mapping.*[*]

Begin by creating a comprehensive list of all the groups that have a stake in the success or failure of the plan. In addition to potential adversaries,

---

[*]*Stakeholder Mapping* is most effective when used in conjunction with the *Four Ways of Seeing* technique described in chapter 7, which examines the problem from the perspective of different key stakeholders.

include potential allies. Also be sure to include employees, suppliers, partners, customers, retailers, distributors, and any other constituency the plan touches. Next, color-code each of these groups as *black*, *white*, or *gray*:

BLACK: competitor/adversary/hard opposition

WHITE: ally/partner/hard support

GRAY: soft opposition/soft support

Sample Stakeholder Mapping Chart

Stakeholder Map for Planned Introduction of Luggage-Handling Robots

Stakeholder	Support	Oppose
Customers		
Shareholders		
Airport Authorities		
Salaried Employees		
Union (Pilots)		
Union (Flight Attendants)		
Union (Baggage Handlers)		
Union (Machinists)		

Once you have done this, look at the grays. These groups are tipping points that could mean the difference between success and failure. Your challenge as a red team is to figure out if there are ways to turn *soft opposition* into *soft support* or *soft support* into *hard support*. Doing so can turn potential adversaries into allies and ensure that those groups that are already on your side not only stay on your side, but actually become active contributors to your plan's success.

That is what Alan Mulally did at Ford. After taking over as CEO in the fall of 2006, he reached out to the automaker's suppliers, dealers, and unions and showed each of these stakeholders how they would become more successful if they helped Ford's turnaround plan succeed. As a result, Mulally was able to negotiate a game-changing contract with the United Auto Workers, convince dealers to remodel their showrooms to boost Ford's brand image, and get parts manufacturers to give the company their best technology and more favorable terms.

Analysis of Competing Hypotheses (ACH)

If your *Argument Dissection* suggests there may be other explanations for a problem, you may want to examine those more carefully through a technique called *Analysis of Competing Hypotheses*, or *ACH*. Developed by the CIA in the 1970s, this method is particularly valuable when you need to make analytical judgments about complex problems and have a good amount of data and other evidence to weigh and consider. I have adapted this step-by-step approach from *The Psychology of Intelligence Analysis,* which was published by the CIA in 1999:

Step 1: Brainstorm the problem and identify all the possible explanations. You can do this informally, or by using one of the *Liberating Structures* described in chapter 5. Be sure to include every possible explanation, no matter how remote it might seem. Only after all the possibilities are on the table should you begin culling those that are not worthy of serious consideration. But be careful when you do. Only eliminate those hypotheses that appear to be *disproved*; hold on to those that are merely *unproven.*

Step 2: Make a list of the evidence for and against each of these hypotheses. For each explanation, the team should ask itself what evidence it would expect to see if this hypothesis were true, and then determine whether that evidence actually exists. If it does, add it to the list. It is also important to note the absence of such evidence. This list can, and often should, include assumptions. Just make sure these are identified as such.

Step 3: Prepare a chart listing all the hypotheses across the top and each significant piece of evidence down the side. Once you have completed this chart, look at each piece of evidence, and put a "✓" under each explanation that piece of evidence is consistent with and an "✗" under each explanation it is inconsistent with. If the evidence neither supports nor refutes a given hypothesis, leave the box below it blank.

Step 4: Once you have evaluated all the evidence, take another look at each explanation in light of this information. Think about whether rewording the hypothesis might make it more consistent with the evidence. If so, rewrite the hypothesis using this new language. Note any changes that makes on the chart. Also, think about whether any new explanations are suggested by the evidence. If any are, add them to the chart. If there is little or no evidence to distinguish between two hypotheses, combine them. Once you have reviewed all the explanations, look at each piece of evidence again. Eliminate any that has a check mark in every column. Since this evidence supports *all* the hypotheses, it has no diagnostic value and can be ignored. At the same time, eliminate any evidence that neither supports nor refutes any of the explanations. Again, it serves no diagnostic purpose. Finally, think about whether any new evidence occurs to you that supports or refutes any of these hypotheses. If so, add it to the chart.*

Step 5: Draw tentative conclusions about the relative likelihood of each of the remaining hypotheses. Work your way down the chart to see

---

*I recommend taking a picture of the chart before making any of these changes so that you can refer back to the original if necessary.

if any of the explanations now seem significantly more or less likely than the others. In doing so, you should seek to disprove hypotheses, rather than affirm them. The one with the most ✗'s beneath it is probably the least likely explanation; the one with the fewest ✗'s is probably the most likely hypothesis. The check marks are far less significant, because a single piece of evidence that refutes a hypothesis can be enough to reject that explanation if that evidence is strong enough—even if there are many pieces of evidence that support it. Rank the remaining explanations from most likely to least likely, based on the number of ✗'s beneath each one. As you work through the list, be on guard against the cognitive biases described in chapter 3. Confirmation bias is a particular threat to this sort of analysis, so it is important to objectively consider all of the evidence before you, and then draw the best conclusion possible about which explanation is most likely to be correct. The chart should not dictate the conclusion, but rather serve as a guide to help you compare the strengths and weaknesses of each hypothesis.

Sample ACH Chart

Question: How will Company Z react to our new quantum computer?

Hypothesis 1: *Z is already developing its own quantum computer and is also ready to bring its product to market.*

Hypothesis 2: *Z is already developing its own quantum computer and will rush its program once we announce ours.*

Hypothesis 3: *Z is not developing its own quantum computer, but will begin doing so once it learns about ours.*

Hypothesis 4: *Z is not interested in quantum computing.*

Evidence	H1	H2	H3	H4
Z has said publicly that it believes "quantum computing is the future"	✓	✓	✗	✗
Z tried to purchase a Canadian quantum computing start-up last summer				✗
Z hired that company's CTO last fall	✓	✓	✗	✗
That individual resigned three months later and has not been replaced	✗			
Z has hired 27 new computer engineers in the past three months, including several recent graduates who have participated in quantum computing research	✗	✓	✗	✗
Z still has 17 open positions listed on its website for engineers with experience in quantum computing	✗	✓	✗	✗
Z rushed the development of its own quad-core computer after we launched ours and brought its first one to market six months later		✓		
CONCLUSION: Hypothesis 2 is most likely correct				

Step 6: Look at how sensitive your conclusion is to a few critical pieces of evidence; consider the consequences for your analysis if that evidence is wrong, misleading, or subject to a different interpretation. Stress-test

the key pieces of evidence that drive your analysis in one direction or another. If you have any concerns that your organization may be in denial about something, now is the time to voice them. If there is any chance some of the information you are evaluating is designed to purposely deceive or mislead, now is the time to consider that possibility as well. You may want to examine the original source material, rather than relying on someone else's interpretation of it. You may also decide additional research is necessary before committing to one hypothesis.

Step 7: Report your conclusions. Make sure you include an analysis of the relative likelihood of all the other explanations that could not be categorically rejected. Explain why you feel your choice is the most likely to be true. This is important, because decision makers need to know that alternative explanations exist. It may be helpful to assign a percentage value to each hypothesis to reflect the red team's assessment of how likely or unlikely each explanation is.

Step 8: Identify milestones for future observation. These should be developments that suggest events are taking a course different from what would be expected if your explanation is correct.*

"Analytical conclusions should always be regarded as tentative," writes former CIA analyst Richards Heuer, the chief architect of *ACH*. "The situation may change, or it may remain unchanged while you receive new information that alters your appraisal. It is always helpful to specify in advance things one should look for or be alert to that, if observed, would suggest a significant change in the probabilities. . . . Specifying in advance what would cause you to change your mind will also make it more difficult for you to rationalize such developments, if they occur."

If you have an in-house red team, have it watch for these signposts of

*Xerox's Palo Alto Research Center has developed software to make *ACH* easier. It is available for download from the company's website: http://www2.parc.com/istl/projects/ach/ach.html.

change. Your team can also help make the most of the results of a *Key Assumptions Check* or *String of Pearls Analysis* by continuing to monitor the plan's assumptions as it is being executed. If any of your assumptions turn out to be false, examine your plan again and see if it is still possible to achieve the desired aims. If not, reassess your strategy instead of continuing to pursue a course of action that is unlikely to succeed.

Regardless of whether your red team is external or internal, standing or ad hoc, it can use the tools described in this chapter to identify faulty logic and flawed thinking, explore alternative explanations that challenge groupthink and conventional wisdom, and close the gaps in your organization's strategies and plans. By combining these tools with the imaginative techniques I will introduce in the next chapter, they can save your organization from making the sort of catastrophic blunders that put companies out of business.

CHAPTER 7

Thinking the Unthinkable: Imaginative Techniques

No plan extends with any certainty beyond the first contact with the enemy.

—Helmuth Karl Bernhard Graf von Moltke

In 2000, Netflix CEO Reed Hastings and his executive team flew to Dallas and walked into the headquarters of the video rental giant Blockbuster with a proposal. Netflix was still struggling to find its footing in the video rental business, and while Hastings and company knew the future was online, they also wanted to establish a physical presence where their subscribers could pick up and drop off movies. They also knew Blockbuster was struggling to find its way onto the Internet. So Netflix offered to run Blockbuster's online business in exchange for Blockbuster giving Netflix a place in its stores.

"They just about laughed us out of their office," recalled former Netflix chief financial officer Barry McCarthy.

Blockbuster's executives kept laughing, too. They laughed when Hastings returned with an offer to sell Netflix to Blockbuster for $50 million, and they laughed when he came back with the same offer a year later. Their chuckling continued as more and more consumers opted to rent their movies online from Netflix or from video vending machines operated by Redbox. The Blockbuster guys were still laughing when their operating income withered and their company plunged into the red.

"Neither Redbox nor Netflix are even on the radar screen in terms of competition," Blockbuster CEO Jim Keyes declared in December 2008, dismissing Wall Street's concerns about those competitors with still more laughter.

Blockbuster filed for bankruptcy less than two years later. By the time its last store closed in November 2013, Netflix was worth almost $20 billion.

The collapse of Blockbuster has been held up as a cautionary tale, a warning to business leaders everywhere of the consequences of not taking new competitors seriously. It certainly is that, but it also shows what can happen when a company fails to understand its own customers.

"At least initially, they thought we were a very small niche business," said McCarthy. "And that was very much to our advantage."

But Netflix was more than just a small niche business even back in 2000. Netflix was the answer to customers' biggest gripe about Blockbuster, and the video rental business in general: late fees. It was a problem Hastings had experienced firsthand after he rented *Apollo 13* and forgot to return it.

"It was six weeks late and I owed the video store forty dollars. I had misplaced the cassette. It was all my fault. I didn't want to tell my wife about it. And I said to myself, 'I'm going to compromise the integrity of my marriage over a late fee?'" Hastings would later tell the *New York*

Times. "On my way to the gym, I realized they had a much better business model. You could pay thirty or forty dollars a month and work out as little or as much as you wanted."

Netflix was born out of this realization that, as much as people loved renting movies, they hated video rental companies because of those hefty, compounding fees. Blockbuster not only failed to recognize the damage these fees were doing to its brand image, but had made the revenue generated by these fines the cornerstone of its business model. It was that failure to understand what its customers disliked about renting movies that put Blockbuster out of business every bit as much as the catastrophic failure of vision that lay behind its dismissal of the repeated offers from Netflix. Blockbuster might have avoided both blunders if it had used a red teaming technique called *Four Ways of Seeing.*

Four Ways of Seeing

Developed by Colonel Steve Rotkoff, *Four Ways of Seeing* is a simple but remarkably revealing technique that can yield valuable insights into the way competitors, customers, and other key constituencies view your company, your industry, and one another. Used early enough, this information can help your planners formulate strategies that address the challenges and opportunities presented by these key constituencies. Alternatively, the red team can use this technique after a plan has been formulated to ensure it takes into account the sensitivities and expectations of all of the stakeholders.

A *Four Ways of Seeing* exercise begins by identifying the most significant groups that may be affected by your plan or strategy using the *Stakeholder Mapping* technique described in the previous chapter. Once you have developed that list, create a quad chart for each of the groups that you want to analyze more closely:

How X views X	How Y views Y
How X views Y	How Y views X

X is your company or organization. Y is the group you are analyzing. It could be your customers, a key competitor, government regulators, a trade union, a supply partner, a retailer, a prospective acquisition, your employees, or even another division within your organization. It can be as general or as specific as your time allows and your plans require. Instead of just looking at your customers as a whole, you could do separate charts for your North American customers, South American customers, European customers, and customers in the Asia-Pacific region. You could do one chart for competitors in general or separate charts for each of your major rivals. It all depends on how much granularity is relevant to the strategy you are developing.

Once you have created your grid, start in the upper left-hand corner of the chart and, working together as a group, think of how your company views itself. Consider your values, your goals, and the characteristics that shape your actions. Are you conservative, or willing to take risks? Do you dominate your industry, or live in fear of bigger players? Are you proactive, or reactive? Are you innovative, or struggling to keep up with the changing marketplace? Be honest. The point here is not to develop marketing material or write boilerplate for a press release, but rather to make an unflinching assessment of your organization that enables meaningful analysis. Your website may describe your company as "innovative," but if most employees would disagree with that statement, then leave that off the chart. At the same time, do remember that the question here is not so much about what your organization *actually is,* but rather what it *believes it is.* As a red teamer, you may recognize that your company is not the most innovative player in its space, but if that is what your organization tells itself and most employees believe it to be true, then by all means write "innovative" in the upper left-hand corner.

During my red team training with the U.S. Army, we practiced *Four Ways of Seeing* by looking at the major players in the Iranian nuclear negotiations that were then under way in Vienna. Some of my classmates, understandably jaded after multiple deployments to the Middle East, offered some pretty scathing descriptions of the United States. Our instructor kept reminding us that the point was not to describe how America actually behaves, but how the nation views itself in the world.

When you have finished with your own organization, move on to the upper right-hand quadrant and think about the group you are analyzing. How do they see themselves? What do they stand for? What do they want? What do they value? What do they fear? Remember, your job is not to describe their behavior or your opinion of them, but to describe that group's own view of itself. Put yourself in their shoes and really try to look at these questions from that group's perspective, not your own.

Next, move down to the lower left-hand quadrant and think about how your organization views that group. Again, be brutally honest. If you are analyzing business partners or employees, forget about what your official messaging says and think about what people in your organization *actually say* about them behind closed doors. If you view your franchisees as cash cows to be milked for every penny they are worth, admit it. If you think the union is greedy, write the word "greedy" in the box. If you think your production partner is incompetent, make sure that is duly noted.

Finally, move over to the lower right-hand box and consider how the group you are analyzing views *you*—not how you *hope* they view you, how you *wish* they would view you, or how they *would* view you if they only understood the real you, but what they *really think* about you, your products or services, your motives, and your ultimate aims. Be ruthless. If you try to sugarcoat it, your analysis will be of little value.

Sample Four Ways of Seeing Chart

How Does Our Company View Itself?	How Does the Union View Itself?
Innovative	Defender of the workers
Fair negotiator	Shrewd negotiators
We care about our employees	Cares about its members
Job/wealth creator	Job/wealth protector
Optimistic about our future	Worried about its future
How Do We View the Union	**How Does the Union View Our Company?**
Outdated	Outdated
Corrupt	Greedy
Milks our employees for dues	Takes advantage of our members
Impedes our progress/growth	Impedes our progress/growth
Makes unreasonable demands	Makes unreasonable demands

When you have finished filling in the final square, study the chart and identify all the disconnects that exist among the four quadrants. Think about how you can help bridge these divides or, if appropriate, how you can exploit them. Consider the ramifications for your plan and discuss how changes to your strategy might help you address the challenges you see in the chart—or take advantage of the opportunities.

Repeat this process for each group or subgroup you have decided to examine. There is no need to keep filling out the upper left-hand quadrant; as long as you are looking at how each group relates to your own organization you only have to do that once. However, it may be useful to explore how different groups see one another. If so, X will be one group and Y will be another, and your own organization will not be part of the equation.

Alternatively, you can create one big chart that includes all the players you want to consider. Instead of just 4 perspectives, you can create a 4-by-4 chart that includes 16, an 8-by-8 chart that examines 64, or a 16-by-16 table that embraces a whopping 256 different ways of seeing. Once again, it all comes down to how much time you can allocate to the process and the nature of the problem you are red teaming.

If Blockbuster had conducted a *Four Ways of Seeing* analysis of its customers, it might have discovered just how much damage those exorbitant late fees were doing and eliminated them.* The company might also have learned just how keen those customers were to avoid a trip to the video store. If Blockbuster had looked at how those same customers viewed Netflix, it might have realized its competitor had found a better way of meeting their needs and written that check for $50 million.

Unfortunately, Blockbuster was also hamstrung by a staggering lack of vision. The world was changing, but like so many other old economy companies, it failed to see how those changes would transform its business. A technique called *Outside-In Thinking* might have helped overcome that myopia.

---

*Blockbuster did ultimately eliminate late fees in response to the growing competition from Netflix, but it was too late.

Outside-In Thinking

When we think about a problem, we usually start with the issue at hand and work our way out from there. There is nothing wrong with that approach, but by starting with where we are instead of where the larger world is heading, we can miss important opportunities, just as Blockbuster did. *Outside-In Thinking* is designed to avoid this. As the name suggests, it is a form of analysis that begins with the broader environment and works its way back in to the issue the red team is working on. It is a simple, four-step process:*

Step 1: Begin by developing a list of all the major forces—social, economic, technological, political, and even environmental—that could have an impact on the problem, but over which your organization has little or no influence. These could include anything from the global economy and geopolitical developments to a new technology or consumer trend.

Step 2: Figure out which of these forces your company might be able to exert some influence over. This might include customers, suppliers, business partners, policy makers, industry organizations, or even markets, consumer trends, and emerging technologies.

Step 3: Consider how each of these actors could potentially affect the problem positively or negatively. For example, a trade union could thwart your plan by refusing to support key elements, or help ensure success by giving the initiative its enthusiastic support.

Step 4: Think about how your organization might be able to influence these actors and nudge them in a direction that would help you achieve your strategic goals, or at least avoid potential problems down the road. In the case of the trade union, that might be as simple as sitting down

---

*The U.S. Army teaches this as a three-step process. I have added the fourth step to help companies take full advantage of it.

with organization's leadership and explaining your plan or as complex as offering concessions in other areas.

If Blockbuster had conducted this sort of analysis, it might have recognized the impact the Internet was having on consumer behavior and realized its existing business model would soon be supplanted. Armed with those insights, Blockbuster might have begun work on its own online service sooner. As it was, Blockbuster realized this far too late, giving Netflix years to perfect its model and build its customer base.

Admittedly, it is not always easy to see how such trend lines might develop. Fortunately, there is another technique called *Alternative Futures Analysis* that can help.

Alternative Futures Analysis

While red teaming cannot provide you with a crystal ball, *Alternative Futures Analysis* can reveal the different ways a strategy could unfold, allowing your organization to plan for the worst even as it prepares for the best. This method is particularly helpful in situations that are highly complex or shrouded by a high degree of uncertainty.

Start by brainstorming or using *Outside-In Thinking* to develop an exhaustive list of the forces and factors that could shape the way your plan unfolds when it is executed. Then, use one of the *Liberating Structures* described in chapter 5 to whittle that list down to the two variables that are most in question and that could have the biggest impact on the final outcome. For example, my class was tasked with analyzing the U.S. Army's new plan for "Army University," a major overhaul of all the service's education initiatives, from basic training to the Army War College, that was designed to make all the instruction soldiers received more easily transferable to the civilian world. Our class decided the two biggest variables would be how much care the army took in rolling out the new initiative and how much buy-in there was from civilian licensing authorities and accreditation organizations.

Next, identify the two most relevant values for each of the two variables. In our case, those were *rapid rollout* and *deliberate rollout*, and *full accreditation* and *limited accreditation*. Once you have done that, create a simple chart that plots those two variables against those two values. That will result in four quadrants, each representing a different way that the strategy or situation could unfold.

Our chart looked like this:

Sample Alternative Futures Analysis Chart

Rapid with Full Accreditation

- Initial wins
- Unsustainable processes (or no processes)
- Uncertain resourcing (budget does not meet needs)
- Lose accreditations
- Faculty trained but only certified with status quo systems
- Initial personnel billets taken from operational units
- Speed requires $$$

Deliberate with Full Accreditation

- Fully realized and sustainable strategic plan
- Clear communications strategy
- Soldiers and academia understand what ArmyU is
- Process vs. personality-based enterprise
- Policies in place
- Programs/opportunities for all military occupational specialties
- Proof of acceptance

Full — *Acceptance/Accreditation* — *Limited*

Rapid — Pace of Phasing — *Deliberate*

- Costs dramatically increase
- Everything is a priority
- Reputations not established
- Overpromise and underdeliver
- Higher accreditation costs $$$
- Broken talent management system

- Moderate improvement in key areas (curriculum, etc.)
- DoD accepts universal transcript
- No support from the force
- Unexpected costs due to reliance on civilian institutions
- Government funding reduced
- No widespread buy-in outside the military

Rapid with Limited Accreditation

Deliberate with Limited Accreditation

Once you have created your chart, have the red team think about each of these four possible futures and describe it in as much detail as possible. What will be the consequences for your organization in each of these four cases? What will be the consequences for your competitors, for your customers, or for other key stakeholders? What new challenges and opportunities will be created? Also think about what would have to occur in order to reach each of these end states. Try to identify signs that you can watch for as the situation develops or the plan is executed that suggest it is heading in one of these four directions. If any of the outcomes are undesirable, your organization should modify its plan to help ensure it unfolds in a more favorable direction and perhaps even develop contingency plans to deal with the possibility it might not. If any of the outcomes would create new opportunities, you should come up with a plan to exploit them. Either way, the *Alternatives Futures Analysis* will provide a useful road map.

In risky situations that have many possible outcomes, the army sometimes uses a more detailed and comprehensive version of this method. Instead of relying on just a red team, it also brings in outside experts with deep knowledge of the issues under review. And instead of looking at just two variables, it analyzes many different alternatives and end states. This approach can be expensive and take several days, but if the stakes are high enough, it can also be well worth the investment. Situations that might warrant this sort of detailed analysis include the emergence of a new competitor or disruptive technology, the imposition of new regulations, or similarly dramatic changes that could fundamentally alter your business environment.

Pre-Mortem Analysis

Not all red teaming techniques require such a significant commitment of time and resources. *Pre-Mortem Analysis* is an incredibly powerful tool developed by cognitive psychologist Gary Klein. A proper

Pre-Mortem takes about an hour to complete, but you can do a quick and dirty one in as few as fifteen minutes. *Pre-Mortem Analysis* is easy to understand, simple to use, and can quite literally save your company from disaster.

You are no doubt familiar with the concept of a *postmortem* analysis, in which a team is convened *after* a plan has failed to figure out *why* it failed. A *Pre-Mortem Analysis* works the same way, but it is far more useful because it takes place *before* a plan is executed, while there is still time to fix it and avoid failure. If there are weaknesses in the plan, or if a strategy could create unanticipated consequences, a *Pre-Mortem Analysis* will help the red team identify them. While it might sound similar to a murder board, risk analysis, failure analysis, or other techniques with which you may already be familiar, *Pre-Mortem Analysis* is actually quite different. Those methods are designed to assess the chances of a plan failing and reduce the risk of failure to acceptable levels. *Pre-Mortem Analysis* assumes the plan has failed and is concerned with figuring out the causes for that failure. This is significant, because those other methods rarely force people to really contemplate what failure looks like.

Klein developed this technique after recognizing that people often become overconfident when they have decided on a plan. *Pre-Mortem Analysis* is designed to counter that dangerous tendency:

> *The attitude of complacency and the false sense of security is punctured, at least temporarily, and is replaced by an active search aimed at preventing trouble later on. You get to show off your smarts through the quality of the problems you can find. You might predict problems with the plan's concept, the timetable, the financial resources, or with the makeup of the team itself. In our experience, we have found a much higher level of candor in this exercise than in more passive attempts at self-critiquing.*

Pre-Mortem Analysis works like this:

Step 1: Have the red team review the strategy or plan.

Step 2: Contemplate disaster. Tell the team to look into the future and imagine the plan has failed—not just fallen short of expectations or missed its mark, but failed spectacularly and in a way that will cause real damage to the organization. If you are red teaming a marketing plan, imagine that it has not just failed to enhance perception of your brand or product but actually turned people against it. If you are contemplating a merger, imagine that it has not only failed to achieve the expected synergies but has also ended up destroying your core business. If you are analyzing a potential investment, imagine that it has not only failed to yield the desired returns, but has also become a financial black hole that is rapidly consuming what little is left of your original stake.

Step 3: Figure out how and why this happened. Have each member of the red team ponder that question and write down all the possible causes for this fiasco on a note card. How much time you devote to this step depends partly on the complexity of the plan and partly on how likely the group is to speak its mind. Klein advocates limiting this period of reflection and writing to just two or three minutes. He believes that time pressure can improve the analysis because people who are working against the clock are less likely to censor themselves. The army recommends giving red team members twenty to thirty minutes to ponder the plan and think about the different ways it could fail. That helps focus the discussion and keeps the team from straying too far away from the realm of possibility, but it also allows sufficient time to really elaborate on these different pathways to failure. The army's approach allows team members to get creative and develop detailed narratives that often reveal more than simple bullet points ever could. Both approaches have merit; choosing the best one for your red team will depend on the personalities of its members. If they are not afraid to express their concerns, give them more time. If they are less inclined to candor, set the timer for two minutes.

Step 4: Consolidate the lists by having each member of the red team share the first thing he or she came up with, then work your way around the room, adhering to the red teaming rule that everyone speaks once before anyone speaks twice. Once everyone has shared an idea, return to the first team member and have that person share the next idea on his or her list. If someone else has already shared the same idea, either skip over it or elaborate on their narrative. Keep going until everyone has exhausted all of their ideas or until those being suggested start to border on the absurd. At Fort Leavenworth, our rule of thumb was: *When someone mentions aliens or giant meteors, it's time to stop.*

Step 5: Use *Dot Voting* or one of the other *Liberating Structures* in chapter 5 to identify the three most likely factors that could cause the plan to fail. Then work together as a team to suggest ways the plan could be altered or improved to mitigate these possibilities.

Step 6: Periodically review the list as the plan is being executed to make sure none of the scenarios the team identified appear to be emerging.

In 2014, the U.S. Army used *Pre-Mortem Analysis* to figure out how the United States could lose a major war in 2030. The resulting report is still shaping American military strategy and planning.

The team laid out a nightmare scenario that began with an earthquake in Indonesia in 2028 and ended two years later with what was left of a U.S. expeditionary force in Iran being evacuated to Dubai with the help of Saudi jetliners in what the authors referred to as "America's Dunkirk." During the two years in between, a downsized U.S. military struggles to respond to the humanitarian crisis in Indonesia and Iranian attempts to close the Straits of Hormuz in retaliation for Western support of Kurdish separatists. When the United States seizes the port city of Bandar Abbas to reopen the Persian Gulf, Iranian troops armed with cheap shoulder-launched surface-to-air missiles made ubiquitous by advances in 3-D printing technology blow American helicopters out of the sky. As American soldiers are about to be overrun by Iranian troops, they call in airstrikes that also kill many civilians, and the whole horrific incident is broadcast live by Russian news drones. It becomes the most watched television event of the year after the 2030 World Cup. But the Iranians don't just watch; they use facial-recognition software to identify the troops involved in this "atrocity." Their names and home addresses are published on extremist websites as a prominent Shi'ite cleric calls for revenge. A few days later, a terrorist bomb blows up an elementary school in North Carolina where several of the soldiers' children are enrolled. Meanwhile, hackers sympathetic to the Iranian cause break into U.S. government computer networks and publish the names and addresses of Army Reservists being called up to fight. Many refuse to report for duty, and America is unable to maintain its beachhead in Iran.

This entire scenario was based on extrapolating recent, real-world geopolitical developments and the latest advances in technology one step into the future. It was hardly science fiction, and the army took the study's warnings very seriously. As a result of this analysis, the army is now working to ensure it has the means of countering—or at least coping with—the cascade of events described in the report.

It is important to stress that *Pre-Mortem Analysis* is not about courting disaster. It is about identifying the ways in which a strategy could fail in order to make sure that failure does not occur. Nor should it be viewed as a negative exercise. Just because a plan has weaknesses does not mean it is a bad plan. It may, in fact, be the best of all possible plans. But as with red teaming in general, *Pre-Mortem Analysis* can help make it a *better* plan. This is important because, in some cultures, merely discussing the possibility of a catastrophe makes people uncomfortable. However, I have found that, by stressing the positive, proactive purpose of *Pre-Mortem Analysis*, it can be used effectively by any organization in any country. My clients have found this technique to be quite revealing, and many of them have made substantial adjustments to their strategies or plans as a result of the insights they gained from this mental simulation.

Klein, too, has had great success teaching this method to companies. He cites several examples in a 2007 *Harvard Business Review* article:

> *In a session held at one Fortune 50–size company, an executive suggested that a billion-dollar environmental sustainability project had "failed" because interest waned when the CEO retired. Another pinned the failure on a dilution of the business case after a government agency revised its policies.*
>
> *In a session regarding a project to make state-of-the-art computer algorithms available to military air-campaign planners, a team member who had been silent during the previous lengthy kickoff meeting volunteered that one of the algorithms wouldn't easily fit on certain laptop computers being used in the field. Accordingly, the software would take hours to run when users needed quick results. Unless the team could find a workaround, he argued, the project was impractical. It turned out that the algorithm developers had already created a powerful shortcut, which they had been reluctant to mention. Their shortcut was substituted, and the project went on to be highly successful.*
>
> *In a session assessing a research project in a different organization, a senior executive suggested that the project's "failure" occurred because there had been insufficient time to prepare a business case prior to an upcoming corporate review of product initiatives. During the entire 90-minute kickoff meeting, no one had even mentioned any time constraints. The project manager quickly revised the plan to take the corporate decision cycle into account.*

Pre-Mortem Analysis is so valuable that I believe it should be part of any red teaming exercise. A number of organizations already advocate its use as part of any project planning process, including the Armstrong Institute for Patient Safety and Quality at John Hopkins University.

"Even if you only have fifteen minutes to spare, you have time for a quick *Pre-Mortem Analysis*," advised Colonel Kevin Benson, when one of the Special Forces majors in my class asked about the minimum amount of time required for effective red teaming. "If you've been ordered to secure a village, gather your men together before you go in, have them take a knee, and ask them, 'If this whole thing goes to hell, how is it going to go to hell?' Just doing that can be enough to save you from a world of grief."

Being Your Own Worst Enemy*

This method harks back to the very beginning of military red teaming. *Being Your Own Worst Enemy* is, in essence, a role-playing exercise in which the red team assumes the role of a competitor or other adversary and then tries to figure out how they would react to your organization's proposed strategy or plan. It is all about getting inside your opponent's head, so if you have employees who have worked for your rival or who have other direct, firsthand knowledge of how they think and act, it would be worth making those people part of the red team for the purpose of this exercise.

In *Being Your Own Worst Enemy*, the red team leader acts as a facilitator, rather than as a participant. Once the team is in place and has been briefed on the process, begin feeding them information about your company's strategy in drips and drabs, trying to mimic how your competitor might learn about your company's plan as it plays out in the real world. If there are multiple phases to the plan, only make the team aware of the first one initially. If your strategy involves feints or misdirection, present those with a straight face and no hint of insincerity. Under no circumstances should you hand the red team a copy of the plan and ask them how your

*The U.S. Army simply calls this method *Threat Emulation* or simply *Traditional Red Teaming*.

opponent might react to it. The whole point of this exercise is to force the red team to react to the same limited information your adversary is likely to possess. Ask the team to think about how your rival would perceive this incoming information and react accordingly. What steps could your opponent take to counter your moves? What plans might the other side already have in place? How might those change when confronted with these new developments? For example, if your company is planning on introducing a new line of running shoes, your competitors might cut the price on their products or respond with a new line of their own. The important thing is to remember that your organization's actions do not take place in a vacuum; too often, planners assume that they do.

Make this exercise as immersive and realistic as possible. Both the CIA's Red Cell and Israel's *Ipcha Mistabra* have their analysts adopt the persona of their adversary when doing this sort of analysis. They might present their report in the form of a communiqué from the president of Syria to his general staff or as an entry from a terrorist leader's personal journal. To the extent possible, you should have your red team do this, too. Have team members write their reports from the point of view of the other side, using its own lingo, logos, and fonts. The deeper the red team dives into its role, the better.

The purpose of *Being Your Own Worst Enemy* is not to explore all the possible courses of action your adversary might take but rather the most likely one, based on the red team's objective analysis of its past behavior and current predilections. The red team leader or a designated scribe should keep careful notes about how the scenario unfolds and include those in the final report. That will help leadership and planners better assess the risks and opportunities.

Some companies use this approach to red team major bids before submitting them to prospective clients. To do that, give your proposal to the red team, ask them to imagine that they are that customer, and then ask them to figure out why they would reject your proposal. Encourage them to be ruthless in their rejection, but also as specific as possible. Then ask your sales team to rewrite their proposal addressing the concerns surfaced by the red team. I know of several firms that already do this when they bid on government contracts, and they have all told me that it has greatly increased their win rate.

Some companies already do this as a matter of practice. One major corporation I worked with created "strategy rooms" for each region and for each of its major competitors. These are staffed by senior strategists who do their best to *be* that country or competitor, and they paper the walls of their rooms with as much information and intelligence as they can find. During each month's board meeting, the company's directors visit one of these rooms and spend a couple of hours comparing their plans to their competitors', looking for both weaknesses and opportunities.

The insurance company I referred to in chapter 4 took *Being Your Own Worst Enemy* even further.

"Our CFO told us, 'Your job is to sink the company as fast as you can. Ready, set, go!' We actually found two ways of putting ourselves out of business—and one of our competitors has actually started pursuing one of those strategies," said the company's red team leader, who asked to remain anonymous for competitive reasons. "This has been the reason why our company has been as successful as we have been. It's also a lot of fun. The one thing our executive leadership had to get used to is that we take great relish in our job!"

SWOT Analysis

This technique is borrowed from the business world and is taught at many business schools, so you may already be familiar with it. *SWOT Analysis* is designed to identify and evaluate a plan's strengths, weaknesses, opportunities, and threats. A *SWOT Analysis* is most valuable when conducted early in the planning process. That allows the red team to share its findings with the planning staff while there is still time to factor that information in to their calculus. You can also conduct a *SWOT Analysis* of a group, a business unit, or even your entire company.

Step 1: As with *Four Ways of Seeing*, a *SWOT Analysis* begins by drawing a quad chart:

Step 2: Starting in the upper left-hand corner, list all the strengths of the strategy or group being analyzed. What does it have going for it? What augurs for its success? What makes this plan superior to other options or gives this company an advantage over its competitors?

Step 3: Move to the upper right-hand quadrant and list all the weaknesses. What worries you about this plan? What are the organization's shortcomings or blind spots? What disadvantages does the strategy or group have compared to other options or other competitors?

Step 4: Move to the bottom left-hand corner and list all the opportunities. What could be gained if the plan succeeds? What could the group exploit to its advantage? What more could be done to ensure success or future growth?

Step 5: Move to the bottom right-hand square and list all the threats to the strategy or organization. What could cause it to fail? What forces are working against it? Who is seeking to thwart it? Where could the plan fall apart? How could the company's progress be derailed? What dangers exist in the competitive environment or marketplace?

Step 6: Once the red team has finished populating the chart, study the results and share them with the organization's planning staff.

Sample SWOT Analysis *Chart*

PROPOSAL: *We should purchase Company X, our largest competitor*

Strengths	Weaknesses
Our market share will double	Our debt will increase substantially
We will become the dominant player in the market	We will end up with too many employees
We will enjoy greater economies of scale	We will have to postpone our plan to expand into new business areas
We will be able to offer more competitive pricing	

Opportunities	Threats
We could dominate the market	Our cultures could clash
We could gain important new customers	We will have to integrate two different management teams
We could increase margins	Some customers could use this as an opportunity to explore other options

If you are red teaming a situation that involves multiple actors, it may be useful to do a *SWOT Analysis* chart for each of them, assessing the situation from the perspective of each of these different groups.

While not as robust as some of the other red teaming tools, a *SWOT Analysis* can be a good place to start a red teaming exercise—particularly when the team is struggling to figure out the best way to tackle a problem. But when it's answers you need, there is no better tool than *Five Whys*.

Five Whys

This powerful problem-solving technique was actually developed by Toyota and is often used as part of the Six Sigma process. But the way *Five Whys* is used in red teaming is a little bit different from what you might be familiar with. Instead of using this technique to resolve quality or production issues, red teams use *Five Whys* to get at the root cause of strategic problems.

Toyota founder Sakichi Toyoda first suggested this deceptively simple approach, which was later codified in the 1950s by legendary quality guru Taiichi Ohno, who had made *Five Whys* part of the vaunted Toyota Production System. The technique should be familiar to anyone with small children: When confronted with a problem or question, ask "Why?" five times to discover its real cause. Ohno often explained *Five Whys* with the following example:

1. "Why did the robot stop?"

   The circuit has overloaded, causing a fuse to blow.

2. "Why is the circuit overloaded?"

   There was insufficient lubrication on the bearings, so they locked up.

3. "Why was there insufficient lubrication on the bearings?"

The oil pump on the robot is not circulating sufficient oil.

4. "Why is the pump not circulating sufficient oil?"

The pump intake is clogged with metal shavings.

5. "Why is the intake clogged with metal shavings?"

Because there is no filter on the pump.

Source: *Toyota Motor Corporation.*

Ohno used to say, "The root cause of any problem is the key to a lasting solution." In his example, simply oiling the robot might get it back up and running, but it would not solve the problem. Cleaning the pump intake would help in the short term, but once it became clogged again, the problem would return. The real solution is revealed by the fifth why: Add an oil filter to the pump to prevent it from clogging in the future.

Many companies besides Toyota use the *Five Whys* technique, including Amazon. CEO Jeff Bezos is reportedly a big fan. Former Amazon employee Pete Abilla witnessed that firsthand in 2004 when, during a visit to one of the company's sprawling distribution centers, Bezos learned that an employee had seriously injured his finger.

When Jeff learned of this during a meeting, he was very disturbed and got very emotional—angry at first, then felt very bad for this associate and his family. Then, he did something remarkable. He got up, walked to the whiteboard, and began to ask the Five Whys *(I quote the below from memory):*

Why did the associate damage his thumb?

Because his thumb got caught in the conveyor.

Why did his thumb get caught in the conveyor?

Because he was chasing his bag, which was on a running conveyor belt.

Why did he chase his bag?

Because he placed his bag on the conveyor, but it then turned on by surprise.

Why was his bag on the conveyor?

Because he used the conveyor as a table.

So, the likely root cause of the associate's damaged thumb is that he simply needed a table, there wasn't one around, so he used a conveyor as a table. To eliminate further safety incidences, we need to provide tables at the appropriate stations or provide portable, light tables for the associates to use.

These examples show how effective *Five Whys* can be in addressing problems on the factory floor. The same approach can also be used to tackle the tough strategy questions that are often assigned to red teams. The results can be surprising.

One of the companies I work with was trying to figure out why it kept missing its sales targets for Fortune 500 companies. Increasing its business with these large corporations was a key element of the company's growth strategy, but it kept falling short of its mark, even though it was having no problem hitting its sales goals for small and midsize businesses. Before I came in, the concern was that there was something about the company's core products that big corporations found unappealing, and executives were struggling to figure out what that might be. However, by using *Five Whys*, we discovered that the root of the problem lay elsewhere.

Our analysis unfolded like this:

WHY 1: *Why can't our salespeople sell to Fortune 500 companies?*

Because they aren't sophisticated enough to sell to these large companies.

WHY 2: *Why aren't they sophisticated enough to sell to these large companies?*

Because they don't have the proper training.

WHY 3: *Why don't they have the proper training?*

Because our franchisees aren't willing to pay for it.

WHY 4: *Why aren't our franchisees willing to pay for it?*

Because they are undercapitalized.

WHY 5: *Why are they undercapitalized?*

Because our franchise agreements don't allow them to retain enough of their revenue.

You can see that what began as a question about sales ended up exposing a serious problem with the company's franchise model. As a result of this revelation, my client modified its franchise agreements to allow its franchisees to retain more of their income, provided they invested that money in employee training. That ended up being a win for the franchisees and a win for the company.

Five Whys and the other imaginative techniques described in this chapter can provide powerful insights into not only the true nature of your business problems, but also the future of your business itself. These tools can help you better understand your customers, competitors, and other important stakeholders. And they can help you avoid the sort of mistakes that cost Blockbuster so dearly.

However, if you want to really stress-test your strategies and push your plans to the limit, then you need to be willing to rip them to shreds. You can do that by using the contrarian techniques I will describe in the next chapter.

CHAPTER 8

Challenging Everything: Contrarian Techniques

Conflict is the gadfly of thought. It stirs us to observation and memory. It instigates to invention. It shocks us out of sheep-like passivity, and sets us at noting and contriving.

—John Dewey

By the spring of 2007, the U.S. housing market was in trouble. A worrying number of Americans were defaulting on their mortgages. Most of these were subprime loans that would never have been approved a decade earlier. But the housing market was hot, and home prices kept going up, so lending requirements kept going down. And when the bubble finally burst, the financial services companies that had backed these questionable loans were left holding the bag.

Until March of that year, Lehman Brothers had been the darling of Wall Street. *Fortune* magazine had named Lehman the most admired company in the securities industry—ranking it higher than Goldman Sachs, Morgan Stanley, and Merrill Lynch. In February, the company's stock had hit a record high of $86.18 a share, giving Lehman a market capitalization of almost $60 billion. But on March 13, a day before the firm was scheduled to announce its first-quarter earnings, shareholders began to panic, and Lehman's stock posted its biggest one-day decline in five years. It was a sign of things to come, but it went unheeded. The next day, after reporting better-than-expected results, Lehman's chief financial officer, Chris O'Meara, told analysts that concerns about his company's exposure to the increasingly shaky subprime mortgage market were overblown. Lehman was monitoring the situation carefully, he promised, adding that the risks posed by those rising delinquencies were "well contained."

"The subprime business itself is not going to create a big event in the economy," O'Meara declared confidently on a conference call with Wall Street's best and brightest. "The credit quality elsewhere is very strong."

Not only that, but Lehman actually saw real upside potential in the growing number of subprime defaults.

"We expect to see various opportunities from the market dislocation," O'Meara said tantalizingly.

By the time the call was over, Lehman's shares were on the rebound. UBS analyst Glenn Schorr spoke for most of his peers when he expressed relief at O'Meara's reassuring analysis: "We all breathe a little easier."

And so Lehman's march toward the precipice continued, with the rest of the global economy following close behind.

With the help of a red team, it could have turned out so much differently for Lehman. Other companies with even less access to the real numbers were able to discern the risk while there was still time to react. One of them was Ford, whose chief economist conducted her own analysis a month before O'Meara shrugged off investor worries and concluded that the growing problems in the subprime mortgage sector had the "potential . . . to generate systemic risk" to the entire economy. As a result, Ford took steps to shore up its balance sheet and became the only American automaker to weather the coming storm—at least without going bankrupt and being bailed out by the American taxpayers. But

Lehman's leaders seemed unwilling to even consider such possibilities. A red teaming technique called *What-If Analysis* would have helped them to do that.

What-If Analysis*

As its name implies, this method is designed to explore the consequences of an event that may have a low probability of occurring, but that would have a major impact if it did occur. Nobody besides a hard-core pessimist likes to contemplate events that would wreak havoc with their best-laid plans, so most planners are quick to point out how unlikely those events are and change the subject. But what if they are wrong, as O'Meara was about Lehman's subprime mortgage business? *What-If Analysis* is designed to cut through those objections and force the organization to take an unflinching look at what would happen if such game-changing events actually occurred. Unlike *Pre-Mortem Analysis*, which is concerned with *how* disaster might strike, *What-If Analysis* is all about determining the *consequences* of a calamity. Armed with that knowledge, a company can—and should—create contingencies to deal with these possibilities or, better yet, modify its plan to lessen the likelihood of them happening in the first place. You can also use this technique to look at potential positive developments that, though unlikely, would be a boon for your company if they did occur. That way, you will be better positioned to take advantage of those opportunities.

What-If Analysis works like this:

Step 1: Start by having the red team imagine an event that would have a major impact on the plan or strategy under review. It is important to

---

*What I refer to as *What-If Analysis* is actually a combination of three different techniques taught by the U.S. Army: *What-If Analysis*, *High-Impact Low-Probability Analysis*, and *Signposts of Change*.

describe this event in as much detail as possible. For example, if you were an investment bank that had bet big on subprime mortgages, you might describe a scenario in which the collapse of the U.S. housing market leads to the failure of several major financial institutions, triggering a meltdown of the entire global economy.

Step 2: Think about all the different ways this event could impact your organization, your competitors, key stakeholders, and the business environment as a whole. Make a comprehensive list for each of these areas.

Step 3: Figure out one or more plausible ways that this event could occur. Describe each of these scenarios in as much detail as possible as well, taking care to identify significant turning points or other observables that would signal a change in this direction. Map these different pathways out on a whiteboard or butcher paper, showing how one development leads to another, and how each of these events could impact your organization.

Step 4: Think about potential triggers that might push events in one direction or change their momentum. What could lead to a sudden change in direction? What could cause progress toward a particular end state to accelerate or decelerate rapidly? Note these on your map.

Step 5: When you are finished, study your map and identify all the signposts of change. Make a list of these so that you can watch for them as the situation actually unfolds.

Step 6: Develop a list of factors that would encourage a positive outcome or, at least, deflect a negative outcome. As you do, note any actions the organization could take to influence events in these directions.

A *What-If Analysis* can be particularly valuable in situations in which your organization's decisions are based on limited information or unprovable assumptions. For example, if your main competitor brought in a new CEO who promptly sacked the entire senior leadership team and announced a major restructuring, that would almost certainly have major implications for your company, but it would not be immediately clear what those might be. A *What-If Analysis* could help you figure that out. Similarly, you might have received reports that your competitor is about to launch a major new product line but are not sure exactly what it will be or when it will hit the market. Again, a *What-If Analysis* can help your company prepare for that. It is designed to keep you from being blindsided by events and allow your organization to develop effective hedges against an uncertain future. And in today's rapidly changing world, the future is usually uncertain and the way forward is often unclear.

Us vs. Them Analysis*

One way to help find the best way forward for your company is by using a technique I call *Us vs. Them Analysis*. This approach is designed to help an organization evaluate two different, competing courses of action. It has been used by the U.S. military since at least the early 1960s, and has proven to be an effective tool for deciding between two alternatives. *Us vs. Them Analysis* requires a significant commitment of time and personnel, so it is best reserved for contentious decisions that will have a major impact on the direction of your company. That said, it can be particularly helpful in settling long-standing disagreements within your organization. For example, if part of your senior leadership wants to aggressively expand into South America and another faction feels the money needed to do that could be better spent modernizing your North American factories, you could use *Us vs. Them Analysis* to fully explore both of these proposals and determine which one is most likely to help your company achieve its long-term goals.

*This technique is sometimes referred to as *Blue Team/Red Team Analysis*.

Though time-consuming, an *Us vs. Them Analysis* is a simple, straight-forward process. Assign each of the two competing proposals to a different group and then have each team make the best, most compelling case possible for their idea. If you have more than two competing proposals, you can create additional teams to represent each of them—provided you have enough people. Give each of the teams a fixed amount of time to conduct their research and encourage them to bolster their case with as much objective evidence from as many different sources as possible. Once the deadline arrives, have each team present its proposal to your senior leadership team, which should act as a jury and decide between them, based on which team presented the most compelling argument supported by the best evidence.

If your red team has enough members, it can conduct an *Us vs. Them Analysis* itself. Simply divide the team up into two or more groups. However, you can also include the organization's regular planning staff in this process. If you do, make sure each of the groups includes members of both the red team and the regular staff. If there are people in your company who have well-established positions in favor of one of the alternatives, assign them to the team responsible for representing the *opposing* view. Doing so will not only force them to think critically about their own position, but also ensure that the group red teams itself.

While the outcome of an *Us vs. Them Analysis* is unlikely to please everyone, it should at least make those who support the losing side feel like their point of view was given full consideration. If your organization is grappling with a really contentious and divisive issue, that alone can make it worth doing.

Devil's Advocacy

Even when everyone in your company agrees that there is only one clear course of action, it still makes sense to question that plan. And there is no better way to do that than through *Devil's Advocacy*. It is probably the oldest weapon in the red teaming arsenal, and certainly one of the most powerful.

Devil's Advocacy dates back to the Renaissance when the Roman Catholic Church began to worry that the process of saint-making had gotten a little, well, loosey-goosey. In the early 1500s, in keeping with the increasingly rigorous standards of the day, Pope Leo X decided the time had come for the Church to take a more skeptical approach to canonization. He called for the creation of a new office, that of the *promotor fidei*, or "promoter of the faith,"* which would be tasked with challenging all nominations for sainthood in order "to prevent any rash decisions concerning miracles or virtues of the candidates for the honours of the altar." The head of this office soon became one of the most powerful officials in the Sacred Congregation of Rites. He also received a new, less formal title: *advocatus diaboli,* or "devil's advocate." His job was to act as a sort of spiritual prosecutor:

> *All documents of beatification and canonization processes must be submitted to his examination, and the difficulties and doubts he raises over the virtues and miracles are laid before the congregation and must be satisfactorily answered before any further steps can be taken in the processes. It is his duty to suggest natural explanations for alleged miracles, and even to bring forward human and selfish motives for deeds that have been accounted heroic virtues.*

Once the devil's advocate got to work, the number of new saints being created dropped dramatically, as rational explanations were found for supposed miracles and purported good deeds turned out to be nothing more than blatant self-promotion.**

---

*Though Leo X was the first to call for the formation of this office, it was not formally established until 1587 by Pope Sixtus V.

**Pope John Paul II effectively defanged the devil's advocate in 1983 as part of an effort to streamline the canonization process, and the number of new saints skyrocketed once again.

As I described in chapter 1, the Israelis adapted *Devil's Advocacy* to their needs after the 1973 Yom Kippur War and used it to take a similarly skeptical view of military intelligence. So did the U.S. Central Intelligence Agency and, later, the U.S. Army.

In red teaming, *Devil's Advocacy* works much the same way it did in the Catholic Church. However, instead of arguing that a candidate for sainthood is actually a sinner, the red team's job is to take a belief or assertion that is central to the organization's strategy and make the most compelling case possible that the opposite is true. If your company believes sales of its new running shoes are weak because people are running less, the red team should try to prove that running remains as popular as ever. If your company is putting together a plan to purchase XYZ Corporation, the red team should try to show why purchasing XYZ Corporation would be an unmitigated disaster. If your company believes the collapse of the subprime mortgage market is no cause for alarm, the red team should try to show just how dangerous that could prove. The red team does not have to be right—and just like a high school debate team, it does not have to believe in the position it is taking. The conclusion your organization has already reached may, in fact, be correct. But by conducting a rigorous *Devil's Advocacy* analysis, you will find out if that is really the case. If there are flaws in the prevailing thinking, *Devil's Advocacy* will reveal them. It is one of the most effective ways to expose faulty reasoning, uncover important information that was overlooked or misinterpreted, and find any gaps that exist in the initial analysis.

Devil's Advocacy is a simple process that can take as much time as necessary or as little as you can spare. Start by having the red team review all the information the organization's regular staff used to reach its conclusion or develop its working hypothesis. Then try to use this same data to build an argument that contradicts the original explanation. The red team should also conduct its own research and try to discover new evidence that supports its contrarian argument. Remember, the task of the red team is not necessarily to find the *right* answer but simply to prove that the current solution is *wrong*. Once the red team has completed its analysis, it should present its findings to senior leadership, taking special care to highlight evidence that was discounted or disregarded by the original planners, as well as any weak assumptions upon which the original analysis relied.

U.S. Army National Guard Colonel Jeanne Arnold was well trained in *Devil's Advocacy* and ready to apply it when she deployed to Afghanistan in 2008 to lead the red team for the 82nd Airborne Division. But the 82nd Airborne was not quite ready for her. She had two strikes against her: She was a woman and, though she had wings on her chest, they were the wrong kind. Hers were pilot's wings—she had originally joined the army to fly helicopters—not the jump wings that were a badge of honor for the paratroopers of this fabled division. Now, as she watched the 82nd Airborne's chief of staff frowning as he studied her orders, Arnold realized that being assigned to fill the newly created post of resident red team leader was strike three.

"What exactly do you *do*?" he asked her.

Arnold did her best to explain what a red team was and how it could help, but it was clear the chief of staff just did not get it. He thought Arnold was a glorified anthropologist and started telling her about the new strategy General David Petraeus was proposing to enlist the Afghan tribes in America's war on terror. In Iraq, the general had persuaded rural Sunni militias to join the fight against al-Qaeda by circumventing the Shi'ite-dominated central government in Baghdad and working directly with local tribal leaders. Now Petraeus was running both wars and hoped a similar approach could be successful in Afghanistan.

"General Petraeus wants us to try the same tribal strategy here that's working in Iraq," the airborne officer told Arnold. "Why don't you tell us something about the tribes we don't already know."

So that is exactly what Arnold and her team did—and they did it by conducting a *Devil's Advocacy* analysis of Petraeus's tribal strategy. That analysis showed why it was unlikely to work in Afghanistan. Arnold's red team studied the Afghan tribes and quickly realized their egalitarian structure was very different from the hierarchical social organization of Arab tribes, such as those Petraeus had worked with in Iraq. There, American forces were able to win over tribal leaders by funding projects in their communities. In return, these sheikhs ordered their militias to support the Coalition's effort to drive al-Qaeda from their territory. But Afghan tribal leaders did not have that kind of authority. This and other important differences meant Petraeus's tribal strategy was doomed to fail in Afghanistan.

Though Arnold's commanders initially bristled at her findings, the failure of early efforts to buy Afghan tribal leaders demonstrated that the concerns raised by the red team were well founded. Arnold's analysis made its way to General Petraeus, who was already a fan of red teaming. He abandoned the tribal strategy, and when he turned the Afghan war over to General John Allen three years later, Petraeus advised his successor to have a red team analyze *his* new plan before making it public. General Allen offered the same advice to General Joseph Dunford when he took over command of the international forces in Afghanistan in 2013.

Some of the most innovative—and disruptive—companies are those that constantly question everything they do. Amazon has this sort of contrarian thinking built into its DNA. From the beginning, Jeff Bezos has challenged his executives to challenge him, as well as pretty much everything the company does or plans to do. There is just one important caveat for Amazon executives: Make sure you have the data to back it up.

Some of the most critical thinking comes from Amazon's secret in-house benchmarking team, which is tasked with studying the company's different business units and comparing their performance to internal and external competitors. These are sensitive reports that often include sharp criticisms and difficult recommendations, so the benchmarking team goes to great pains to ensure they have considered every possible objection before submitting them to senior management.

"We have someone who takes the role of the devil's advocate," one of the team's leaders told me. "They're there to ask all the really hard questions. Their job is to basically poke holes in the work we've done."

The benchmarking team members welcome this criticism because it allows them to prepare for the questions they know will start flying furiously when the final report is presented to the business unit leader and other senior executives.

"We kind of beat it up internally first. If there are gaps in our data, the devil's advocate will ask, 'Why weren't you able to get this?' They try to anticipate all the questions the business leader might ask. They've been through enough of these reviews to know," the Amazon executive explained. "It's really helpful. Sometimes we have our own blind spots as far as what the business is doing or some of the realities of that business. Having a devil's advocate review the report first helps us make sure we've done everything we can on our end to get all the data we need to support our recommendations, as well as make sure we're not missing anything and have really gotten to the core of the problem."

Many great business leaders have an innate ability to assume this contrarian role. Professors Jeffrey Dyer, Hal Gregersen, and Clayton Christensen discovered this during their six-year study to uncover the origins of disruptive business strategies.

"Innovative entrepreneurs like to play the devil's advocate," they wrote when sharing their findings in a 2009 *Harvard Business Review* piece, offering several examples to support that conclusion:

> *Innovators constantly ask questions that challenge common wisdom or, as Tata Group chairman Ratan Tata puts it, "question the unquestionable." Meg Whitman, former CEO of eBay, has worked directly with a number of innovative entrepreneurs, including the founders of eBay, PayPal, and Skype. "They get a kick out of screwing up the status quo," she told us. "They can't bear it. So they spend a tremendous amount of time thinking about how to change the world. And as they brainstorm, they like to ask: 'If we did this, what would happen?'"*
>
> *Most of the innovative entrepreneurs we interviewed could*

remember the specific questions they were asking at the time they had the inspiration for a new venture. Michael Dell, for instance, told us that his idea for founding Dell Computer sprang from his asking why a computer cost five times as much as the sum of its parts. "I would take computers apart . . . and would observe that $600 worth of parts were sold for $3,000." In chewing over the question, he hit on his revolutionary business model. . . .

"My learning process has always been about disagreeing with what I'm being told and taking the opposite position, and pushing others to really justify themselves," [eBay founder] Pierre Omidyar told us. "I remember it was very frustrating for the other kids when I would do this." Asking oneself, or others, to imagine a completely different alternative can lead to truly original insights.

Innovators are not the only ones who rely on contrarian thinking. The folks who fund them often do as well. When I described *Devil's Advocacy* and *What-If Analysis* to my friend Norbert Gottenberg, a former recruiting partner at Kleiner Perkins Caufield & Byers, he said these techniques sounded a lot like the methodology the legendary Silicon Valley venture capital firm used to vet prospective investments.

"We used to really grill entrepreneurs. We would bombard them with questions: What are the risks? What does commercial success look like? What are you really going to need in terms of continued funding? What other technologies are out there that could compete with yours? Who's going to eat your lunch?" Gottenberg explained. "The partners would look at all their assumptions and try to poke holes in them. The vetting system is designed to identify all the competitive threats and all the impediments to success. The partners would say, 'This is how it could all blow up.' They'd try to shoot down that entrepreneur—because they couldn't invest in the next big thing if they had already spent their money on a company that was not quite it."

The whole process could take hours—sometimes days. Entrepreneurs who could withstand this scrutiny and successfully address all of the partners' concerns often walked away with checks for tens of millions of dollars. They include Google, Uber, Twitter, and Amazon. Those who withered under the Kleiner Perkins spotlight got a handshake and directions to the next venture capital firm on Sand Hill Road.

Scott Weber and his colleagues at Vaughan Nelson also use *Devil's Advocacy* to evaluate their investment strategies.

"Instead of asking ourselves how we can make money off this investment—which is what most firms do—we ask ourselves how we could *lose* money," he told me. "You get pregnant with the deal, and it's hard to overcome that bias. *Devil's Advocacy* helps us do that."

Imagine if Lehman Brothers had applied this sort of contrarian analysis to its subprime mortgage strategy back in 2007. Imagine what it could do for your business today.

CHAPTER 9

Putting It All Together

*Nobody can really guarantee the future. The best
we can do is size up the chances, calculate the risks
involved, estimate our ability to deal with them
and then make our plans with confidence.*

—Henry Ford II

There is no "right way" to red team. The techniques employed by
a red team and the order in which they are used will depend on
the nature of the problem, the time available, where the organization
is at in its planning process, and the resources it is able to devote to red
teaming.

If you are analyzing a potential merger, then an *Analysis of Competing Hypotheses* is not going to add much value. If your company must
make a decision on a proposed deal by 5:00 p.m., then there is no point
starting a *String of Pearls Analysis*, which takes time to do right. If you
are still trying to figure out why you keep missing your sales targets in
Europe, then there is nothing for the devils on your red team to advocate against. And if your red team has only three members and cannot

enlist other staff, then an *Us vs. Them Analysis*, which requires more people, is probably off the table.

That is why I say red teaming is as much an art as it is a science.

A big part of the art lies in knowing which tools to use, and when to use them. Think of the red teaming tool kit as a golf bag. In it, there is a driver, woods, irons, wedges, and a putter. Every golfer carries most of these clubs, and most golfers carry all of them. Success on the links comes from knowing how to use these clubs correctly. But that is only part of the formula. A good golfer must also know when and where to use them. On a short par 3, a skilled golfer might use only two clubs—a seven iron and a putter. On a long par 5, he or she might use a driver, fairway wood, an iron, a wedge, and a putter.

The art of red teaming also depends on knowing when to stop.

As I stated earlier, red teaming must never be allowed to get in the way of action when action is required. But just because a decision is not required immediately does not mean a red team should be allowed to continue poking and prodding a problem ad infinitum. Red teamers must guard against that temptation—red teaming just enough, and no more. But how do you know when you have red teamed just enough? Usually, there will be an external time restraint. A decision will have to be made. A trigger will have to be pulled. In the absence of such hard stops, the red team should set a deadline for itself. Having a deadline focuses the mind and keeps the analysis—and the analysts—from getting lost in the proverbial weeds.

"Red teaming is best done iteratively," says the British Ministry of Defence in its *Red Teaming Guide*. "It should be conducted throughout the project, with red team products being available in time to inform key decisions. The tasks given to red teams are likely to cover complex problems. It is also important that the red team focuses on the key issues. Red teams should contribute quality thinking rather than quantity."

So what does an actual red teaming exercise look like? Let's consider some real business problems and think about how a red team might have helped solve them.

The Cheeseburger Nobody Wanted

In the 1990s, American consumers were becoming increasingly health conscious and more sophisticated when it came to their tastes in food. That was bad news for McDonald's, which had for decades dominated the fast-food scene with its menu of high-calorie, high-fat, and highly sweetened products. Sugar-addicted children still loved their Happy Meals, but sales at existing locations were slumping as grown-ups looked elsewhere for a quick bite. So, in 1996, McDonald's announced what the company called its "biggest new-product introduction since the Big Mac"—the Arch Deluxe.

As the company's white-coated "head chef" described in one of the original television ads, the Arch Deluxe was supposed to be "a symphony of tastes," featuring a stone-ground mustard sauce, peppered bacon, and a potato roll. "The burger with the grown-up taste," as McDonald's called it, was supposed to appeal to adults. To prove it, the company aired other ads showing kids grimacing and turning up their noses at the new sandwich.

"We have identified a market portion that we're not doing a good job in," one franchisee told the *Wall Street Journal*. "Strategically, I think we're headed in the right direction."

McDonald's was actually headed for one of the biggest product disasters in fast-food history. Not only did the Arch Deluxe fail to attract the more sophisticated, grown-up consumers the company was angling for, but it also cost McDonald's a whopping $300 million in wasted development and marketing costs. As the Arch Deluxe was quietly removed from the menu, McDonald's same-store sales continued to sag, along with the corporation's shares. A headline in the *Journal* on September 4 of the same year said it all: "New McDonald's Burger Cools Stock as It Fizzles on the Menu."

"The trouble was that nobody goes to McDonald's for sophistication, they go for convenience. Part of this convenience is knowing exactly

217

what to expect," explains marketing expert Matt Haig in his book *Brand Failures*. "Most people who walk into a McDonald's restaurant know what they are going to order before they reach the counter. They don't want to be bombarded with a million and one variations on what is essentially the same product—a hamburger."

So, how could red teaming have helped McDonald's avoid this super-size brand blunder?

If you were leading a McDonald's red team when the Arch Deluxe was first conceived back in 1995 and were asked to analyze this new product strategy, you might have started with a *Four Ways of Seeing* analysis to get a better understanding of how different consumer cohorts viewed the company and its products. That might have revealed the breadth of the chasm McDonald's would have to bridge to connect with the consumers it was targeting. A *Key Assumptions Check* would have underscored just how much the Arch Deluxe's success depended on the company's ability to close that gap. McDonald's spent a good deal of time and energy testing its new hamburger with likely consumers, and claimed half of them said they would order another one. That does not sound like a ringing endorsement. But even if it was good enough, the company failed to subject its whole "up-market" strategy to similar testing. *Devil's Advocacy* could have exposed just how misguided that plan was, and a *Pre-Mortem Analysis* could have revealed the consequences its failure would have for McDonald's brand image and share price. By bringing all these techniques to bear on the problem, McDonald's might have saved itself a few hundred million dollars—money it could have spent on developing new fast-food offerings that appealed to its existing customer base and gave those people more reasons to visit the Golden Arches more often. America might have been a little fatter for it, but so would McDonald's balance sheet.

Face Palm

Remember Palm? That was the company that, in the late 1990s, introduced the first genuinely useful personal digital assistant, or PDA. It may be a stretch to call the PalmPilot the iPhone of its day, but for tech-savvy business folks, it came close. Soon legions of executives were keeping track of their calendars and contacts on a small, electronic computer they could carry in their pockets. The top-of-the-line models could even do e-mail. But then came the BlackBerry, followed by the iPhone, and by 2010 Palm was a company that had been left behind in a market it helped create. So it came as a bit of a surprise when Hewlett-Packard announced in April of that year that it was buying Palm for $1.2 billion.

That seemed like a lot of money to pay for a company that had seen its already meager share of the global smartphone market drop to just 1.5 percent the year before. If that was not bad enough, Palm had just issued a profit warning and was burning through more than $200 million in cash a quarter. But HP had money to burn—and a burning desire to muscle its way into the mobile computing and smartphone markets.

Hewlett-Packard CEO Mark Hurd wanted to use Palm's proprietary operating system, webOS, to transform HP's bread-and-butter printers into Internet devices, though no one was exactly sure why. He also wanted a device that could compete head-to-head with Apple's new iPad, which Palm dutifully delivered less than a year later. The fact that journalists were not allowed to actually touch the HP TouchPad when it was unveiled in February 2011 was cause for some concern, but it looked good enough from a distance to persuade some that HP's acquisition actually made sense—at least until the product went on sale that summer. The TouchPad was heavy, slow, and felt unfinished. It proved such an unmitigated disaster that HP killed the tablet just forty-nine days later. HP also canceled the other Palm-designed products it had been planning to introduce and announced that webOS would be open sourced. In February 2012, HP sold off what was left of Palm to LG Electronics for an undisclosed sum—a deal so small that both companies assured investors it would have no material impact on their financials.

If HP had asked a red team to review the Palm deal before signing on the dotted line, it might have begun with a *Key Assumptions Check*, followed by a *Probability Analysis* to gauge how risky the acquisition might be for the company. The red team could then have taken the riskiest assumptions and used *Pre-Mortem Analysis* to look at how these might fail to pan out and *What-If Analysis* to look at what that failure would mean for HP. A *SWOT Analysis* would have also been useful. If that assessment was done honestly, it would have revealed just how far Palm had fallen behind in the mobile computing business HP was so eager to enter. Finally, the red team could have conducted a *Devil's Advocacy* exercise arguing against the proposed acquisition. That might have given HP's board pause, even if it failed to dissuade Hurd, who resigned a month after the Palm acquisition was completed.

Any Taxi Company in the World

The ride-hailing service Uber went live in San Francisco in the summer of 2010. A year later, it expanded to New York. It was in Paris six months after that, and taxi companies all over the world were in trouble. Five years before, it had not mattered how dirty their taxis were or how disheveled their drivers looked. Suddenly, in city after city, it did. And for many of them, it was too late to do anything about it.

If you owned a small taxi company in a city that Uber had not yet reached, those developments might have given you real anxiety. But if you were clever, they might also have spurred you to reevaluate your business and your plans for its future. While you probably could not have afforded an actual red team, you could have gathered your senior staff together and red teamed the problem yourselves.

If you did, you might start by using *Four Ways of Seeing* to take an unflinching look at how your customers view you and how they are likely to view Uber. This might reveal some real opportunities to improve your service while you still could. Then you might conduct a *Pre-Mortem Analysis* to figure out exactly how Uber could put you out of business, paying special attention to the key areas where your company might be able to steer events in a different direction. Then you could use the information you gleaned from these exercises to develop a plan for coping with this new threat. Once that was finished, you could conduct a *Key Assumptions Check* to make sure that plan was realistic and fine-tune it as necessary.

There is no guarantee that red teaming would save your taxi company, but at least it would give you a fighting chance. And if your red teaming analysis revealed you did not even have that, then it would give you time to come up with Plan B.

Formal Red Teaming Models

Several of the military organizations that have embraced red teaming have developed manuals to use as field guides for red team leaders and members. Because militaries, as a rule, like to do things "by the book," these manuals include step-by-step directions on how to red team a strategy or plan. There are a couple of problems with these paint-by-numbers approaches to red teaming. First, because they are designed for military strategies and plans, the steps they call for are far more exhaustive than most business problems merit and require more time than most businesses can spare. The second problem is that the best military red teams do not rigorously adhere to these procedures. In fact, Colonel Steve Rotkoff says even the tools themselves should be modified as needed.

"You're creating an environment that encourages divergent thought, and that gets people thinking about the process itself—which is good and desirable," he explains.

Still, some people like to have a road map. For those who do, there is no better one than the structured approach developed by the British Ministry of Defence. I include it here as a point of reference. However, even the British caution that it should be used only as a rough guide:

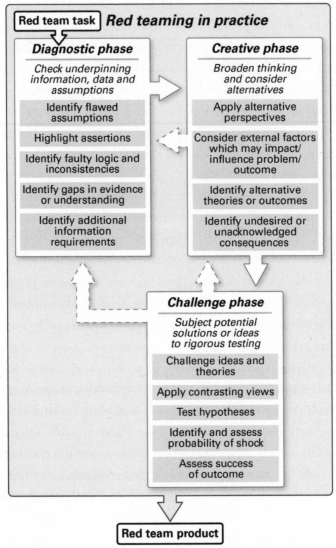

Used with permission from the British Ministry of Defence

Producing a Useful Product

As you can see, the British red teaming road map ends with a finished product. This is important, because if the red team fails to report its findings in a way the rest of the organization can use, then it is of little value. Just what that product looks like will depend on the needs of your organization and the nature of the problem that has been assigned to your red team, but there are some important considerations a red team should always keep in mind:

Be realistic. A red team's results need to take into account the realities and limitations of the organization it serves. You should never assume an unlimited budget or ignore other resource constraints. Nor should you fail to make good recommendations simply because they are too costly to implement today. If there are elements of the strategy or plan under review that are "off-limits," the red team should be informed of this ahead of time, and it should respect these conditions. Just remember that such restrictions limit the red team's ability to conduct a thorough analysis.

Provide a concrete action plan. If the red team recommends specific changes to the organization's plan, it should provide a phased implementation strategy that allows the organization to begin moving in the right direction *right now*. This should be as specific as possible, and it should always include a time element. Otherwise, it will be too easy to ignore. Recommending that your company "add more quality inspectors" is a lot less effective than recommending that it "double the number of quality inspectors on Lines 3 and 4 by the end of the third quarter."

Make it measurable. The red team's recommendations should include specific metrics your organization's leadership can monitor to measure its progress toward the objectives identified by the red team. This is one of the most important lessons I learned from legendary CEO Alan Mulally. "You can't manage what you can't measure," he would often tell me, paraphrasing Peter Drucker. "The data sets you free!" Technology can help. Today many aspects of a company's operations are tracked and monitored in real time. This data can not only provide important inputs for your red teaming analysis, but can also help your company ensure the red team's recommendations are being carried out. However, it is important to choose the *right* metrics. Too often, we simply measure those things that are easy to measure. That can do more harm than good. For example, if you measure the number of vehicles pulled off an assembly line for quality issues and set a goal of reducing that number, your factory workers may simply let vehicles pass that should be pulled and fixed. A better metric would be the number of vehicles returned to dealers in the first ninety days for warranty claims.

Flag signposts of change. The red team's report should include a list of things the organization should be on the lookout for as it executes its plan or implements its strategy. These are developments that suggest either things are unfolding as planned, or that they are headed in an unintended or undesirable direction. Either way, these indicators are important and should be featured prominently in your report. For example, if you conducted a *Pre-Mortem Analysis* and found one way your company's plan to introduce a new line of running shoes might fail was through the inability of your suppliers to keep up with the increased demand for rubber, then you should call that out in your report as something to watch out for as production ramps up.

Offer solutions. The red team should suggest ways of offsetting negative developments or mitigating potential failures. For example, your red team should not just note how much the success of the plan depends on the ability of your rubber suppliers to keep up with the increased demand; the team should also suggest your company identify one or more additional suppliers it could call upon if the primary vendor runs short, and make sure agreements are inked with those companies before production begins.

Identify constraints and limitations. If there were elements of the strategy that were declared off-limits, the red team should make this clear in its report, as well as noting any additional restrictions or limitations that were imposed on its analysis. If requested data or other evidence was not provided, that should be noted as well. And if the red team did not have the time or resources necessary to fully evaluate parts of the plan, make that clear in the final report, so the limitations of your analysis are visible to the powers that be.

Describe the methodology. Your report should include a list of all the tools and techniques used by the red team in its analysis, as well as an explanation of why these particular approaches were employed. Provide a brief summary of the key findings each of these methods yielded, and explain how these factored into your final analysis. Doing so will not only make your arguments stronger and your conclusions more compelling, but also help your organization's planning staff understand how they can improve their work in the future.

Include sources and supporting evidence. Attach any supporting data, relevant reports, or other evidence the red team used to reach its conclusions with your final report. Also include a list of any outside sources or subject matter experts who were consulted as part of the red teaming process. Again, this will lend credence to your findings and allow decision makers to better evaluate your conclusions.

Communicate effectively. Most important of all, the red team needs to communicate its findings in a clear, constructive, and collegial manner.

Communication Is Key

The best red teaming analysis in the world is worthless if nobody pays attention to it. For red teams to be effective, they need to be heard. And for red teams to be heard, they need to share their findings in a way that allows the organization's senior leadership to listen to what the red team has to say. That is why effective communication is an essential part of effective red teaming. And effective communication starts not with speaking, but with listening.

Your red team needs to listen to your organization's leadership and understand what its expectations are for each red teaming analysis. If your company has already decided on a course of action, but wants to know how it could fail, then do not waste time trying to develop alternative courses of action. Simply conduct a *Pre-Mortem Analysis*, or use *Devil's Advocacy*, to expose the weaknesses in that plan. If those weaknesses are significant, you might want to suggest that other options be considered, but do not take it upon yourself to do so without being asked. Similarly, if senior leadership declares parts of the strategy you are analyzing are off-limits, then critiquing those elements is only going to damage your reputation and make it that much harder for those executives to embrace red teaming.

Effective communication also means presenting your findings in a constructive manner.

Remember, just because a plan has flaws does not necessarily mean it is a bad plan. If your red team takes great glee in ripping a plan to shreds without offering viable suggestions to address its weaknesses and shortcomings, it will succeed only in making the planning staff defensive. For example, instead of smugly pointing out that your company's plan to introduce a new running shoe line fails to account for the fact that its current rubber supplier is already having trouble keeping up with existing demand, suggest that additional sources for rubber be found before moving forward.

This is not to suggest the red team should not be critical or contrarian. That is its job, after all. But a red team does that job most effectively when it is done in a collegial manner.

One way to maintain good relations between the red team and the rest of your organization is to be thoughtful about the ways in which the red team's findings are presented and shared. Because part of a red team's job is to critique plans and strategies, the red team should, as a rule, not report its findings in regular staff meetings or other open forums. Doing so could provoke a defensive response from the staff that developed the original plan or strategy, and the briefing is likely to devolve into a debate. Your organization's regular staff should absolutely be encouraged to respond to the red team's findings, but only after the red team presents those findings directly to your senior leadership. Because the red team must also offer alternative, outside-the-box analyses, any red teaming documents disseminated in your organization should be clearly labeled as such. The U.S. Central Intelligence Agency is careful to do this so that anyone who reads the reports produced by its Red Cell understands they are based on contrarian analysis, and designed to provoke critical thinking.

Making Use of the Red Team's Findings

Once the red team has completed its analysis and delivered its report, it is up to the organization's leadership to decide what to do with the results. If you are one of those leaders, there are some important things you must keep in mind to make the most of your red team's work.

First, you must remember that the red team's role is not to come up with a better plan, but to make the existing plan better. You must also remember that the red team is supposed to be critical and contrarian, not necessarily *right*. The red team's work is not designed to supplant the work of the company's regular planning staff, but to be weighed alongside it.

As a leader, you should never take the red team's findings as gospel, but you should always take them seriously. Sometimes, the concerns raised by the red team will be so significant that you may decide to abandon your plan entirely. For example, if your company is considering a proposed merger, and the red team identifies several ways in which that marriage could do irreparable harm to the company's future, you may decide it just is not worth the risk. However, you should never reject a plan or strategy simply because your red team finds fault with it. Rather, consider how serious the threats or weaknesses exposed by the red team are for the plan's success. Also consider any steps the red team has suggested to mitigate these shortcomings or counter these dangers. If you still think the strategy is worth pursuing, ask your planning staff to address the red team's concerns. If your planners can modify their proposal to deal with those issues, or create contingencies to deal with any unintended or undesirable consequences, then by all means move forward with the plan. However, I do suggest you keep an eye on the areas flagged by the red team. Or, better yet, have the red team do that for you.

Whenever possible, the red team should remain engaged in the project or initiative so that it can provide additional insights and watch for any signposts of change identified in its analysis. Perhaps the best way to ensure that happens is to schedule regular progress reviews, and ask the red team to present an update as part of them. That has the added benefit of ensuring the red team remains invested in your organization's success, rather than allowing it to become a clique of professional gadflies. If there is confusion as to why the plan is not proceeding as expected, the red team may be able to help figure out why.

CHAPTER 10

The Rules of Red Teaming

Most people would rather die than think; many do.

—Bertrand Russell

By now, I hope it is apparent just how powerful red teaming can be and what a difference it can make for your company. By applying the tools and techniques I have explained in this book, your organization can plan better, compete more effectively, innovate more proactively, and become one of the disruptors in your industry, rather than one of the disrupted. But as effective as red teaming is, it is not without its challenges. And knowing how to deal with those challenges is just as important as knowing how to red team.

Business red teaming is still in its infancy. In my work with companies here and abroad, I have learned some important lessons by trial and error. I have asked my clients what worked and what did not. And I have discussed what I have learned with red teaming experts from the military and intelligence communities around the world. What follows are the most important takeaways from those conversations, starting with the most important red team rule of all:

Rule 1: Don't Be a Jerk

The U.S. Army's first red team was a disaster. By the time the training program at Fort Leavenworth was ready for its first class in 2006, the United States had been at war for more than four years. Recruiters were having a hard time meeting their quotas for America's all-volunteer fighting force. There was no draft, and soldiers could only stay in combat zones for so long before being rotated out. As a result, the army found it-self struggling to keep up with the demand for troops. Red teaming was starting to look like a luxury the military might not be able to afford. So National Guard members were used to fill most of the red teaming slots that had been created.

That solved the personnel problem, but it created a new one.

The National Guard has a very different culture from the regular army, and many full-time soldiers look down their noses at these "week-end warriors." The first red team rookies sent to Iraq did little to change their mind. After reporting for duty at Coalition headquarters in Baghdad, they asked for a separate workspace so that their thinking would not be "infected" by that of the regular planning staff. They also informed senior commanders they would not be wearing uniforms, since they did not want to let rank interfere with their discussions. Several of the red team members were denied security badges as a result. Reports soon began filtering back to Fort Leavenworth, and they were not encouraging.

"We will have to see how it goes in Iraq," Colonel Greg Fontenot told the *Los Angeles Times* in January 2007. "I know we are doing the right thing. I don't know if we are doing it the right way."

It turned out they were not. The rules of red teaming were still being written, but Colonel Steve Rotkoff, who replaced Fontenot when he retired as head of the army's red teaming program, says that first group broke every single one of them—including his most important rule of all.

"Don't be an asshole! If there is one red teaming rule you should never break, that is it," Rotkoff cautions. "You can be smart. You can be critical. You can be contrarian. You can be right. But don't be a jerk about it."

Not being a jerk about it can be challenging, because red team members can be a difficult bunch. The same traits that make them effective analysts—a quick intellect, a skeptical perspective, and a questioning nature—can make them seem arrogant and aloof, particularly when they are right. That is why it is essential that every red team member guard against these traits and instead develop an attitude of cooperation and collegiality.

I often tell my clients that red teaming is a form of "tough love" for companies, because it makes them better by pushing them harder, by asking difficult questions, and by challenging the status quo. If these things were easy, they would already be doing them. But they are not easy, and because of this, it is easy for a red team to find itself at odds with the rest of the organization. That is why an effective red team will always strive to be part of the solution, not part of the problem. How? By remembering that it is only successful if it makes the rest of the organization successful, too. And a red team can only do that if it works *with* the rest of the organization, rather than *against* it.

That does not mean red team members should avoid conflict, because conflict is inherent in the red teaming process. A red team should never compromise the integrity of its work to avoid hurting someone's feelings or, worse, for the sake of internal politics. But a red team should go out of its way to present its findings as respectfully and constructively as possible.

Good leaders know that there is nothing intrinsically wrong with conflict. Some, such as legendary Intel CEO Andy Grove, have actively encouraged it. Grove believed what he called "constructive confrontation" was key to his company's success:

Dealing with conflict lies at the heart of managing any business. As a result, confrontation—facing issues about which there is disagreement—can be avoided only at the manager's peril. The issue can be put off, it can be allowed to fester for a long time, it can be smoothed over or swept under some rug. But it is not going to disappear. Conflicts must be resolved if the organization is to go forward. Constructive confrontation accelerates problem solving. It requires that participants be direct. . . . It pushes people to deal with a problem as soon as possible, keeping it from festering. It encourages all concerned to concentrate on the problem, not on the people caught up in it.

"Constructive confrontation does not mean being loud, unpleasant or rude, and it is *not* designed to affix blame," Grove said. "Attack the problem, not the individual."

This is precisely how red teams must approach their work. To borrow a line from that great master of interpersonal relations Dale Carnegie, they need to learn how to *disagree agreeably.*

Red teams also need to be sensitive to the impact their work has on other members of the organization. A red team's report can be painful to read—particularly for those who helped draft the plan it is critiquing. Behind closed doors, the red team may have fun doing that, but it should never take such relish in its work in an open forum. Red teams and red team members need to be humble. A certain level of irreverence is a desirable quality in a red teamer, but not if it reaches the level of being a smart-ass.

Rule 2: Red Teams Must Have Top Cover

I have talked about this before, but it bears repeating: Successful red teaming requires the support and engagement of an organization's senior leadership. Otherwise, it is too easy to subvert the red teaming process, or simply ignore the results.

In a business setting, a red team will be most effective when it reports directly to the CEO and enjoys his or her full support. In practice, that will not always be possible. Red teams can still be effective when they report to the head of a department or division, as long as their scope is limited to those areas. If the red team tries to tackle problems outside of those areas, it is bound to find itself in conflict with other senior executives.

"A red team without top cover is merely a group of dissidents putting their careers at risk," warns Rotkoff.

If your red team does not report to the top of your organization, then it should do whatever it can to include senior leadership in its work. The red team should solicit the management's input before beginning any red teaming exercise in order to make sure the leadership's concerns are addressed and any limitations it might feel the need to impose are respected. The red team should also share its findings with those executives directly—preferably by inviting them to sit in on the final briefing, but at least by giving them a copy of the final report.

Bad things can happen if you do not do this. A British Ministry of Defence red team, for example, was asked to analyze a proposal by a senior government official. It found serious problems with the plan and recommended substantial changes. When the government official was then asked by his own superior if he had submitted his proposal to a red team review, he assured his boss he had. However, he did not share the red team's concerns. The plan was approved, and it ended up being a disaster—a disaster for which the red team was partially blamed!

Rule 3: Red Teaming Only Works If You Let It

Even when red team members conduct themselves blamelessly, it can still be a challenge to get the entire organization to embrace red teaming and take the red team's recommendations to heart. In the military, resistance to red teaming has come largely from officers who do not fully understand what red teaming is or why it is necessary. Once they are briefed on red teaming, that resistance usually dissipates. Successful units also tend to resist red teaming. They think that because they have been successful in the past, they know what it takes to be successful in the future. That is the sort of thinking that led to the collapse of the American automobile industry.

Most organizations—whether they be militaries, government agencies, publicly traded corporations, private companies, or even nonprofits—are hierarchical, and hierarchies often have a hard time taking a critical look at their own strategies and plans. Hierarchies tend to encourage compliance and reward conformity, rather than encouraging questions and rewarding innovation. Instead of the proverbial grease, the squeaky wheel often gets marginalized or invited to seek opportunities elsewhere. Moreover, people within hierarchies tend to resist any sort of critical review, because they worry such scrutiny might provide ammunition for careerist peers or ambitious subordinates. Organizations, or factions inside organizations, that do not want to take a hard look at their plans and processes will sometimes try to game the red team by limiting the scope of its analyses, withholding important information, or denying access to people and data. An experienced red teamer will have no trouble recognizing this, but circumventing these restrictions can be a challenge. This is yet another reason why it is essential that red teams have the support of the organization's senior leadership. A red team leader should not hesitate to make the executive who ordered a red teaming analysis aware of any interference or lack of cooperation. Similarly, those responsible for red teams must be prepared to remove such roadblocks if they want their red team to fulfill its mission.

It is hard to red team effectively if the red team is not allowed to look at all aspects of a company's operations. It can be done, but only with the proviso that the results may not be as complete as they would have been if everything had been open to critical analysis. That is understandably challenging for many organizations. Some companies will want to take sensitive issues, such as those involving personnel or trade unions, off the table. But a red team needs the freedom to look at all aspects of the business in order to conduct a thorough analysis.

Sometimes, that will simply not be possible. The board of directors may have already vetoed a particular course of action. Regulatory requirements or union contracts may limit a company's options. In situations such as these, it is important to remain mindful of the adage, *Don't let the great be the enemy of the good.* We live and work in a world where available courses of actions are often limited by politics, personalities, or purse strings. Red teaming within predefined lines is still better than not red teaming at all—unless those lines are put in place to shape the outcome of the red teaming exercise.

A particularly egregious example of how a red teaming exercise can be subverted took place in 2002, when the U.S. Department of Defense conducted one of the largest and most expensive war games in history. Millennium Challenge 2002 was no tabletop simulation. It cost $250 million and included thousands of actual troops, aircraft, and even warships. It was designed to simulate a future conflict between the United States, represented by the Blue Team, and a fictional Persian Gulf country, represented by the Red Team. That country was a stand-in for Iran, and the man tapped by the Pentagon to lead the Iranian forces was retired U.S. Marine Corps Lieutenant General Paul Van Riper. Arrayed against him was not only the combined military might of the U.S. Army, Air Force, Navy, and Marines, but also a panoply of future military technologies, some of which have yet to actually be deployed. Van Riper had to make do with the Iranian arsenal as it then stood. But he and his Red Team proved more than up to the challenge.

Like most recent wars, this one began with an ultimatum, and lines being drawn in the sand. As the Blue Team rattled its sabers and prepared to launch an invasion, Van Riper took a page out of the World War I playbook and used motorcycle couriers to mobilize his forces, rendering the Blue Team's sophisticated surveillance systems useless. He then launched a preemptive strike just ahead of the deadline set by the fictional American president. Within hours, most of the U.S. naval task force was at the bottom of the Persian Gulf. Van Riper's Red Team overwhelmed the American ships with a chaotic air and sea assault that included everything from low-flying jets to suicide speedboats laden with explosives and piloted by fanatical skippers. The mock war was over before it had even started.

At least, it should have been.

Instead, the generals running the war game simply resurrected the Blue Team's fleet, then told Van Riper to move his forces so that the Americans would have an easier time taking the beaches. But even with these advantages, the Blue Team kept running into trouble. So, as the days went on, the referees kept changing the rules in Blue's favor. The Red Team was told to leave its vulnerable antiaircraft systems out in the open where they could be more easily targeted and destroyed, and Van Riper was forbidden to use the chemical weapons in his arsenal as he had planned. The entire exercise had become a farce, a farce the general refused to sanction with his continued participation. Halfway through the three-week event, Van Riper resigned as Red Team leader and began drafting a memo to senior leaders at the Pentagon, telling them "it was in actuality an exercise that was almost entirely scripted to ensure a Blue 'win.'"

When that memo was leaked to the press, it became a major embarrassment—one the Pentagon spent months trying to live down.

Even when a red teaming exercise is allowed to proceed without such gross interference, the process can still be subverted by simply ignoring the red team's results. Once again, the best way to guard against this is by ensuring the red team has the blessing of senior management and reports its findings directly to the top of the organization. But there are other, more creative steps red teams can take to ensure their results are taken seriously. For example, the CIA's Red Cell has become adept at marketing itself and its products inside the agency. Red Cell reports often feature eyebrow-raising headlines to make sure they get read. The group also employs a part-time graphic designer to add catchy info-graphics to its products. It even presented one of its reports as a graphic novel. This shows what is possible when a red team red teams the problems of red teaming!

Of course, not all red teams want or need that sort of attention. In a business setting, it is often better for a red team to keep a low profile. And it is important to remember that there is such a thing as too much attention. Just ask the head of NATO's alternative analysis program, Johannes de Nijs. His problem is finding the time to handle all the requests for red teaming his organization receives.

"Either people haven't heard about us, or they overwhelm us with work," de Nijs told me. "There is nothing in between."

Rule 4: Don't Red Team Things to Death

There is such a thing as red teaming an issue or idea to death. The most effective red teams are those that have figured out how to red team just enough, but no more than necessary to solve the problems they are tasked with analyzing. Ineffective red teams waste time plunging down one rabbit hole after another.

If you are asked to red team your company's plan to introduce a new line of running shoes, concentrate on stress-testing that plan. Do not use this assignment as an opportunity to explore whether a new line of hiking boots might not be more profitable or to question whether your company should be in the shoe business in the first place. If you are asked to analyze a proposed merger with XYZ Corporation, focus on the risks and opportunities of that tie-up. Do not use it as an opportunity to reevaluate your company's entire business strategy.

It is counterproductive for a red team to analyze every decision an organization makes. Constant red teaming can be stressful and demoralizing for employees who have their every move questioned and challenged. That is not the point of red teaming, nor is it an effective use of red teams.

A red team should be used strategically and selectively. It should be brought in to analyze important decisions, major deals, and overarching strategies. It should be called on when problems cannot be satisfactorily solved through regular means. If you have an in-house red team and it is not occupied with one of these tasks, then it should be asked to work on big-picture issues or analyze the competitive landscape. You should never allow your red team to become an internal police force that spends its days looking over the shoulders of other employees and pointing out their mistakes.

Nor should you exhaust your red team.

Red teaming is hard work. A formal red teaming process using the tools and techniques I have described in this book can be intense, mentally draining, and—particularly if you are red teaming yourself—emotionally exhausting. Red teaming makes you think a lot harder than you are probably used to. Red teaming requires you to not just answer tough questions but also to question your answers—and then question *those* answers, too. Red teaming demands intellectual self-discipline, analytical persistence, and emotional resilience.

I learned this the hard way the first time I led an actual red teaming exercise for a client. We had scheduled a couple of all-day sessions to analyze the company's new business strategy. The first several hours went well, but by late afternoon, it was all starting to blur together for me. Reluctantly, I threw in the towel about 4:00 p.m., went back to my hotel, and fell right asleep without even taking off my suit. When I shared this experience with the head of the British Ministry of Defence's red teaming program, Brigadier Tom Longland, I could almost hear him shaking his head on the other end of the line.

"If you are doing this properly, ninety minutes is about the maximum that you can usefully do in one [red teaming] session," he told me. "What we do is two sessions in the morning and one session in the afternoon, ninety minutes each. Because of the way it is set up here, in the gaps we go back to our desks and pretend to work. But the truth, if you are doing it properly, you are absolutely bushed—because you are having to think and concentrate and you are having to listen to what each person is saying and weighing that against the knowledge that you've got of ideas that you are looking at. And then, of course, you are having to think about how to organize your own arguments. And, of course, here inside the red team, no prisoners are taken. It is quite tiring. I was in the army for thirty years, and I never worked as hard as I do as when we do a concept test session."

So learn from my mistake, and take Longland's advice: Limit yourself to three ninety-minute red teaming sessions a day. Sometimes a looming deadline will make that impossible. But even then, you should still adhere to the ninety-minute rule and be sure to take at least a thirty-minute break in between each session.

Rule 5: Red Team Your Red Team

Red teaming should never become routine. Red teaming is all about looking at things differently, so you need to avoid the tendency to approach every problem the same way and with the same techniques. That can be a challenge, because when we find an approach that works, we tend to keep repeating it. And when we do, we start to get lazy and less alert to the dangers of bias and groupthink.

A red team should always challenge itself. It should always encourage its members to voice different perspectives and conflicting views. Longland encourages his red team members to cultivate a thick skin.

"When you are red teaming, you do not own an idea. Ideas get attacked, often quite brutally. You must not take it personally," he advises. "We can have the most furious argument about something, but when the red team leader looks at his watch and sees that it is half past twelve, then we all go off together and have a very nice lunch."

As I have said before, rotating people in and out of a red team can help it keep its edge. Just be sure new team members understand the principles of red teaming and how to use the various tools and techniques.

Mixing up the way the team uses those tools and techniques is also a good idea. If you approach every problem the same way, you run the risk of making red teaming a bureaucratic exercise rather than the game-changing tool it should be. In addition, using the same methods over and over again can yield red teaming reports that read remarkably similar to one another, making them easier to ignore.

Red teaming can start to become routine for others in your company as well, and that can create its own challenges. Once red teaming becomes part of an organization's planning process, staff planners may start to anticipate the objections of the red team. This is not necessarily a bad thing; it may make them better planners. But it can become a problem if they start trying to game the system. If the most obvious objections are consistently addressed by the planning staff before a proposal is submitted for alternative analysis, the red team may become less skeptical and, therefore, less rigorous in its analysis. For example, if the planning staff figures out that the red team is always going to raise issues about suppliers' ability to keep up with increased demand, it could address those concerns in its proposal without actually addressing them with the suppliers. The red team should ask for proof. It should always remain critical, even of the most well-crafted plans. That is the red team's job, and it can only do it by digging deep.

Rule 6: You Don't Always Have to Be Right— But You Can't Always Be Wrong

As I have said before, you cannot judge a red team by its track record of success, because a red team is not in the business of predicting the future. Red teams do not have to be right. They need to be able to be wrong in order to do their job effectively.

Consider the following scenario: You ask your red team to analyze a proposed merger with XYZ Corporation. The red team does a contrarian analysis of the deal, and the analysis reveals all the different ways the tie-up could spell disaster for your company. But you decide to go ahead with the merger anyway, and the marriage turns out to be a resounding success for both companies.

Has the red team failed?

Not at all. It has done exactly what it was supposed to do. It has thought critically about your plan, identified all the ways in which it could go wrong, and—hopefully—made your senior leadership weigh those possibilities before signing off on the deal. Ideally, the red team's analysis will also have given you warnings signs to watch out for that could alert you to trouble during the subsequent reorganization.

In his study of the CIA's Red Cell, Micah Zenko said agency sources "described the unit as resembling a home-run hitter for whom you learn to live with the strikeouts. 'For every seven duds, you get three brilliant pieces. So you have to learn to live with the duds and not try to smother [the Red Cell] with traditional oversight that would kill its creativity.'"

Gauging the success of a red team or red teaming exercise is easy for participants but often difficult for those who did not take part in the process. After I helped the senior leadership team of Dale Carnegie & Associates red team their turnaround plan, each of the executives was convinced the new version of their plan did a far better job of addressing the company's fundamental challenges than the original draft had. But if you were not part of the process and had not seen the original plan, how would you know that? And if you did not know that, how would you assess the red team's effectiveness?

I believe red teams and red team members should be judged by the conversations they stimulate among the company's senior leadership, by how much more food for thought they provide for those discussions, and by how useful their insights are when it comes time to make important decisions. Any red team that gets people thinking and provides new perspectives to decision makers has done its job. Any red team that gets people thinking about something they would not have thought about before has done it well.

However, if a red team is always wrong, that creates its own problems.

A red team that is always wrong will never be taken seriously. Its warnings will be ignored. Its reports will go unread. Its members will lose their credibility. For that reason, red teams do need to pay attention to their track record and make sure that they hit the ball out of the park, at least occasionally.

If your red team is incapable of doing that, then it is doing something wrong. Because while red teams do not need to be right, they do need to be credible. If the red team misunderstands the problem it was asked to solve, recommends actions that have already proven unsuccessful, or suggests alternatives that are ethically, legally, or financially impossible, it will lose its credibility.

Rule 7: Don't Give Up

Sometimes, red teaming can be a lonely occupation—particularly if you are red teaming in an organization that does not want to learn, to change, and to grow.

Red teaming is about getting at the truth, and the truth is often quite complicated. Remember the Cynefin Framework from chapter 5? As we discussed, many of the problems red teams are assigned to analyze lie in its *Complex* quadrant, where the game pieces are interconnected. Red teaming is adept at tackling these tough issues, but the solutions to such problems rarely come in the form of quick fixes or easy answers. And, too often, those are the only solutions an organization wants to hear.

Many companies like simple solutions that do not require too much effort to implement. They prefer short-term fixes that offer immediate results, even if they do little to address the underlying problem. They are less interested in long-term solutions that require a coordinated effort to implement and that often take time to move the needle in a big way. But as Peter Senge warned in *The Fifth Discipline,* "The easy way out usually leads back in."

If your work as a red teamer falls on deaf ears, it is easy to get discouraged and demoralized. That is why the U.S. Army teaches its red teamers to always think about what it calls *My 15 Percent.* The idea is simple: Whether you are a general or a private, a senior executive or just another cog in the corporate machine, there are things you can do to improve the performance of your unit, your department, and by extension, your entire organization.

"We all retain a certain amount of power to affect what we do. We control our own attitude and approach, how we interact with other people, how we prioritize and use our time. But people tend to think they have no control. The idea with *My 15 Percent* is to flip that on its head," explains Rotkoff. "It is simply a matter of asking, 'What can I do to make a small difference? What can I do to make things a little better? What can I do to light a candle?' The idea is not to fix the problem, but just to improve the situation. Of course, when you start to get a lot of people inside an organization thinking this way, it can change everything for the better."

CHAPTER 11

Go Forth and Red Team

The most courageous act is still to think for yourself. Aloud.

—Coco Chanel

When our class completed the Red Team Leaders training course at Fort Leavenworth, we celebrated our graduation not inside the walls of the former prison, but in the old officers' club on the base golf course where General Dwight Eisenhower used to re-create. As on my first day at Fort Leavenworth, I was the odd man out in my civilian dress. My classmates had reverted to their combat attire, and the graduates of other red team training classes were similarly decked out in khaki, brown, and olive drab. At the podium stood retired Colonel Gary Phillips, head of the U.S. Army Training and Doctrine Command's Intelligence Directorate, which ran the University of Foreign Military and Cultural Studies and its red team training program.

"You've now been trained and given tools to challenge senior officers. And it's going to take courage for you to use them," he told us. "It's going to take courage for you to say, 'Sir, we need to stop and think about that.'"

As a business red teamer, you will need that same sort of courage, because you need to be able to say the same thing to senior executives. You will need the courage to speak truth to power. You will need the courage to point out the flaws in a plan, even if it was written by your boss, or your boss's boss. You will need the courage to explain why "the way we've always done things around here" is not necessarily the best way, and you will need the courage to suggest a better alternative. Red teaming is not for the faint of heart. It is not for those who are afraid to ruffle a few feathers. Red teaming is for those determined to make a real difference in the organizations they serve. It is for men and women who sleep better at night knowing that they helped solve a problem, find a solution, or avert a catastrophe.

This book has given you the tools and techniques you need to conduct a comprehensive red teaming analysis. I firmly believe there is no corporation, company, business, or nonprofit that cannot benefit from that. You are now in a position to help your organization succeed like never before, to save millions and make even more, to become a disruptive force in your industry instead of one of the disrupted. But as Gary Phillips told our graduating class, you must summon the courage to use what you have learned in order for what you have learned to make a difference.

Phillips also said those in charge need to muster the same sort of courage if they want to see red teaming succeed in their organizations.

"Perhaps more important is the courage you are going to require when you become senior leaders yourselves—the courage to take advice from someone who is junior to you, the courage to allow your views to be challenged and not get angry about it," he continued. "You've got to figure out how to convince people that you will listen to them, you will take what they say to heart, and you will act on it. And that takes courage. It takes courage to get past your ego. You can't get angry about it. You can't lash out at them. You can't kill the messenger—because you know what happens when you kill enough messengers? The messages stop coming."

Whether you are running a business, running a division, or running a department, you need the courage to submit your best-laid plans and strategies to critical review. You need the courage to solicit contrarian perspectives that challenge the prevailing wisdom inside your organization. You need the courage to red team. Because asking for a red teaming analysis *is* an act of courage, as is listening to the results. You may not always like what you hear. You may decide *not* to act on the red team's recommendations—and you may be justified in doing so. But you still need to hear what the red team has to say.

And you need to hear it now.

Are you thinking about a major acquisition? Red team it. Are you planning a major expansion? Red team it. Are you facing a new competitor or disruptive technology? Red team it. Are you getting ready to launch a new marketing campaign or a corporate reorganization? Red team it. If nothing else, I recommend your company consider red teaming its entire business strategy every three to five years, just to make sure it is still viable.

"Change before you have to," advised former General Electric CEO Jack Welch. Today, everybody has to change—constantly. For most businesses, each day brings new challenges and new opportunities. Red teaming can help you deal with the challenges and take advantage of the opportunities better than any business method I have encountered. Because while red teaming cannot predict the future, it sure can help you prepare for it.

Red Teaming Yourself

You now are aware of the biases and logical fallacies we all fall victim to in our daily lives, and you know that you are not immune to them. If you cannot recognize your own biases and identify the logical fallacies in your own arguments, how can you expect others to listen when you try to point out theirs?

You also know that the perspective from which we view a problem can have a big impact on how we approach it. That is why it is important for each of us to understand our own frame of reference. We cannot escape that frame, but we can recognize it and acknowledge it. By doing so, we can mitigate its effects on our analysis.

Those who are able to look critically at themselves, their assumptions, and their beliefs are also better able to see things others may have missed. In *Superforecasting*, the authors sought to identify the qualities the best prognosticators shared. The most important ones, it turned out, were not analytical skill or intelligence, but involved the ability to be self-critical and open-minded.

"A brilliant puzzle solver may have the raw material for forecasting, but if he doesn't also have an appetite for questioning basic, emotionally charged beliefs he will often be at a disadvantage relative to a less intelligent person who has a greater capacity for self-critical thinking. It's not the raw crunching power you have that matters most. It's what you do with it," they discovered. "For superforecasters, beliefs are hypotheses to be tested, not treasures to be guarded."

Unfortunately, most people lack the courage to do this. They are not willing to challenge their beliefs, question their assumptions, or even analyze their own arguments. But to be effective at red teaming, that is precisely what you must do.

When was the last time you read something you completely disagreed with? I mean really *read* it, all the way to the end—not just stumbled upon it, rolled your eyes, and closed the book or clicked on something else. When was the last time you listened to someone whose views were diametrically opposed to your own? I mean actually heard them out, not just shook your head and walked away or changed the channel. When was the last time you took a hard look at something you adamantly believed and asked yourself how you could be so sure it was true?

These are prerequisites for effective red teaming. They are also things each of us should do as a matter of course. Socrates famously said, "The unexamined life is not worth living." In terms of red teaming, he was not far off. I am not suggesting you become a latter-day René Descartes, closeting yourself in a room with a fireplace, a piece of wax, and the certainty only of your own existence. But I am asking you to apply the same critical approach to yourself that you apply to your company, your organization, and its strategies and its plans.

The Red Teaming Insurgency

On May 16, 2016, the U.S. Joint Chiefs of Staff issued *Joint Doctrine Note 1-16*, which mandated the use of red teams across all branches of the American military to "help commanders and staffs think critically and creatively; challenge assumptions; mitigate groupthink; reduce risks by serving as a check against complacency and surprise; and increase opportunities by helping the staff see situations, problems, and potential solutions from alternative perspectives."

This was the most powerful endorsement yet of red teaming in the U.S. military. The practice of red teaming also continues to expand in other nations' militaries and intelligence agencies. And red teaming is gaining traction among businesses, as well.

I have shared the same tools and techniques that I have shared with you with companies all over the world. These businesses have used red teaming to stress-test turnaround plans, to reorganize their corporate structures, to vet investment targets, to formulate their pitches to investors, to strengthen their bids before submitting them to clients, and to figure out how to find the upside in a slowing global economy.

Red teaming is quickly becoming a movement, albeit a quiet one spreading slowly by word of mouth. With this book, I hope to turn up the volume, and make sure every company is aware of red teaming, understands its benefits, and has an opportunity to use this game-changing approach to improve its strategies and make better decisions.

With the methods you have learned in this book, you can help your organization do just that. You can help your business, your corporation, or your nonprofit stress-test its strategy, perfect its plans, flush out hidden threats, identify missed opportunities, and avoid being sandbagged by unexpected events or new competitors. But once again, you can only do these things if you have the courage to use what you have learned.

At our graduation ceremony, Colonel Steve Rotkoff described red teaming as an insurgency—an insurgency that is transforming the way the army makes important decisions, the way it plans, the way it formulates strategy; an insurgency that is making the entire organization more competitive, more agile, and better able to cope with a rapidly changing world.

"You are now part of that insurgency," he told us. "Now, go forward, and spread the word!"

Welcome to the insurgency.

Acknowledgments

Any thanks for helping make this book happen must begin with my agent, Stuart Krichevsky, and my editor, Roger Scholl. After the publication of my first book in 2012, I struggled to find the right subject for my next one. Both men spent countless hours on the telephone with me going over various ideas and dutifully shooting them down one by one. Roger did me an immense favor by rejecting my first idea as an unworthy follow-up to *American Icon,* encouraging me to find something more suitable, and promising Crown would still be there for me when I did. Stuart bent his own rules to take me on as a client without a product to pitch, and while there may have been many times over the next couple of years that he regretted that decision, he never let me know it. Instead, he confidently assured me we would find the right book. When I discovered red teaming, we all knew that we had. That was when the real fun began. For the next two years, Stuart and Roger provided invaluable guidance and support as I studied this innovative approach to planning and strategy, then helped me distill down what I had learned into the book you have just read.

Thanks to everyone else at Crown for believing in this project and helping to make it a success, including Tina Constable, Campbell Wharton, Carisa Hays, Ayelet Gruenspecht, Megan Peritt, and so many others, too numerous to name. Thanks to my agent in the United Kingdom, Felicity Rubinstein, as well as to my editor, Zoe Bohm, and everyone else at Little, Brown in London. Thanks, too, to Manami Tamaoki, my agent in Japan, and to everyone at Hayakawa Publishing. And thanks to my outside publicist, Johanna Ramos-Boyer, and my social media manager, Dan Blank.

Acknowledgments

Of course, this book would never have happened without the gracious assistance of the U.S. Army, which allowed me to become the first person from outside government to attend its Red Team Leader course at the University of Foreign Military and Cultural Studies at Fort Leavenworth. The army would never have let me do that without the intervention and persistent support of two retired colonels, UFMCS director Steve Rotkoff and his boss, Gary Phillips. They were responsible for convincing the army to allow me to attend their program, rightly believing it would help give the outside world a new appreciation for the sort of cutting-edge thinking that is going on in the American military today. But my gratitude to Steve does not stop there. A tireless evangelist for red teaming, he gave up several weekends to be my private tutor during my time at Fort Leavenworth, as well as my tour guide in the greater Kansas City area. Steve continued my red teaming education after I returned to Michigan, offering additional insights, sharing his firsthand experiences, and serving as a sounding board for my own ideas.

I also want to thank my able instructor at UFMCS, retired Colonel Kevin Benson, as well as my classmates: Kyle Baer, Shawn Campbell, Chad Corbin, Timothy Driscoll, Thomas Dysinger, Brian Hatalla, John Luckie, Andrew Miller, Steven Patterson, Jacob Prater, Daniel Riesenberger, and Ebony Thomas. Each of your stories deserves its own book. Thank you all for putting up with me as I wrote this one. And many thanks to everyone else who made my time at Fort Leavenworth so enjoyable and worthwhile, including General Robert Brown, Colonel Curt Taylor, and the entire faculty of UFMCS, many of whom went above and beyond in sharing their own red teaming experiences and aiding me in my research.

I also am indebted to the red teaming experts from other military services around the world who have so generously offered their insights and assistance, including retired Brigadier Tom Longland and his team at the Development, Concepts, and Doctrine Centre, in the United Kingdom; Defence Academy in Shrivenham; Johannes de Nijs at Allied Command Transformation Headquarters in Norfolk; Kristy Hill of the New Zealand Defence Forces; and Eytan Buchman, formerly of the Israeli Defense Forces. I also want to thank the director of the U.S. Marine Corps' red team training program retired Colonel Ray Damm for inviting me to Quantico, and all the red teamers who shared their perspectives with me during my time there, especially retired Lieutenant General Paul Van Riper.

I am also grateful to Dr. Daniel Kahneman and Dr. Gary Klein for taking the time to explain their theories to me in person and for listening to mine. And thanks to Karimah Sweet and the other members of the mathematics department at Oakland University for checking my arithmetic.

Thanks are also due to my friends and associates from the business world and elsewhere who have allowed me to share these ideas with them and helped me examine them through the lens of their own experiences, especially Justin Foster, Norbert Gottenberg, Joe Hart, Mark Horn, James McKeough, Gavin McMahon, Hedieh Mirahmadi, Alan Mulally, Harry Murakami, and Alex Pascal.

Special thanks are due to my parents, Billie Crowley and Ned Hoffman, for a lifetime of support and encouragement; to my coach, Gary Ranker, for his generous guidance; and to my able assistant Emily Lawrence, who spent so much time scheduling interviews, tracking down sources, proofreading copy, and helping to keep this entire project from unraveling. Her suggestions helped make this book better, as did those of my other readers, Kevin Benson, John Luckie, Gavin McMahon, Alex Pascal, and Steve Rotkoff. Thank you all again for red teaming this book!

Last, but certainly not least, thanks to my wife, Gretchen Meyer-Hoffman. In the dedication of this book, I referred to her as my personal red team. She is that, but *so* much more—and none of this would have been possible without her.

Bryce G. Hoffman
Fenton, Michigan
November 30, 2016

Appendix

Those interested in honing their critical thinking skills or learning more about how we think and make decisions will find the following books invaluable:

Predictably Irrational: The Hidden Forces That Shape Our Decisions, by Dan Ariely

Sway: The Irresistible Pull of Irrational Behavior, by Ori and Rom Brafman

Asking the Right Questions: A Guide to Critical Thinking, by M. Neil Browne and Stuart M. Keeley

The Logic of Failure: Recognizing and Avoiding Error in Complex Situations, by Dietrich Dörner

Smart Choices: A Practical Guide to Making Better Decisions, by John S. Hammond, Ralph L. Keeney, and Howard Raffia

How We Reason, by Philip N. Johnson-Laird

Thinking, Fast and Slow, by Daniel Kahneman

Seeing What Others Don't: The Remarkable Ways We Gain Insights, by Gary Klein

Winning Decisions: Getting It Right the First Time, by J. Edward Russo and Paul J. H. Schoemaker

The Black Swan: The Impact of the Highly Improbable Fragility, by Nassim Nicholas Taleb

Critical Thinking: An Introduction to Reasoning Well, by Jamie Carlin Watson and Robert Arp

Selected Bibliography

Applied Critical Thinking Handbook (formerly the) *Red Team Handbook*. Version 7. Fort Leavenworth, KS: University of Foreign Military and Cultural Studies.

Ariely, Dan. *Predictably Irrational: The Hidden Forces That Shape Our Decisions*. New York: HarperCollins, 2008.

Booth, Ken. *Strategy and Ethnocentrism*. New York: Holmes & Meier, 1979.

Brafman, Ori, and Rom Brafman. *Sway: The Irresistible Pull of Irrational Behavior*. New York: Doubleday, 2008.

Brookfield, Stephen D. *Developing Critical Thinkers: Challenging Adults to Explore Alternative Ways of Thinking and Acting*. San Francisco: Jossey-Bass, 1987.

Browne, M. Neil, and Stuart M. Keeley. *Asking the Right Questions: A Guide to Critical Thinking*. 8th ed. Boston: Pearson Prentice Hall, 2006.

Clausewitz, Carl von. *On War*. Edited by Michael Howard and Peter Paret. Princeton, NJ: Princeton University Press, 1976.

Claxton, Guy. *Hare Brain, Tortoise Mind: How Intelligence Increases When You Think Less*. New York: Harper Perennial, 2000.

Collins, Jim. *Good to Great: Why Some Companies Make the Leap . . . and Others Don't*. New York: Harper Business, 2001.

Dörner, Dietrich. *The Logic of Failure: Recognizing and Avoiding Error in Complex Situations*. Translated by Robert Kimber and Rita Kimber. Cambridge, MA: Perseus, 1997.

Eagleman, David. *Incognito: The Secret Lives of the Brain*. New York: Pantheon Books, 2011.

Fisher, Glen. *Mindsets: The Role of Culture and Perception in International Relations*. Yarmouth, ME: Intercultural Press, 1988.

Fisher, Roger, and William L. Ury. *Getting to Yes: Negotiating Agreement Without Giving In*. New York: Penguin Books, 2011.

Hammond, John S., Ralph L. Keeney, and Howard Raffia. *Smart Choices: A Practical Guide to Making Better Decisions*. Brighton, MA: Harvard Business Press, 1998.

Harris, Marvin. *Cows, Pigs, Wars, and Witches: The Riddles of Culture*. New York: Random House, 1974.

Harvey, Jerry B. *The Abilene Paradox and Other Meditations on Management*. New York: Jossey-Bass, 1988.

Heuer, Richards J., Jr. *The Psychology of Intelligence Analysis*. Langley, VA: Center for the Study of Intelligence, Central Intelligence Agency, 1999.

Hofstede, Geert, Gert Jan Hofstede, and Michael Minkov. *Cultures and Organizations: Software of the Mind*. 3d ed. New York: McGraw-Hill Education, 2010.

Selected Bibliography

Intelligence Analysis Course Book. Chicksands: UK: Defence College of Intelligence, 2007.

Janis, Irving L. *Groupthink: Psychological Studies of Policy Decisions and Fiascoes.* New York: Houghton Mifflin, 1983.

Johnson-Laird, Philip N. *How We Reason.* Oxford: Oxford University Press, 2009.

Jomini, Baron de. *The Art of War.* Translated by Captain G. H. Mendell and Lieutenant W. P. Craighill. Radford, VA: Wilder, 2008.

Jones, Morgan D. *The Thinker's Toolkit: Fourteen Skills for Making Smarter Decisions in Business and in Life.* New York: Three Rivers Press, 1995.

Kahneman, Daniel. *Thinking, Fast and Slow.* New York: Farrar, Straus & Giroux, 2011.

Klamer, Arjo, Deirdre McCloskey, and Stephen Ziliak. *The Economic Conversation.* London: Palgrave Macmillan, 2014.

Klein, Gary. *The Power of Intuition: How to Use Your Gut Feelings to Make Better Decisions at Work.* New York: Doubleday, 2003.

——. *Seeing What Others Don't: The Remarkable Ways We Gain Insights.* New York: PublicAffairs, 2013.

——. *Sources of Power: How People Make Decisions.* Cambridge, MA: MIT Press, 1998.

Lewis, Michael. *Moneyball: The Art of Winning an Unfair Game.* New York: Norton, 2003.

Lipmanowicz, Henri, and Keith McCandless. *The Surprising Power of Liberating Structures: Simple Rules to Unleash a Culture of Innovation.* Seattle: Liberating Structures Press, 2014.

Marcus, Gary. *Kluge: The Haphazard Construction of the Mind.* Boston: Houghton Mifflin, 2008.

Neustadt, Richard E., and Ernest R. May. *Thinking in Time: The Uses of History for Decision-Makers.* New York: Free Press, 1986.

Plous, Scott. *The Psychology of Judgment and Decision Making.* New York: McGraw-Hill, 1993.

Red Team Handbook. Version 6. Fort Leavenworth, KS: University of Foreign Military and Cultural Studies.

Red Teaming Guide. 2d ed. Swindon, UK: Ministry of Defence, 2013.

Russo, J. Edward, and Paul J. H. Schoemaker. *Winning Decisions: Getting It Right the First Time.* New York: Currency Doubleday, 2002.

Senge, Peter M. *The Fifth Discipline: The Art & Practice of the Learning Organization.* New York: Doubleday, 1990.

Slim, Field-Marshal Viscount William. *Defeat into Victory: Battling Japan in Burma and India, 1942–1945.* New York: Cooper Square Press, 2000.

Sun Tzu. *The Art of War.* Translated by Samuel B. Griffith. Oxford: Oxford University Press, 1963.

Taleb, Nassim Nicholas. *The Black Swan: The Impact of the Highly Improbable Fragility.* 2d ed. New York: Random House, 2007.

Thaler, Richard H., and Cass R. Sunstein. *Nudge: Improving Decisions About Health, Wealth, and Happiness.* New Haven, CT: Yale University Press, 2008.

Watson, Jamie Carlin, and Robert Arp. *Critical Thinking: An Introduction to Reasoning Well.* New York: Continuum International, 2011.

Zenko, Micah. *Red Team: How to Succeed by Thinking Like the Enemy.* New York: Basic Books, 2015.

Notes

Introduction

5 *"It's something that I still think about":* Bryce G. Hoffman, "Bill Ford's Challenge: Stay Lean, Hungry and Innovative," *Detroit News,* February 11, 2010, 1A.

7 *I knew what a devil's advocate was:* Christopher Hitchens, *Hitch-22: A Memoir* (New York: Twelve, 2010), 337.

8 *It turns out there are many different types of red:* Brian Bennett, "Red Team Agents Use Disguises, Ingenuity to Expose TSA Vulnerabilities," *Los Angeles Times,* June 2, 2015, http://www.latimes.com/nation/nationnow/la-na-tsa-screeners-20150602-story.html.

14 *"You have complete authority to be strident":* Bob Woodward, *State of Denial: Bush at War Part III* (New York: Simon & Schuster, 2006), 98.

Chapter 1

28 *Over the next two weeks:* This brief synopsis of the 1973 Arab-Israeli War was taken from a number of different sources, including the books *Duel for the Golan: The 100-Hour Battle That Saved Israel* by Jerry Asher and Eric Hammel, *The 1973 Arab-Israeli War* by David T. Buckwalter, *The Yom Kippur War: The Arab-Israeli War of 1973* by Simon Dunstan, and *The Yom Kippur War: The Epic Encounter That Transformed the Middle East* by Abraham Rabinovich, as well as contemporary reports by *Time* magazine.

29 *Israel's Military Intelligence Directorate:* "The Middle East War," *Armed Forces Journal International* (January 1974), 34.

29 *But he and other members:* David T. Buckwalter, *The 1973 Arab-Israeli War* (Damascus, MD: Penny Hill Press, 2012), 122–23.

30 *A few hours later:* Ibid., 123–24.

30 *Reluctantly, Meir put:* Ibid., 124.

30 *With just hours to spare:* Ibid., 124–25.

31 *By October 1973:* Ibid., 121.

32 *According to a 2007 report:* Yosef Kuperwasser, "Lessons from Israel's Intelligence Reforms," Analysis Paper, The Saban Center for Middle East Policy at The Brookings Institution, no. 14 (October 2007), 4.

33 *The directorate's regular analysts:* Ibid.

34 *The 9/11 attacks:* National Commission on Terrorist Attacks, *9/11 Commission Final Report Executive Summary* (Washington, DC, 2004), http://www.9-11commission.gov.

34   *"Tenent decided to form":* Micah Zenko, "Inside the CIA Red Cell: How an Experimental Unit Transformed the Intelligence Community," *Foreign Policy,* October 30, 2015, http://foreignpolicy.com/2015/10/30/inside-the-cia -red-cell-micah-zenko-red-team-intelligence.html.

34   *According to the CIA:* "History," CIA.com, last modified January 5, 2016, https://www.cia.gov/offices-of-cia/intelligence-analysis/history.html.

34   *Those memos changed the way:* Intelligence Reform and Terrorism Prevention Act of 2004, Public Law 108–458, 118 Stat. 3670 (2004). See section 10A, subsection A.

35   *The U.S. Army developed:* Two American officers developed their own competing versions of *Kriegsspiel* in the 1880s. The first was William Roscoe Livermore's *American Kriegsspiel: A Game for Practicing the Art of War Upon a Topographical Map,* copyrighted in 1879 and published in 1882. The second was Lieutenant Charles Totten of the 4th Artillery Regiment, who in 1880 published *STRATEGOS: A Series of American Games of War Based Upon Military Principles and Designed for the Assistance Both of Beginners and Advanced Students in Prosecuting the Whole Study of Tactics, Grand Tactics, Strategy, Military History, and the Various Operations of War.* Both patterned their war games on the Prussian model, using blue markers to represent friendly forces and red markers to represent the opposing force.

36   *The September 11 terrorist attacks:* Defense Science Board, *The Role and Status of DoD Red Teaming Activities* (Washington, DC, 2003), 1.

44   *Petraeus would later say:* David Petraeus, "5 'Big Ideas' to Guide Us in the Long War against Islamic Extremism," *Washington Post,* April 15, 2016, https://www.washingtonpost.com/opinions/5-big-ideas-to-guide-us-in-the -long-war-against-islamic-extremism/2016/04/15/c145cdde-028a-11e6-9203 -7b8670959b88_story.html.

44   *And it did work:* Associated Press, "Iraqi Surge Exceeded Expectations, Obama Says," *NBC News,* September 4, 2008, http://www.nbcnews.com/ id/26550764/ns/politics-decision_08/t/iraqi-surge-exceeded-expectations -obama-says/#.VzH3VGNMahM.html; Peter Feaver, "Hillary Clinton and the Inconvenient Facts About the Rise of the Islamic State," *Foreign Policy,* August 13, 2015, http://foreignpolicy.com/2015/08/13/clinton-surge-iraq -maliki-obama/.

47   *The success of red teaming:* Kiran Stacey, "'Red Team' to Scrutinize Welfare Reforms," *Financial Times,* September 20, 2012, https://www.ft.com/ content/58709d22-033b-11e2-bad2-00144feabdc0.

Chapter 2

49   *Want of foresight:* Winston Churchill, "Air Parity Lost" (speech, United Kingdom, House of Commons, May 2, 1935), The Churchill Centre, http:// www.winstonchurchill.org/resources/speeches/1930-1938-the-wilderness/air -parity-lost.

49–50   *We've long believed:* Larry Page memo to Google employees, August 10, 2015.